Lecture Notes in Computer Science   8564

Commenced Publication in 1973
Founding and Former Series Editors:
Gerhard Goos, Juris Hartmanis, and Jan van Leeuwen

T0212189

Thorsten Holz   Sotiris Ioannidis (Eds.)

Trust and Trustworthy Computing

7th International Conference, TRUST 2014
Heraklion, Crete, Greece, June 30 – July 2, 2014
Proceedings

 Springer

Volume Editors

Thorsten Holz
Ruhr-University Bochum
Chair for Systems Security
Universitätsstr. 150, ID 2/439, 44780 Bochum, Germany
E-mail: thorsten.holz@rub.de

Sotiris Ioannidis
Institute of Computer Science
Foundation for Research and Technology - Hellas (FORTH)
N. Plastira 100, Vassilika Vouton, 700 13 Heraklion, Crete, Greece
E-mail: sotiris@ics.forth.gr

ISSN 0302-9743　　　　　　　　　　e-ISSN 1611-3349
ISBN 978-3-319-08592-0　　　　　　 e-ISBN 978-3-319-08593-7
DOI 10.1007/978-3-319-08593-7
Springer Cham Heidelberg New York Dordrecht London

Library of Congress Control Number: Applied for

LNCS Sublibrary: SL 4 – Security and Cryptology

Typesetting: Camera-ready by author, data conversion by Scientific Publishing Services, Chennai, India

Printed on acid-free paper

Springer is part of Springer Science+Business Media (www.springer.com)

Preface

This volume contains the proceedings of the 7th International Conference on Trust and Trustworthy Computing (TRUST), held in Heraklion, Crete, Greece, during June 30-July 2, 2014. TRUST 2014 was hosted by the Institute of Computer Science of the Foundation for Research and Technology-Hellas (FORTH-ICS), Greece, and was sponsored by Trusted Computing Group, Intel, and Microsoft.

Continuing the tradition of the previous conferences, held in Villach (2008), Oxford (2009), Berlin (2010), Pittsburgh (2011), Vienna (2012), and London (2013), TRUST 2014 provided a unique interdisciplinary forum for researchers, practitioners, and decision makers to explore new ideas and discuss experiences in building, designing, using, and understanding trustworthy computing systems.

The conference program of TRUST 2014 shows that research in trust and trustworthy computing is active, at a high level of competency, and that it spans a wide range of areas and topics. Papers dealt, for example, with topics such as a large-scale security analysis of the Web, hiding transaction amounts and balances in bitcoins, a security evaluation of specific physical unclonable functions, security aspects of mobile systems, security considerations of TPM 2.0, and location privacy.

In total, 40 papers were submitted in response to the Call for Papers. All submissions were carefully reviewed by at least three Program Committee members or external experts according to the criteria of scientific novelty, importance to the field, and technical quality. After an online discussion of all reviews, ten papers and three short papers were selected for presentation and publication in the conference proceedings. This amounts to an acceptance rate of 32.5%. We also encouraged people to report on work in progress by submitting two page abstracts describing ongoing research. A panel of experts reviewed these submitted abstracts. Nine of these abstracts were selected to be included in these conference proceedings. We hope that these abstracts will convey a sense of the vibrancy and current themes of research in trusted and trustworthy computing. Authors of these abstracts also presented posters of their work at the conference. Furthermore, the conference program contained several keynotes and a panel by leaders in academia, industry, and government agencies.

We would like to express our gratitude to those people without whom TRUST 2014 would not have been this successful, and whom we mention now in no particular order: the general chair Ioannis Askoxylakis, the publicity chair Manolis Stamatogiannakis, the members of the Steering Committee (where Ahmad-Reza Sadeghi deserves a special mention for his continued and valuable advice during the preparation of this conference), the local Organizing Committee, the keynote speakers, and the panel speakers (Jean-Pierre Seifert, Ingrid Verbauwede, and Christian Wachsmann). We also want to thank all Program Committee members and their sub-reviewers; their hard work made sure that the scientific program was of high quality and reflected both the depth and breadth of research in this area. Our special thanks goes to all those who submitted papers, and to all those who presented posters and papers at the conference.

June 2014

Sotiris Ioannidis
Thorsten Holz

Organization

TRUST 2014 was organized by the Institute of Computer Science of the Foundation for Research and Technology-Hellas (FORTH-ICS), Greece.

Steering Committee

Alessandro Acquisti	Carnegie Mellon University, USA
Boris Balacheff	Hewlett Packard, UK
Paul England	Microsoft, USA
Michael Huth	Imperial College London, UK
Andrew Martin	University of Oxford, UK
Chris Mitchel	Royal Holloway, University of London, UK
Sean Smith	Dartmouth College, USA
Ahmad-Reza Sadeghi	TU Darmstadt/Fraunhofer SIT, Germany
Claire Vishik	Intel, UK

General Chair

Ioannis Askoxylakis	FORTH-ICS, Greece

Program Chairs

Thorsten Holz	Ruhr University Bochum, Germany
Sotiris Ioannidis	FORTH, Greece

Publicity Chair

Manolis Stamatogiannakis	Vrije Universiteit Amsterdam, The Netherlands

Local Organizing Committee

Nikolaos Petroulakis	FORTH-ICS, Greece
Theodosia Bitzou	FORTH-ICS, Greece

Program Committee

Magnus Almgren	Chalmers University of Technology, Sweden
Elias Athanasopoulos	FORTH, Greece

Table of Contents

Trust and Trustworthiness

Poster Abstracts

DAA-Related APIs in TPM 2.0 Revisited

Li Xi, Kang Yang, Zhenfeng Zhang, and Dengguo Feng

Trusted Computing and Information Assurance Laboratory
Institute of Software, Chinese Academy of Sciences
Beijing 100080, China
{xili,yangkang,zfzhang,feng}@tca.iscas.ac.cn

Abstract. In TPM 2.0, a single signature primitive is proposed to support various signature schemes including Direct Anonymous Attestation (DAA), U-Prove and Schnorr signature. This signature primitive is implemented by several APIs which can be utilized as a static Diffie-Hellman (SDH) oracle. In this paper, we measure the practical impact of the SDH oracle in TPM 2.0 and show the security strength of these signature schemes can be weakened by 13-bit. We propose a novel property of DAA called forward anonymity and show how to utilize these DAA-related APIs to break forward anonymity. Then we propose new APIs which not only remove the SDH oracle but also support the forward anonymity, thus significantly improve the security of DAA and the other signature schemes supported by TPM 2.0. We prove the security of our new APIs under the discrete logarithm assumption in the random oracle model. We prove that the proposed DAA schemes satisfied the forward anonymity property using the new APIs under the Decision Diffie-Hellman assumption. Our new APIs are almost as efficient as the original APIs in TPM 2.0 specification and can support LRSW-DAA and SDH-DAA together with U-Prove as the original APIs.

1 Introduction

Direct Anonymous Attestation (DAA) is a special group signature scheme that enables remote authentication of a trusted platform which contains a valid TPM [1] while preserving the platform's privacy. Basically, DAA protocol allows a trusted platform called signer to sign arbitrary message and convince a verifier that the message is indeed signed by a valid TPM without leaking the signer's identity. A RSA-based DAA is proposed by Brickell *et al.* [2]. This RSA-based DAA is adopted by TCG and included in TPM 1.2 specification [3]. Since then several ECC-based DAA [4–8] are proposed to achieve better performance and shorter signature length. Some of them are now supported by the latest TPM 2.0 specification [1]. In TPM 2.0, a single TPM signature primitive [9] which can support various signature schemes including DAA and U-Prove is implemented by several DAA-related application programming interfaces (APIs).

An interesting feature of DAA is to provide differing degrees of privacy. While DAA signatures can be totally anonymous, a pseudonymous DAA signature can be linked to another signature by using a specific basename. A DAA signature

T. Holz and S. Ioannidis (Eds.): TRUST 2014, LNCS 8564, pp. 1–18, 2014.

signed by a trusted platform contains a ticket $t = (J,K = J^k) \in G \times G$, where G is a cylic group, k is the DAA secret key of the trusted platform and $J =$ hash(*basename*) if *basename* $\neq \perp$. This ticket is used for linking and rogue tagging: given two signatures, if the two tickets in signatures are the same, then these two signatures are linked.

In some DAA schemes, including the scheme adopted by the TPM 1.2 specification, the TPM simply gets input J and output J^k to the host, thus can be used as a static Diffie Hellman oracle which significantly reduces the security strength of DAA [10]. A security fix is proposed and is adopted by the TPM 2.0 specification [1].

Now in TPM 2.0 specification, TPM gets *basename* as input instead of J and calculates $J =$ hash(*basename*) by itself. It is believed that there is no obvious way that TPM can be used as a static DH oracle even though the security proof of the DAA-related APIs in TPM 2.0 specification is still based on the static DH assumption [9]. Unfortunately, Tolga Acar *et al.* [11] show these DAA-related APIs can still be used as a static DH oracle. Moreover, we find the security proof [9] is not correct either, which is rather disturbing as DAA is one of the few complex cryptographic protocols deployed in real life. Hundreds of millions of computers have been equipped with TPM.

Another important feature of DAA is that the signer, i.e., the trusted platform, is split into two parts: the TPM part and the host part. The TPM is a low speed hardware chip with high security; the host normally is a X86-based PC equipped with powerful CPU but is easy to corrupt. While the security definitions of user-controlled traceability and non-frameability of DAA give the adversary the ability to compromise the host, all the previous definitions and analyses of anonymity of DAA [12, 13] consider a setting that the host and TPM are both honest. This is easy to understand, because if the host of a trusted platform is already corrupted when signing, it can easily reveal its identity together with the signature, so anonymity of the platform can not be preserved.

However, as host is easier to compromise than TPM, the host part of a trusted platform which is honest when signing can be controlled by the adversary later. The adversary can then utilize the APIs provided by the TPM to find out if a given signature was signed by this TPM previously, thus breaks the anonymity. For example, consider an adversary who has gathered DAA signatures sent to a service provider (this is quite reasonable as DAA signatures are not confidential, moreover the adversary can be a malicious service provider itself), by corrupting the host part of a specific user, he may be able to trace all the previous actions of this user, even if the DAA signatures produced by this user are totally anonymous.

1.1 Contribution

In this paper, we provide the following main contributions:

1. We measure the practical impact of the SDH oracle in TPM 2.0. We analyze the Barreto-Naehrig (BN) elliptic curves [14] defined in ISO/IEC 15946-5

[15] which are recommended by the TPM 2.0 specification and show the security strength of DAA can be significantly reduced by about 13-bit in practice.

2. We propose a new property called forward anonymity of DAA. This property assures that even if the host of a trusted platform is corrupted, the anonymity of DAA signatures signed by the platform previously will not be broken. We propose a security definition of forward anonymity based on interactive game and shows attacks against forward anonymity both in the original DAA schemes and in the implementations of these DAA schemes using APIs in TPM 2.0 specification.

3. We propose new APIs which not only remove the static Diffie-Hellman oracle but also support the forward anonymity thus significantly improve the security of DAA. We present security proof of our new APIs under the discrete logarithm assumption in the random oracle model. We prove that both LRSW-DAA [7] and SDH-DAA [16] satisfy forward anonymity using the new APIs under the Decision Diffie-Hellman assumption. Our new APIs are almost as efficient as the original APIs in TPM 2.0 specification and can still support LRSW-DAA and SDH-DAA together with U-Prove [17] as the original APIs.

2 Background

In this section, we briefly introduce the static Diffie Hellman assumption and the DAA-related APIs in TPM 2.0.

2.1 Static DH Assumption

Definition 1. *Static DH oracle. Let G be a cyclic group of prime order n, x is a value in Z_n^*. Given any $p \in G$ as input, the static DH oracle on x outputs p^x.*

Definition 2. *Static DH problem. Let G be a cyclic group of prime order n, x is a value Z_n^*. Given $g, h = g^x \in G$, the static DH problem is to compute x given access to a static DH oracle on x.*

The static DH assumption is that for large n, it is computational infeasible to solve the static DH problem. While the static DH problem is still believed as a computational hard problem, the study of Brown and Gallant [18] shows that static DH problem is easier to solve than the discrete log problem:

Theorem 1. *[18] Given a cyclic group $G = \langle g \rangle$, the order of which is $n = uv+1$, a group member $h = g^x$, there is an algorithm that (1) asks the static DH oracle on x u times, (2) performs at most $2(\sqrt{u} + \sqrt{v})$ scalar multiplications in G and 10 simple arithmetic operations on numbers no larger than n and (3) outputs x.*

2.2   The DAA-Related APIs in TPM 2.0

We briefly recall the DAA protocol and DAA-related APIs in TPM 2.0, more details can be found in [9]. The DAA protocol consists of two subprotocols: the join protocol and the sign protocol. The TPM has an asymmetric endorsement key and a certificate *cert* associated with the public part of the endorsement key *epk*, the secret part of the endorsement key is *esk*.

In the join protocol, 1) the host use TPM2_Create to create the DAA secret key *tsk*, the public key is *tpk*. 2) The host send *tpk* and *epk* to the issuer. The issuer verifies *epk* and responses with an encryption blob *a* of a nonce *c* using *tpk* and *epk*. The host loads *tsk* and calls TPM2_ActivateCredential(*epk, tpk, a*) to get *c*. 3)The host calls TPM2_Sign to generate the schnorr signature on *c* using *tsk*, and sends the signature to the issuer. The issuer verifies the signature and the nonce *c*, then generates the DAA credential *cred* corresponds to *tsk* using *tpk*. The issuer generates a symmetric key *k*, encrypts the DAA credential *cred* using *k* and encrypts *k* using *tpk* and *epk*, then sends the ciphertexts to the host. 4)The host retrieves the symmetric key *k* using TPM2_ActivateCredential then decrypts the credential.

In the sign protocol, given a basename *bsn*, the host works together with the TPM by calling TPM2_Commit and TPM2_Sign to generate the DAA signature. In high level, the final DAA signature can be seen as consists of two parts: a ticket $(J, K) = (H_G(bsn), H_G(bsn)^{tsk})$ which is used for linking, and the information that proves (1) the trusted platform has a valid DAA credential and (2) the ticket and the credential are bound with the same DAA secret key *tsk*. Notice in complex signatures such as DAA, the computation which needs the secret key is only a small part. This part which is generate by TPM2_Commit and TPM2_Sign is actually a self-contained signature primitive.

Now we introduce the DAA-related APIs in TPM 2.0. Let $\mathbb{G}$ be a cyclic group of prime order p and g be a generator. $H : \{0,1\}^* \to Z_p$ and $H_G : \{0,1\}^* \to G$ are two collision-resistant hash functions.

TPM2_Create: The TPM generates a random number k and computes $y = g^k$. The secret key is k, the public key is y.

TPM2_ActivateCredential: Given $epk, pk, eblob$ as input, epk is the public part of endorsement key, pk is a public key, $eblob = \mathsf{enc}_{epk}(pk, k)$ is a blob encrypt under epk, the secret part of the endorsement key is esk:
   1. verify that pk is loaded in TPM, if true then
   2. decrypt $eblob$ using esk and check that k is bound with pk.
   3. output k.

TPM2_Commit: Given $P_1 \in G$, $str \in \{0,1\}^*$ as input:
   1. Verify that $P_1 \in G$.
   2. If $str = \emptyset$, set $P_2 = 1$, otherwise, compute $P_2 := H_G(str)$.
   3. Choose a random integer $r \leftarrow Z_p$.
   4. Compute $R_1 = P_1^r, R_2 = P_2^r$, and $R_2 = P_2^k$ where k is the private key.
   5. Output R_1, R_2, K_2 and a counter ctr which is used for the TPM to find the corresponding random number r in TPM2_Sign, as TPM2_Commit can be execute many times before TPM2_Sign is executed. The counter value is then increased by 1.

TPM2_Sign : Given c_h, m and a counter ctr as input:
1. compute $c := H(c_h, m)$.
2. According to the counter ctr finds the corresponding r, compute $s := r + ck \bmod p$, delete r.
3. Output(c, s).

The signature $(P_1, P_2, R_1, R_2, K_2, c, s)$ produce by TPM2_Commit and TPM2_Sign is a signature of knowledge $SPK\{(k) : K_1 = P_1^k \wedge K_2 = P_2^k\}(m)$. Given $m, K_1 = P_1^k$, the verification of the signature $(P_1, P_2, R_1, R_2, K_2, c, s)$ proceeds as follows:

1. Verify $P_1 \neq 1$.
2. Verify $H(R_1, R_2, m) = c$.
3. Verify $R_1 = P_1^s \cdot K_1^{-c}$ and $R_2 = P_2^s \cdot K_2^{-c}$.

3   Static DH Oracle in TPM 2.0

Tolga Acar *et al.* [11] show these DAA-related APIs can be used as a static DH oracle. In TPM2_Commit API, the input are a group member $P_1 \in \mathbb{G}$, where $\mathbb{G}$ is a cyclic group with prime order p, and a string $str \in \{0, 1\}^*$ that represents the basename, TPM calculates $P_2 = H_G(str)$, the output is $R_1 = P_1^r$, $R_2 = P_2^r$, $K_2 = P_2^x$, x is the DAA secret key. In TPM2_Sign API, the TPM get a input c_h, m from the host, calculate $c = H(c_h, m)$, and output (c, s), $s = r + cx$.

Notice that there is no restriction on the first input P_1, if the host is corrupted, he can send whatever he wants. Now the host (adversary) can get $R_1 = P_1^r$ from TPM2_Commit and he can then get $(c, s = r + cx)$ from TPM2_Sign. Thus he can calculate $Mid = P_1^{cx} = P_1^s / P_1^r$, then he can calculate $P_1^x = Mid^{1/c}$ ($1/c \bmod p$ is easy to calculate as p is a public prime number). Thus TPM can still be used as a static DH oracle.

3.1   Practical Impact of the Static DH Oracle

Theoretically, according to result of [18], for $p = uv + 1$, in the worst case, when there exists $u \approx p^{1/3}$, the adversary who controls the host can query TPM u times and uses about $2(\sqrt{u} + \sqrt{v}) \approx O(p^{1/3})$ group operations to solve the static DH problem. For a 256-bit p, the adversary can query the TPM about 2^{85} times then solve the discrete log problem with $O(2^{85})$ computations instead of $O(2^{128})$ computations. However, as TPM is a low speed device, and according to the algorithm in [18], the static DH query should be asked sequentially, i.e. the adversary has to obtain g^{k^n} then ask the static DH oracle for $g^{k^{n+1}}$, where k is the DAA key, it may be impractical for the adversary to ask for too many static DH oracles using the known technology.

According to preliminary performance figures in [9], on a discrete 40MHz TPM 2.0 chip, a scalar multiplication operation on a 256-bit prime curve takes only 125ms, and according to our benchmark, a scalar multiplication on a 256-bit prime curve takes less than 1 ms on a X86-based PC equipped with an Intel i7-3770M CPU at 4x3.4GHz, so it takes less than 130ms to get the answer to a static DH query using the method described in above subsection. The adversary can then ask the static DH oracle about $1.22 \times 10^8 > 2^{26}$ times in half a year. So the security strength can be significantly weakened by about 13-bit, which means given a 256-bit BN curve, the security strength is now only 115-bit instead of the assumed 128-bit.

Notice that in order to utilize the Brown-Gallant algorithm, the adversary has to find a large $u|p - 1$, p is the order of the elliptic curve group. In the TPM 2.0 specification, it is recommended that DAA be implemented using the Barreto-Naehrig (BN) elliptic curve [14] as defined in ISO/IEC 15946-5 [15]. We present the factorizations of $p - 1$ for the BN curves given in ISO/IEC 15946-5 [15] in table 1.

Table 1. Factorizations of $p - 1$ for BN curves, where p is the group order

BN256	$2 \cdot 2 \cdot 3 \cdot 7 \cdot 7 \cdot 189239 \cdot 24818737 \cdot 6192533153 \cdot 53176290319 \cdot$ 127328277910133303695654392417046642892297
BN224	$2 \cdot 2 \cdot 3 \cdot 13 \cdot 43 \cdot 3539 \cdot 3099193 \cdot 118621 \cdot 21529517 \cdot 105380711 \cdot 247994786597 \cdot$ 5490314800167041813327
BN192	$2 \cdot 2 \cdot 3 \cdot 269 \cdot 124427 \cdot 923526871 \cdot 15942266405279489963 \cdot$ 1061479012505267222401
BN160	$2 \cdot 2 \cdot 3 \cdot 12132793 \cdot 164442871007 \cdot 448873741399 \cdot 135993458106516349$

As shown by the Table 1, every BN curve in the international standard ISO/IEC 15946-5 which is adopted by TPM 2.0 specification has a large $u|p - 1$ which is close to 2^{26}. For example, the 160-bit BN curve which is supposed to provide 80-bit security strength now only provides poorly 67-bit security strength which may be easy to break in nowadays. Moreover, as static DH assumption is a non-standard assumption and has not been studied enough, we do not have the confidence that more efficient algorithms will not be found. If a more efficient algorithm is found, the firmware of TPM may need to be updated which is hard to implement. So obviously, the safest solution is to design new DAA-related APIs that can be proved secure under a weaker assumption, for example, the discrete logarithm assumption.

4   Forward Anonymity

In this section we introduce the notion of forward anonymity and show how the adversary can break forward anonymity both in the original DAA schemes and the implementation of DAA using APIs in TPM 2.0.

All the previous definitions and analyses of anonymity of DAA consider a setting that the host and TPM are both honest. However, we find a DAA protocol which is proved to be secure under former definitions of anonymity may not be able to resist the following attack: the whole platform is honest when signing a signature, after the signature is signed, the adversary wants to find out whether this signature is signed by the platform, so he corrupts the host and gains information stored in the host and the ability to directly communicate with the TPM. Of course, we assume an honest trusted platform will wipe out all the one-time information used in signing after the signature is produced, including the random number and the signature. With these capabilities, the adversary may be able to find out whether the signature was signed by the platform before.

As we know, the host is easier to corrupt than TPM, thus it is not enough to rely on the security of host to achieve anonymity under high level security requirement. It is promising to guarantee anonymity of signatures only under the assumption that the TPM is honest which is reasonable because TPM is designed to resist software attacks and some kinds of physic attacks.

So we propose forward anonymity. Informally, the notion of forward anonymity requires that the following property holds in the DAA scheme: even after an adversary compromised the host of a trusted platform, he finds it hard to find out whether a previous signed anonymous DAA signature (with basename $=\perp$) is signed by this trusted platform as long as the TPM is not corrupted. Notice that generally we can not expect a pseudonymous signature to remain anonymous after the host is compromised, because the adversary with the ability to communicate with TPM can always generate a new signature using the same basename as the pseudonymous signature. Thus by checking whether these two signatures contain the same ticket, the adversary can decide if this pseudonymous signature is generate by the platform.

The notion of forward anonymity is defined via a game played by a challenger $\mathcal{C}$ and an adversary $\mathcal{A}$ as follows, for simplicity, we assume that for each trusted platform there will be only one DAA secret key:

Initial: $\mathcal{C}$ runs Setup and gives the resulting issuer's secret key isk to $\mathcal{A}$. $\mathcal{C}$ publishes the public parameters on a public channel.

Phase 1: The adversary makes the following requests to $\mathcal{C}$:

   Join. $\mathcal{A}$ submits a TPMs identity id to $\mathcal{C}$, who acts as the trusted platform with identity id and executes Join protocol with $\mathcal{A}$.

   Sign. $\mathcal{A}$ submits a TPMs identity id, a message m and a basename bsn to $\mathcal{C}$, who acts as the trusted platform with identity id and execute Sign protocol with $\mathcal{A}$ using message m and basename bsn.

   API. $\mathcal{A}$ submits a TPMs identity id along with the name of the API he wants to use, for example, TPM2_Commit, and the data used in calling the API of his choice to $\mathcal{C}$, who acts as the TPM with identity id and responds with the output of the API. Also the information stored inside the host part of this trusted platform will be output to the adversary.

   Corrupt. $\mathcal{A}$ submits a TPMs identity id to $\mathcal{C}$, who response with the DAA secret key created by this TPM.

Challenge: At the end of Phase 1, $\mathcal{A}$ chooses two TPMs' identities id_0 and id_1, submits the two identities and a message m of his choice to $\mathcal{C}$. $\mathcal{A}$ must not have made any API query or Corrupt query on either id_0 or id_1. For simplicity, we assume that $\mathcal{A}$ has already made Join query on id_0 and id_1, $\mathcal{C}$ chooses a bit b uniformly at random, produce a signature as platforms with identity id_b using m and $bsn = \perp$, then output signatures to the adversary.

Phase 2: The adversary can do what he can in phase 1 except that he can not make any Corrupt query on either id_0 or id_1, notice now he can make API query using id_0 and id_1.

Guess: $\mathcal{A}$ returns a bit b', the advantage of $\mathcal{A}$ is $\mathbf{Adv}(\mathcal{A}) = |\mathbf{Pr}(b = b') - 1/2|$. We say that a DAA scheme satisfies forward anonymity if for any probabilistic polynomial-time adversary $\mathcal{A}$, $\mathbf{Adv}(\mathcal{A})$ is negligible.

In both LRSW-DAA [7] and SDH-DAA [16], even the totally anonymous DAA signature contains a tuple (J, K), $K = J^k$, which is used for rogue tagging. In TPM 2.0, when signing a totally anonymous signature, the host will choose a random string str, then TPM will calculate $J = \mathtt{hash}(str)$ and $K = J^k$. Notice that it is unnecessary to include the random string str in the signature as only the tuple (J, K) is used for rogue tagging. To achieve forward anonymity, it actually *should not be include in the signature*. Otherwise after the host is compromised, given a totally anonymous DAA signature which contains (str, J, K), where $J = \mathtt{hash}(str)$, the adversary can use the string str and the API TPM2_Commit to reconstruct the tuple (J, K), thus can decide whether the signature is signed by this TPM. If only (J, K) is included in the signature, this approach will not work: the adversary can not calculate $bsn = \mathtt{hash}^{-1}(J)$ as $\mathtt{hash}$ is a one-way function.

Note that even only consider user-controlled anonymity as in [12], for totally anonymous DAA signatures with basename= $\bot$, the random string str should not be included in the signature either. In the challenge phase of user-controlled-anonymity game [12], if the adversary $\mathcal{A}$ chooses a basename $bsn = \bot$, then in Phase 2 there is no restriction of basename used in the Sign query. Thus if the totally anonymous DAA signature (with basename=$\bot$) outputted in the challenge phase contains (str, J, K) where $J = \mathtt{hash}(str)$, the adversary $\mathcal{A}$ can submit basename= str in phase 2, thus reconstruct (J, K) which breaks user-controlled anonymity.

Attacks against Forward Anonymity. In the original LRSW-DAA, $(c, s) = SPK\{(k) : K_1 = P_1^k \wedge K_2 = P_2^k\}(m)$ is generated by a single procedure, the random commitments R_1, R_2 are not output to the host. In TPM2.0, this procedure is split into two parts: TPM2_Commit and TPM2_Sign in order to support various signatures, especially the SDH-DAA. However section 3 shows splitting the procedure leads to the result that the TPM can be used as a static DH oracle. In TPM 2.0, DAA protocols can not satisfy forward anonymity because given a challenge DAA signature which contains a ticket (J, K), the adversary can utilize the TPM as the static DH oracle and get $K' = J^k$, k is the DAA secret key. By checking whether $K' = K$, the adversary can find out whether the signature is signed by this TPM.

It is worth noting that in the original LRSW-DAA [7] (of course we move the calculation $J = \mathtt{hash}(basename)$ inside the TPM according to [10]), even though now there is no obvious way that TPM being used as a static DH oracle, the forward anonymity still can not be preserved.

To make this paragraph easy to understand, we use the same notation as in the sign/verify protocol of [7, § 2.3]. In the sign protocol, the input to TPM is $(c, J, S, \mathtt{msg}, \mathtt{bsn})$, where $J = H_1(bsn)$. In our analysis, we delete J as $J = H_1(bsn)$ should be calculate by TPM (or at least verified by TPM). So now the input to TPM is $(c, S, \mathtt{msg}, \mathtt{bsn})$. Given a TPM and a challenge DAA signature which contains a ticket $(\hat{J}, \hat{K})$, $\hat{K} = \hat{J}^{k^*}$ where k^* is the DAA secret key this signature is signed under, the adversary generates three random values $(c, \mathtt{msg}, \mathtt{bsn})$ and output $(c, S = \hat{J}, \mathtt{msg}, \mathtt{bsn})$ to the TPM. The TPM will output $(K = J^k, h, s, n_T)$. (h, s) actually is a signature of knowledge $SPK\{(k) : K = J^k \wedge K' = \hat{J}^k\}(c, \mathtt{msg})$, now K' is *not known* by the adversary. Notice $(h, s) = SPK\{(k) : K = J^k \wedge K' = \hat{J}^k\}$ can only be verified by two pair $(J, K = J^k)$ and $(\hat{J}, K' = \hat{J}^k)$. The adversary can now use the ticket (J, K) and the ticket $(\hat{J}, \hat{K})$ in the challenge DAA signature to verify (h, s), if (h, s) is verified, then the challenge DAA signature is signed by this TPM.

More deeply thinking, we can see the above analysis shows a TPM in LRSW-DAA (even the calculation $J = \mathtt{hash}(basename)$ is moved inside the TPM) provides a weaker kind of Decision Diffie-Hellman oracle: let (g, h) be the DAA public key, given arbitrary tuple $(\hat{J}, \hat{K})$, an adversary can utilize the TPM to decide whether $log_{\hat{J}}\hat{K} = log_g h$.

This attack works because TPM does not check the input $S \in G$. So our analyses of static DH oracle and forward anonymity both show there should be restriction on the first parameter of $\mathtt{TPM2\_Commit}$'s input $(P_1 \in G, bsn \in \{0, 1\}^*)$.

5 The New DAA-Related APIs

5.1 Fix the DAA-Related APIs to Satisfy Forward Anonymity and to Remove the Static DH Oracle

Our target is to revise the APIs without adding much cost and retain the capabilities of the APIs, i.e., the revised APIs should still support LRSW-DAA, SDH-DAA and U-Prove. As pointed out above, there should be restriction on the first input of the $\mathtt{TPM2\_Commit}$. Actually, we step a little further, we will bind $P_1 \in G$ which is the first input of the $\mathtt{TPM2\_Commit}$ with the DAA key $(g, y = g^k)$: now P_1 can only be g or a fixed group member $P \in G_1$ which is bound to the DAA key. Before using $\mathtt{TPM2\_Commit}$ and $\mathtt{TPM2\_Sign}$ to generate DAA signatures, if the P_1 needed by $\mathtt{TPM2\_Commit}$ is different from g, then the host should first output the P_1 to the TPM, who will bind P_1 with the DAA key. After binding, the API $\mathtt{TPM2\_Commit}$ can only use the *same* bound group member $P_1 \neq g$ or g as input.

We propose a new command $\mathtt{TPM2\_DAAbind}$ to bind $P_1 \in G_1$ with the DAA key $(g, y = g^k)$, the input of this command is a pair (P_1, K_1) together with a signature of knowledge $SPK\{(r) : K_1 = y^r \wedge P_1 = g^r\}$ which is generate by the issuer (the join protocol of LRSW-DAA in TPM 2.0 is different from the original scheme [7], it actually adopted the join protocol in [8]: the issuer generates a DAA credential together with a signature of knowledge). The TPM checks the signature of knowledge $SPK\{(r) : K_1 = y^r \wedge P_1 = g^r\}$ and bind P_1 with the DAA key. Only after the DAA key is bound with a group member P_1, can the host call the API TPM2_Commit using the *fixed* $P_1 \neq g$ as a input.

Now we describe the new TPM signature primitive, denoted by tpm.sign*.

Key Generation (TPM2_Create): The TPM generates a random number k and computes $y = g^k$. The secret key is k, the public key is y.

DAA Binding (TPM2_DAAbind): Given a pair (P_1, K_1) and a signature of knowledge $SPK\{(r) : P_1 = g^r \wedge K_1 = y^r\}$, the TPM verifies the signature of the knowledge $SPK\{(r) : P_1 = g^r \wedge K_1 = y^r\}$, if it is valid, then bind k with P_1.

Signing:

  Commit Oracle (TPM2_Commit): Given $P_1 \in G, l \in Z_P, str \in \{0,1\}^*$ as input:
  1. Verify that $P_1 = g$ or P_1 has been bound with k, if both not, abort.
  2. If $str = \emptyset$, set $P_2 = 1$, otherwise, compute $P_2 := H_G(str)$
  3. Choose a random integer $r \leftarrow Z_p$.
  4. Compute $R_1 = P_1^{lr}, R_2 = P_2^r$, and $R_2 = P_2^k$ where k is the private key.
  5. Output R_1, R_2, K_2 and a counter ctr. The random number r is bound with ctr, the counter is then increased by 1.

  Sign Oracle (TPM2_Sign) : Given c_h, m and a counter number ctr as input.
  1. Generate a nonce n_T, compute $c := H(c_h, m, n_T)$.
  2. According to the counter ctr finds the corresponding r, compute $s := r + ck \mod p$, delete r.
  3. Output (c, s, n_T).
  The signature on m is $(P_1' = P_1^l, P_2, R_1, R_2, K_2, c, s, n_T)$, it is a signature of knowledge $SPK\{(k) : K_1 = P_1'^k \wedge K_2 = P_2^k\}(m)$, where $K_1 = P_1'^k$.

Verification: Given a signature $(m, P_1' = P_1^l, P_2, R_1, R_2, K_2, c, s, n_T)$, $K_1 = P_1'^k$, the verification proceeds as follows:
  1. Verify that $P_1 \neq 1$.
  2. Verify that $H(R_1, R_2, m, n_T) = c$.
  3. Verify that $R_1 = P_1'^s \cdot K_1^{-c}$ and $R_2 = P_2^s \cdot K_2^{-c}$.

Our TPM2_Commit is slightly different from the original one, as now $R_1 = P_1^{lr}, l$ is an input number. This difference guarantees that the implementations of DAA protocols and U-Prove using our new APIs is as efficient as using the original APIs which will be discussed thoroughly in section 6.

5.2 Security Proof of the New tpm.sign*

We first point out the mistake in the security proof of the original DAA-related APIs in TPM 2.0 [9] then we present security proof of our new APIs under the discrete logarithm assumption in the random oracle model.

Mistake in the Security Proof of DAA-Related APIs in TPM 2.0. In the proof [9], the simulator $\mathcal{B}$ does not provide the hash query H for the adversary $\mathcal{A}$. Actually, after making a TPM2_Commit query, $\mathcal{A}$ can first query H n times using arbitrary pairs (c_h, m_i), $i \in [1, n]$ and gets answers $h_i = H(c_h, m_i)$, then call the TPM2_Sign using one pair (c_h, m_j), $j \in [1, n]$, however, the simulation of TPM2_Sign have to output the (c, s) which is already fixed in the simulation of TPM2_Commit. So now $c = H(c_h, m_j) \neq h_j$ which means the simulation fails.

In our new API TPM2_Sign, the TPM generates a nonce n_T. By adding a nonce n_T, we fix this problem: now $c = H(c_h, m_j, n_T)$ and $\mathcal{A}$ can not obtain n_T before calling TPM2_Sign as n_T is a newly-generated nonce.

Security Proof of the Our New APIs. We prove the security of our new tpm.sign* using the standard security notion of signature schemes which is existential unforgeability under adaptive chosen message attacks (EUF-CMA). In EUF-CMA model, the attacker is allowed to query the signing oracle adaptively. In our case, it means the attacker is allowed to call the APIs adaptively, i.e., he can call TPM2_DAAbind (bind oracle), TPM2_Commit (commit oracle), TPM2_Sign (sign oracle) as he wishes.

Definition 3. *The tpm.sign* scheme is said to be existentially unforgeable under adaptive chosen message attacks if there is no probabilistic polynomial-time adversary $\mathcal{A}$ with non-negligible advantage in the following game played with a challenger $\mathcal{C}$:*

Initial: $\mathcal{C}$ runs Setup and call TPM2_Create to create the secret key. $\mathcal{C}$ sends systems public parameters params and public key to $\mathcal{A}$

Queries: The adversary $\mathcal{A}$ adaptively makes API queries as he wishes.

Forgery: The adversary $\mathcal{A}$ produces a pair (m^*, σ^*), notice m^* should not be called in TPM2_Sign queries. The adversary $\mathcal{A}$ wins if σ^* is a valid signature.

Our security proof is based on the well-known forking lemma [19] which applies to signatures with the form (σ_1, h, σ_2). Here σ_1 are random commitments; $h = H(\sigma_1, m)$ where H is a hash function.

Theorem 2. *The new tpm.sign* is existentially unforgeable under adaptive chosen message attacks in the random oracle model under the DL assumption.*

Proof: If there is an adversary $\mathcal{A}$ that breaks the new tpm.sign* scheme, i.e., $\mathcal{A}$ outputs a forged signature $(m, P_1, P_2, R_1, R_2, K_2, c, s, n_T)$ after given arbitrary access to TPM2_Create, TPM2_DAAbind, TPM2_Commit and TPM2_Sign, then there exists an algorithm $\mathcal{B}$ which utilize $\mathcal{A}$ to solve the DL assumption. $\mathcal{B}$ is given a pair $(g, h = g^x)$, and $\mathcal{B}$ wants to compute x. Algorithm $\mathcal{B}$ works as follows:

key generation(TPM2_Create): $\mathcal{B}$ sets h as the public key and outputs it to $\mathcal{A}$ and sets $log_g h$ as the corresponding private key x, although $\mathcal{B}$ does not know x.

Bind Query(TPM2_DAAbind): Given a pair (P, K) and a proof of knowledge $PK\{(r) : P = g^r \wedge K = h^r\}$. $\mathcal{B}$ verifies the proof of the knowledge $PK\{(r) : P = g^r \wedge K = h^r\}$, if it is right, stores (P, K). Due to the soundness of proof of knowledge, we have $K = P^x$.

Hash Query: There are two hash functions modelled as random oracles: H_G and H.

  H_G: Given a input str, if the str is not queried before, $\mathcal{B}$ generates a random number r, calculated $H_G(str) := g^r$, store $(H_G(str) = g^r, r)$ in the hash list of H_G, if the str has been queried, return the former answer.

  H: Given a input x, if x has been queried before, return the former answer. If x has not been queried, choose a random number r and add the (x, r) to H's hash list.

Commit Query(TPM2_Commit): If $\mathcal{A}$ makes a commit query with (P_1, l, str) as input, $\mathcal{B}$ first check if P_1 is equal to g or has been bound to the DAA key using TPM2_DAAbind, if not, returns fail. $\mathcal{B}$ calls the H_G oracle to get $P_2 = H_G(str) = g^r$ and the random number r. Now $\mathcal{B}$ knows $K_1 = P_1^x$ and $K_2 = h^r = P_2^x$. $\mathcal{B}$ chooses at random c and s and computes $R_1 := P_1^{ls} \cdot K_1^{-lc}$ and $R_2 := P_2^s \cdot K_2^{-c}$. $\mathcal{B}$ outputs (R_1, R_2, K_2) and a counter number ctr. $\mathcal{B}$ stores (c, s, ctr) Then $\mathcal{B}$ increases the ctr by 1. It is direct to see this simulation of commit query is perfect.

Sign Query(TPM2_Sign): $\mathcal{A}$ makes a sign query on m, the input are (c_h, m) and a counter number ctr. If ctr is not used before, $\mathcal{B}$ retrieves (c, s, ctr). Then $\mathcal{B}$ generates a random number n_T, and sets $c := H(c_h, m, n_T)$, store $((c_h, m, n_T), c)$ into the hash list of H, then output the (c, s, n_T), ctr is marked as used. Notice the failure only occurs if $H(c_h, m, n_T)$ has been queried before and the answer is $c' \neq c$. However, it is direct to see the chance this failure happens is negligible, because n_T is a newly-generated nonce by the TPM.

Forgery: $\mathcal{A}$ produces a signature $(m, \tilde{P}_1, \tilde{P}_2, \tilde{R}_1, \tilde{R}_2, \tilde{K}_2, c, s, n_T)$. According to the forking lemma, we can use $\mathcal{A}$ to output two signature $\sigma_1 = (m, \tilde{P}_1, \tilde{P}_2, \tilde{R}_1, \tilde{R}_2, \tilde{K}_2, c, s, n_T)$ and $\sigma_2 = (m, \tilde{P}_1, \tilde{P}_2, \tilde{R}_1, \tilde{R}_2, \tilde{K}_2, c', s', n'_T)$. We have $\tilde{R}_1 \cdot \tilde{K}_1^c = \tilde{P}_1^s$ and $\tilde{R}_1 \cdot \tilde{K}_1^{c'} = \tilde{P}_1^{s'}$. So $\tilde{K}_1^{c-c'} = \tilde{P}_1^{s-s'}$, thus we can calculate the discrete logarithm $x = (s - s')/(c - c')$. Notice calculating $x = (s - s')/(c - c')$ does not need to know $\tilde{K}_1 = \tilde{P}_1^x$.

Therefore, under the discrete logarithm assumption, the new `tpm.sign`* is secure.

6   Applications and Implementation of the New TPM.Sign* APIs

Now we show how to use our modified DAA APIs to implement LRSW-DAA [7], SDH-DAA [16]and U-Prove [17]. Then we present how our APIs can be implemented, particularly TPM2_DAAbind. Details about how to use the original APIs to implement LRSW-DAA, SDH-DAA and U-Prove can be found in [9].

6.1 Applications of the New APIs: DAAs and U-Prove

The LRSW-DAA Protocol

Join: The host calls TPM2_Create to get the $tpk = g^{tk}$, where tk is the DAA secret key. Then host proceeds the same as the join protocol using the original APIs. The host gets the DAA credential (A, B, C, D) which is a CL-LRSW signature on tk together with a proof of knowledge $\sigma_I = PK\{(r) : B = g^r \wedge D = tpk^r\}$ from the issuer. The host binds B with the DAA key tk by calling TPM2_DAAbind(B, D, σ_I) and stores the credential (A, B, C, D).

Sign: Given a nonce n_V, a message m, the host generate a random number $l \in Z_p$, calls TPM2_Commit(B, l, bsn). The TPM first checks that B is bound with tk, then outputs $R_1 = B^{lr}, R_2 = H_G(bsn)^r, K = H_G(bsn)^{tk}$. The host then uses the random number l to randomize the credential: $(R, S, T, W) = (A^l, B^l, C^l, D^l)$, notice that $R_1 = S^r$. The host calculate $c_h = H_3(R, S, T, W, J = H_G(bsn), K, R_1, R_2, n_V)$ and calls TPM2_Sign(c_h, m) to get a TPM signature $(c, s_f, n_T) = PK\{(k) : W = S^{tk} \wedge K = J^{tk}\}$. The final DAA signature is $(R, S, T, W, J, K, c, s_f, n_v, n_T)$.

The SDH-DAA Protocol

Join: The join process is almost the same as LRSW-DAA except that there is no need for the host to execute TPM2_DAAbind because when signing the first input of TPM2_Commit will always be g which is part of the DAA public key.

Sign: Given a nonce n_V, a message m, the host calls TPM2_Commit$(g, 1, bsn)$. The TPM first checks that g is part of the public key, then outputs $R_1 = g^r, R_2 = H_G(bsn)^r, K = H_G(bsn)^{tk}$. The host generate random numbers $a, r_x, r_a, r_b \leftarrow Z_p$, calculate $b = ax \mod p$, $T = Ah_2^a$, then uses R_2 to generate the random commitments used in the final proof of knowledge: $R_2' = e(R_2 T^{-r_x} h_2^{r_b}, g_2) e(h_2, w)^{r_a}$. The host calculate $c_h = H_3(J = H_G(bsn), K, T, R_1, R_2', n_V)$ and calls TPM2_Sign(c_h, m) to get a TPM signature (c, s_f, n_T). The host calculate $s_x = r_x + cx$, $s_a = r_a + ca$, $s_b = r_b + cb$, the final DAA signature is $(J, K, T, c, s_f, s_x, s_a, s_b, n_v, n_T)$.

U-Prove Using the New APIs. U-Prove is a pseudonym system based on the blind signatures and zero-knowledge proofs. In the U-Prove 1.1 specification, it is proposed that a U-Prove token can be protected by a hardware device. By using a hardware device, the leaked U-Prove token still can not be used unless the hardware device is also controlled by the adversary. Moreover, the hardware device can produce a ticket which is the same as in the DAA protocol to provide user-controlled linkability: the tickets generated by the same device key and basename are the same.

Using our new APIs to protect the U-Prove token is almost the same as using the original APIs [9]. While the input of the original TPM2_Commit is (g_d, str), the input of our new API TPM2_Commit is now $(g_d, 1, str)$. There is no need to execute TPM2_DAAbind as g_d is part of the TPM public key.

6.2   Efficiency Analysis

We have two targets: first the runtime performance of various protocols using the new tpm.sign* should still be as good as using the original tpm.sign, second the revised API should still be easy to be implemented in the TPM, as TPM is just a cheap chip.

Notice our newly added API actually have little influence on the run time performance of protocols including various DAA schemes and U-Prove. The host has only to run the new command TPM2_DAAbind once after the join protocol and then he can call TPM2_Commit and TPM2_Sign an arbitrary number of times.

The revise API TPM2_Commit is almost as efficient as the original TPM2_Commit: in the new API TPM2_Commit(P_1, l, str), the only operation added is now the TPM need to calculate $l \cdot r$ first, where $l, r \in Z_p^*$. Calculating $l \cdot r$ takes much less time than calculating a point multiplication in an elliptic curve. In our new API TPM2_Sign, the only operation added is generating a nonce n_T which is also very efficient. The computational workload of the host part using our APIs is the same as using the original APIs.

Implementing the new command TPM2_DAAbind will not add much cost to TPM as it only uses operation in G_1 which has already be implemented in TPM for supporting TPM2_Commit. Moreover, TPM 2.0 supports ECC Schnorr signature validation while the verification of $SPK\{(r) : P_1 = g^r \wedge K_1 = y^r\}$ in TPM2_DAAbind is similar to the verification of Schnorr signature. Thus extending the verification of Schnorr signature to support verification of $SPK\{(r) : P_1 = g^r \wedge K_1 = y^r\}$ would not be hard to implement.

The binding of P_1 with the DAA key is also easy to implement. Notice TPM 2.0 is able to protect the integrity of the key object by using a key hierarchy, so what we need to do is just adding the P_1 into the key object. Now the key object contains a new entry called daabind. When the object (DAA key) is not bound to any $P_1 \in G_1$, daabind equals to zero; if the object has been bound to a P_1, daabind equals to P_1. The detail of TPM2_DAAbind is as follows, we adopt the notation in [9]:

1. Given a DAA key pair tk = (tpk = (g, h), tsk), where tpk is the public key and tsk is the secret key, before TPM2_DAAbind is executed, the key blob of tk is tk* = (tsk)$_{SK}$ || tpk || MAC_{MK}((tsk)$_{SK}$ || tpk.name). tpk.name is a message digest of the public portion of tk. The integrity of the key object tk is protected by a message authentication code (MAC) using a MAC key MK and the secret key tsk is encrypted by a secret key SK, both SK and MK are derived from the parent key of tk: $(SK, MK) = KDF$(parentK). Thus the secrecy and integrity of tk is protected by the key hierarchy.

2. Given a pair (P, K) and a signature of knowledge $SPK\{(r) : P = g^r \wedge K = h^r\}$. TPM verifies the signature of the knowledge $SPK\{(r) : P = g^r \wedge K = h^r\}$, if it is right, generates a new key blob tk$_n^*$ which binds tk with P as follows. First TPM pads the tpk: tpk$_n$ ← tpk || P, then generate the new key name tpk$_n$.name = hash(tpk$_n$), finally generate the MAC for binding: MAC_{MK}((tsk)$_{SK}$ || tpk.name). TPM outputs the new key blob tk$_n^*$ = (tsk)$_{SK}$ || tpk$_n$ || MAC_{MK}((tsk)$_{SK}$ || tpk$_n$.name).

7   Forward Anonymity in the New TPM.Sign* Scheme

In this section, we prove that both LRSW-DAA and SDH-DAA satisfy forward anonymity using the new APIs under the Decision Diffie-Hellman assumption. Both LRSW-DAA and SDH-DAA utilize the bilinear pairing $e : G_1 \times G_2 \rightarrow G_T$. We prove the forward anonymity of LRSW-DAA and SDH-DAA under the G_1-Decisional Diffie-Hellman (DDH) assumption. The DDH assumption on G_1 is often known as the External Diffie-Hellman (XDH) assumption.

Theorem 3. *Under the $G_1 - DDH$ assumption, the implementation of LRSW-DAA using the new* tpm.sign* *satisfies forward anonymity. More specifically, if there is an adversary A that succeeds with a non-negligible probability to break the forward anonymity game, then there is a polynomial-time algorithm B that solves the $G_1 - DDH$ problem with a non-negligible probability.*

Proof: If there exists a adversary $\mathcal{A}$ that breaks the forward anonymity of LRSW-DAA, then we can build a polynomial-time simulator $\mathcal{B}$ that breaks the $G_1 - DDH$ problem as follows. The input to $\mathcal{B}$ is a tuple $(u, v = u^a, w = u^b, z = u^c) \in G_1 \times G_1 \times G_1 \times G_1$, where (a, b) are independent uniform random elements in Z_p, and either $c = ab$ or c is also a independent uniform random element in Z_p. By interacting with $\mathcal{A}$, $\mathcal{B}$ wants to find out whether c equals ab or c is a random element.

We first give a overview of the security proof. $\mathcal{B}$ first select a special trusted platform S^*, the secret key f of which is $a = log_u v$, however $\mathcal{B}$ does not know a. $\mathcal{B}$ creates the other trusted platform by honestly executing the Join protocol with $\mathcal{A}$. $\mathcal{B}$ uses the pair (u, v) to simulate the answers to queries about the trusted platform S^*. In the challenge phase, if $\mathcal{A}$ select S^* as one of the two challenge platform S_1, S_2, then $\mathcal{B}$ choose the bit b so that $S^* = S_b$, and calculate the challenge signature sig_c using the pair (w, z), so if $log_w z = log_u v$ then sig_c is a valid DAA signature signed by S^* and $\mathcal{A}$ should have advantage in deciding b, if $log_w z \neq log_u v$ then sig_c is actually a valid DAA signature signed under the DAA secret key $b^{-1} c$ which is independent of S_1 and S_2, so $\mathcal{A}$ can not have any advantage guessing b or may simply abort the game. So $\mathcal{B}$ can utilize $\mathcal{A}$ to judge whether $c = ab$. $\mathcal{B}$ works as follows:

Setup: choose (G_1, G_2) as a bilinear group pair of prime order p with generator $g_1 = u$ and g_2 respectively and a bilinear paring $e : G_1 \times G_2 \rightarrow G_T$. The gpk is $G_1, G_2, G_T, e, g_1 = u, g_2, p, H_G, H, H_3$, in which H_G is used by TPM in TPM2_Commit, H is used by TPM in TPM2_Sign, H_3 is used by host to generate c_h. $\mathcal{B}$ choose two random number $x, y \leftarrow Z_P$ as the issuer's secret key, and calculate $X = g_2^x, Y = g_2^y$ as the issuer's public key. $\mathcal{B}$ sends issuer's secret key and gpk to $\mathcal{A}$.

Hash queries: H_G and H are modeled as random oracles. $\mathcal{B}$ response to the hash queries about H_G and H the same as in the proof of theorem 2.

API queries:

- TPM2_Create: Given a TPM's identity T_i, If $T_i \neq T^*$ then $\mathcal{B}$ honestly execute this API, i.e. generates a secret key x and sets the public key $Y = u^x$; if $T_i = T^*$, $\mathcal{B}$ sets v as the public key and outputs it to $\mathcal{A}$

and sets $log_u v$ as the corresponding private key x, although B does not know x.

- TPM2_DAAbind: $\mathcal{B}$ act the same as in the proof of theorem 2.
- TPM2_Commit queries: Given a TPM's identity T_i, $P_1 \in G_1, bsn \in \{0,1\}^*$, $l \in Z_p$ as input, If $T_i \neq T^*$ then $\mathcal{B}$ honestly execute this API using the DAA secret key; if $T_i = T^*$, $\mathcal{B}$ act the same as in the proof of theorem 2.
- TPM2_Sign queries: Given a TPM's identity T_i, if $T_i \neq T^*$ then $\mathcal{B}$ honestly execute this API using the DAA secret key; if $T_i = T^*$, $\mathcal{B}$ act the same as in the proof of theorem 2.

Join queries: Given a trusted platform's identity T_i, $\mathcal{B}$ honestly execute the Join protocol with $\mathcal{A}$ by calling (the simulated) TPM2_Create, TPM2_Commit and TPM2_Sign queries described above, $\mathcal{B}$ stores the DAA credential obtained from $\mathcal{A}$.

Sign queries: Given a trusted platform's identity T_i, a message m, a nonce n_V, a basename bsn, $\mathcal{B}$ extracts the credential (A, B, C, D) then execute the Sign protocol by calling the TPM2_Commit query and TPM2_Sign query together to generate a valid DAA signature

Corrupt queries: Given a trusted platform's identity T_i, If $T_i \neq T^*$ then $\mathcal{B}$ outputs the DAA secret key. If $T_i = T^*$ then output "**Abort 1**".

Challenge: In the challenge phase, $\mathcal{A}$ output a message m, nonce n_V, two trusted platforms' identities T_1 and T_2. If $T^* \notin \{T_1, T_2\}$, then $\mathcal{B}$ quits and outputs "**Abort 2**". Otherwise, $\mathcal{B}$ chooses bit b such that $T_b = T^*$, and generate the challenge signature σ^* using w, z as follows:

1. $\mathcal{B}$ chooses a random $r \leftarrow Z_p$ and sets $J := w^r$ and $K := z^r$.
2. $\mathcal{B}$ generate the CL-LRSW credential $(A, B, C, D) \leftarrow (w, w^y, w^x \cdot v^{xy}, v^y)$ for (w, v). It is direct to see (A, B, C, D) is a valid CL-LRSW signature for $log_w v$.
3. Using a random number $l \leftarrow Z_p$, $\mathcal{B}$ calculate $(U, S, T, W) = (A^l, B^l, C^l, D^l)$.
4. $\mathcal{B}$ chooses at random c and s and computes $R_1 := S^s \cdot W^{-c}$ and $R_2 := J^s \cdot K^{-c}$. $\mathcal{B}$ calculate $c_h = H_3(R, S, T, W, n_V, R_1, R_2, J, K)$, generate a nonce n_T and set $H(c_h, m, n_T) = c$. If $H(n_T, c_h, m)$ has been queried before, $\mathcal{B}$ quits and outputs "**Abort 0**".

The final challenge signature is $(R, S, T, W, J, K, c, s, n_T, n_V)$. It is direct to see if $log_w(z) = log_u(v)$ then the challenge signature is a valid signature of trusted platform T^*; if not, then the challenge signature is a valid signature corresponds to DAA secret key $log_w(z)$ which is independent of $\{T_1, T_2\}$, so $\mathcal{A}$ can not have any advantage in deciding b.

Output. In the end, $\mathcal{A}$ outputs $b \in \{0, 1\}$ as the guess for b or aborts without any output. If $b = b$, then $\mathcal{B}$ outputs 1, which means that $z = u^{ab}$. Otherwise $\mathcal{B}$ outputs 0, which means that z is a random element in G_1.

We now analysis the probability that $\mathcal{B}$ does not abort in the above game. There are three case that $\mathcal{B}$ may abort, we discuss each case as follows:

Abort 0. The chance that this type abortion happens is $O(1/p)$, where p is a large prime, so the probability is negligible.

Abort 1. Notice that $\mathcal{A}$ can not corrupt all the trusted platforms, so the probability that this abortion does not happen is at least $1/q_j$.

Abort 2. This abortion does not happen if in the challenge phase, $\mathcal{A}$ chooses T^* as one of the $\{T_1, T_2\}$, so the probability that this abortion does not happen is at least $1/q_j$.

So the the probability that $\mathcal{B}$ does not abort in the above game is at least $1/q_j$, (if the **Abort 2** does not happen, then **Abort 1** should not happen, as the trusted platforms chosen in challenge phase must not be corrupted).

Let ε be the advantage of $\mathcal{A}$ in breaking the forward anonymity game. Assume that $\mathcal{B}$ does not abort when simulating the above game, if $z = u^{ab}$, then $\mathcal{B}$ simulate the game perfectly, so $\mathcal{A}$ will still have the same advantage in winning the forward anonymity game. If z is a random member in G_1, then the challenge signature is a valid signature corresponds to DAA secret key $log_w(z)$ which is independent of $\{T_1, T_2\}$, so $\mathcal{A}$ can not have any advantage in deciding b. So if $\mathcal{B}$ does not abort, then he can break the $G_1 - DDH$ assumption with advantage at least $\varepsilon/2$.

Theorem 4. *Under the $G_1 - DDH$ assumption, the implementation of SDH-DAA using the new* tpm.sign* *satisfies forward anonymity. More specifically, if there is an adversary $\mathcal{A}$ that succeeds with a non-negligible probability to break the forward anonymity game, then there is a polynomial-time algorithm $\mathcal{B}$ that solves the $G_1 - DDH$ problem with a non-negligible probability.*

Proof: The basic idea of this proof is analogous to that of theorem 3. The key point is that $\mathcal{B}$ can simulate all the queries which has been proved above. Due to the page limit, the proof will be presented in the full version.

8 Conclusion

In TPM 2.0, a single signature primitive is proposed to support various signature schemes including DAA, U-Prove and Schnorr signature. This signature primitive is split into two parts (TPM2_Commit and TPM2_Sign) and there is no restriction on the input of TPM2_Commit. However, this gives too much ability to the outside, thus these APIs can be utilized as a static Diffie-Hellman oracle and forward anonymity can not be satisfied. We propose new APIs which not only remove the static Diffie-Hellman oracle but also support the forward anonymity thus significantly improve the security of DAA and the other signature schemes supported by TPM 2.0. Our new APIs are almost as efficient as the original APIs in TPM 2.0 specification and can still support LRSW-DAA, SDH-DAA and U-Prove. We believe our research actually shows the importance of reducing the potential attack surface, i.e., limiting the ability provided to the outside, the ability should be just sufficient to be functional.

Acknowledgments. We thank the anonymous reviewers for their valuable comments. This work has been supported by the National Natural Science Foundation of China (under grants No.91118006 and No.61202414) and the National 973 Program of China (under grants No.2013CB338003).

References

1. Trusted Computing Group: TCG TPM specification 2.0 (2012),
   https://www.trustedcomputinggroup.org
2. Brickell, E., Camenisch, J., Chen, L.: Direct anonymous attestation. In: Proceedings of the 11th ACM CCS, ACM, pp. 132–145 (2004)
3. Trusted Computing Group: TCG TPM specification 1.2 (2003),
   https://www.trustedcomputinggroup.org
4. Brickell, E., Chen, L., Li, J.: A new direct anonymous attestation scheme from bilinear maps. In: Lipp, P., Sadeghi, A.-R., Koch, K.-M. (eds.) Trust 2008. LNCS, vol. 4968, pp. 166–178. Springer, Heidelberg (2008)
5. Chen, X., Feng, D.: Direct anonymous attestation for next generation TPM. Journal of Computers 3(12), 43–50 (2008)
6. Chen, L., Morrissey, P., Smart, N.P.: DAA: Fixing the pairing based protocols. Technical report, Cryptology ePrint Archive, Report 2009/198 (2009)
7. Chen, L., Page, D., Smart, N.P.: On the design and implementation of an efficient DAA scheme. In: Gollmann, D., Lanet, J.-L., Iguchi-Cartigny, J. (eds.) CARDIS 2010. LNCS, vol. 6035, pp. 223–237. Springer, Heidelberg (2010)
8. Brickell, E., Chen, L., Li, J.: A (Corrected) DAA scheme using batch proof and verification. In: Chen, L., Yung, M., Zhu, L. (eds.) INTRUST 2011. LNCS, vol. 7222, pp. 304–337. Springer, Heidelberg (2012)
9. Chen, L., Li, J.: Flexible and scalable digital signatures in TPM 2.0. In: Proceedings of the 2013 ACM CCS, pp. 37–48. ACM (2013)
10. Brickell, E., Chen, L., Li, J.: A Static Diffie-Hellman Attack on Several Direct Anonymous Attestation Schemes. In: Mitchell, C.J., Tomlinson, A. (eds.) INTRUST 2012. LNCS, vol. 7711, pp. 95–111. Springer, Heidelberg (2012)
11. Acar, T., Nguyen, L., Zaverucha, G.: A TPM Diffie-Hellman oracle. Technical report, Cryptology ePrint Archive: Report 2013/667 (2013)
12. Brickell, E., Chen, L., Li, J.: Simplified security notions of direct anonymous attestation and a concrete scheme from pairings. International Journal of Information Security 8(5), 315–330 (2009)
13. Chen, L.: A DAA scheme requiring less TPM resources. In: Bao, F., Yung, M., Lin, D., Jing, J. (eds.) Inscrypt 2009. LNCS, vol. 6151, pp. 350–365. Springer, Heidelberg (2010)
14. Barreto, P.S.L.M., Naehrig, M.: Pairing-friendly elliptic curves of prime order. In: Preneel, B., Tavares, S. (eds.) SAC 2005. LNCS, vol. 3897, pp. 319–331. Springer, Heidelberg (2006)
15. ISO/IEC: ISO/IEC 15946-5:2009 information technology – security techniques – cryptographic techniques based on elliptic curves – part 5: Elliptic curve generation
16. Brickell, E., Li, J.: A pairing-based DAA scheme further reducing TPM resources. In: Acquisti, A., Smith, S.W., Sadeghi, A.-R. (eds.) TRUST 2010. LNCS, vol. 6101, pp. 181–195. Springer, Heidelberg (2010)
17. Microsoft: U-Prove cryptographic specification v1.1 (2013),
   http://www.microsoft.com/u-prove
18. Brown, D.R., Gallant, R.P.: The static Diffie-Hellman problem. IACR Cryptology ePrint Archive, 306 (2004)
19. Pointcheval, D., Stern, J.: Security arguments for digital signatures and blind signatures. Journal of cryptology 13(3), 361–396 (2000)

Continuous Tamper-Proof Logging Using TPM 2.0

Arunesh Sinha[1], Limin Jia[1], Paul England[2], and Jacob R. Lorch[2]

[1] Carnegie Mellon University, Pittsburgh, Pennsylvania, USA
{aruneshs,liminjia}@cmu.edu
[2] Microsoft Research, Redmond, Washington, USA
{pengland,lorch}@microsoft.com

Abstract. Auditing system logs is an important means of ensuring systems' security in situations where run-time security mechanisms are not sufficient to completely prevent potentially malicious activities. A fundamental requirement for reliable auditing is the integrity of the log entries. This paper presents an infrastructure for secure logging that is capable of detecting the tampering of logs by powerful adversaries residing on the device where logs are generated. We rely on novel features of trusted hardware (TPM) to ensure the continuity of the logging infrastructure across power cycles without help from a remote server. Our infrastructure also addresses practical concerns including how to handle high-frequency log updates, how to conserve disk space for storing logs, and how to efficiently verify an arbitrary subset of the log. Importantly, we formally state the tamper-proofness guarantee of our infrastructure and verify that our basic secure logging protocol provides the desired guarantee. To demonstrate that our infrastructure is practical, we implement a prototype and evaluate its performance.

1 Introduction

Run-time security mechanisms often are not sufficient to completely prevent malicious activities. Under such circumstances, auditing system logs is an important means of ensuring systems' security. A fundamental requirement for reliable auditing is the integrity of log entries. Adversaries may benefit significantly from tampering with log entries; for instance, malware may erase log entries recording its installation or presence in order to avoid detection and subsequent removal by anti-malware software. Or, an authorized insider may view private customer data in violation of company policy, then remove evidence of his malfeasance from the access log so that audits do not detect it.

There has been much work on developing tamper-proof logging protocols [1–5]. These protocols aim to attest to the integrity of logs as well as detect tampering of logs by the adversary. Some provide tamper-proofness by online commitments of current log state [3]; others store logs in secure memory [4]. Some use the TPM monotonic counter to attest to the integrity of every log entry [2]; others use hash chain based approach [1]. However, these schemes do not meet the stringent

T. Holz and S. Ioannidis (Eds.): TRUST 2014, LNCS 8564, pp. 19–36, 2014.

requirements for tamper-proof logging in today's computing environment. Next we explain these requirements through a realistic scenario.

Consider a scenario, where the organization, by means of auditing, aims to enforce policies such as, "confidential documents stored on company-owned devices must never be transferred to an external USB storage device." The organization mandates that all employee devices, such as laptops and iPads, run an application that monitors actions relevant to the policy. The logging infrastructure needs to protect audit logs on these devices. Since many of these devices are often offline, the *first requirement* is that the integrity of the audit log is not dependent on continuous connectivity to a central server. Adding a log entry should not require connection to a server. Further, the device could power off, then restart with no connectivity to the network (e.g., the device is turned on during flight). Consequently, a *second requirement* is that the logging infrastructure needs to preserve its continuity across power cycles without contacting a remote server.

It is difficult to segregate security-relevant events from security-irrelevant ones. The logging process is often required to capture a large variety of events from many processes (e.g., OS, browser). Therefore, a *third requirement* is that logging should be fast enough to support high-frequency log updates. Finally, devices have only limited disk space. The *last requirement* is that the logging infrastructure should work with limited disk space for storing logs.

All aforementioned schemes lack at least one of the features required for our application: they lack support for either offline tamper-proofness [3, 5]; or large logs on the order of gigabytes [4]; or continuous logging across power cycles [1, 6]; or high frequency logging [1, 2, 4, 7, 8]. In this paper, we present a logging infrastructure that satisfies all of these requirements. The security guarantee of our logging infrastructure is based on a *forward integrity* adversary model [9], where the adversary can obtain administrative privileges and take complete control of the system. Our infrastructure ensures that the adversary's actions leading up to the action of compromising the machine will be logged and cannot be tampered with, and therefore, can be detected.

Our logging infrastructure is mainly composed of two entities: a logger and a verifier. Initially, the logger and the verifier share a secret key. As the system executes, the logger generates a new key for every new log entry, and uses the key to compute the HMAC of the log entry in order to attest to the log entry's integrity. The key sequence is generated as a *hash chain*; the initial key is known only to the logger and verifier, similarly to the scheme by Schneier et al. [1]. At any given time point, only the key on top of the chain is used; older keys are deleted from memory. When an adversary takes control of the system, it cannot find old keys in memory. The hash-chained key sequence ensures that, without knowledge of the initial key, old keys cannot be derived from the key currently stored in memory. Thus, the adversary cannot produce valid HMACs for earlier log entries.

To allow high-frequency logging, our hash chain is constructed in software, instead of the PCR registers in the TPM. This greatly reduces the time required to append a log entry. Furthermore, we develop mechanisms that allow *truncation* of the log after verification and allow a verifier to efficiently verify any subset of the log. As a result, our infrastructure works with limited disk space.

One of the main novelties of our infrastructure, compared to Schneier et al. [1], lies in leveraging TPM 2.0 features to maintain the continuity and secrecy of the key chain *across a power cycle*. Specifically, we use the ability to seal data to values of a TPM monotonic counter, which TPM1.2 does not allow. At system shutdown, we create a *blob* by sealing the last key before powering off to the value of a TPM monotonic counter. Upon device restarts, the logger can recover the key by unsealing the blob. Our creation of *use once and discard* blobs for logging is a novel use of TPM 2.0's sealing to a monotonic counter feature.

In addition to the design and prototype implementation of our infrastructure, we formally verify the tamper-proofness property of the basic protocol, which we consider as one of our key contributions. We believe this is the first formal proof of security for a logging protocol. The analysis brings out a number of assumptions that the system must satisfy to ensure tamper-proofness.

The rest of the paper is organized as follows. We define the adversary model and review TPM 2.0 features in Section 2. Our logging protocols are presented in Sections 3 and 4. Section 5 details the verification steps of the basic protocol. We describe our prototype implementation and evaluation results in Section 6. Section 7 discusses related work.

Due to space constraints, we omit details of several definitions and verification steps, which can be found in our companion technical report [10].

2   Overview

Review of TPM2.0. We list features of TPM2.0 that are key to ensuring tamperproofness property of our protocols [11].

NV Memory. TPM 2.0 allows for a larger non-volatile memory than TPM 1.2. Its expected size is more than a megabyte.

Monotonic NV Counter. Any memory slot in NV memory can be tagged as a monotonic counter, which can only be incremented; it starts with a value greater than the maximum of all counters that ever existed in this TPM.

Enhanced Authorizations. TPM 2.0 provides enhanced authorization by defining authorization policies, which can be the conjunctions and disjunctions of basic policies. Basic policies include checking whether an NV memory location stores a specified value and whether a PCR contains a specified value. These authorization policies can be used to implement data sealing.

Power Failure Counter. TPM 2.0 has a special 32-bit NV monotonic counter *resetCount* that can be modified by the TPM only. This counter is incremented on a power failure, and thus provides a count of the number of power failures.

Adversary model. We consider an adversary that controls processes that reside on the same machine as the logging process. We assume that the adversary never controls the hardware, i.e., she cannot snoop on electrical signals, or conduct side-channel attacks by observing physical signals like power consumption. We distinguish between two phases of a system that runs our logging infrastructure. These two phases are separated by the event that the adversary takes control of the machine by gaining root privilege. We assume that in the first phase, the adversary does not have root privileges.

3   The Basic Protocol (Protocol A)

In this section, we present our basic protocol (Protocol A), and provide informal arguments for its tamper-proofness.

3.1   Protocol Description

Protocol A specifies the behavior of four entities: the logger, the verifier, the TPM, and the OS. We call each entity a role in the protocol. We explain the logger program, as it is the most complex component and uses novel TPM features. We briefly discuss the verifier program and omit the OS and TPM.

Logger. The logger uses a sequence of keys $(key(0), key(1),...key(n))$ to produce HMACs of the log data, which arrives sequentially. We annotate each key with the index i of its position in the sequence. The key sequence is a hash chain starting with secret $key(0)$, which is a secret shared between the logger and verifier. The nth key is the hash of the $n-1^{th}$ key: $key(n) = hash(key(n-1))$.

The logger has four phases: startup, logging, shutdown, and verification.

Startup. At machine startup, a sealed key object (sealed blob containing the key) is stored in a designated location *sKeyLoc* on the hard disk. This blob is sealed to the current value of the monotonic TPM counter. Initially, the first sealed key object for $key(0)$ is set up by the administrator. Subsequent sealed key objects are stored by the logger during shutdown.

The logger first acquires locks on its memory locations, the disk location *sKeyLoc* storing the sealed key object, and the disk location *fileLoc* storing the log. These locks prevent any attacker without root privileges from reading from and writing to these locations. They are implemented using mechanisms such as process memory isolation and access control in the file system. On a system restart, these locks are released. Next, the logger unseals the sealed key object to obtain the current key and then increments the TPM counter. At this point, the sealed key object can no longer be unsealed.

Logging. After startup, the logger, upon receiving new log data, (1) produces an HMAC of the data using the current key $key(k)$, (2) writes the log data and HMAC to disk, (3) generates $key(k + 1)$ by computing the hash of the old key $key(k)$, and (4) irretrievably erases the old key from the RAM.

The logger does not use the hash chain feature that TPM offers via PCRs. Instead, it computes the hash in software, which vastly improves the logger's performance, because hashing in memory is much faster than using PCRs.

Shutdown. Upon receiving a shutdown notification, the logger finishes processing the queue of logs, and then seals the current key to the current monotonic TPM counter value and writes the sealed key object to disk. This phase ensures that when the machine starts up again, there is a sealed key object stored on disk. Protocol A requires the shutdown module of the OS to guarantee that the logger is able to finish its shutdown phase before the machine is powered off.

Verification. The verification phase is triggered by a verification request from an external verifier; a nonce is sent with such a request. Upon receiving such a request, the logger sends back the log entries (log data and HMACs) stored on disk, and the HMAC of the nonce using the current key.

Verifier. The verifier initiates the verification phase by sending a nonce along with the verification request to the logger. Upon receiving log entries containing both log data and its HMAC and the HMAC of the nonce using the last key, the verifier checks the HMAC of each log entry and the HMAC of the nonce. The verifier has the initial shared secret and can generate all the keys.

3.2   Informal Argument for Tamper-Proofness

We explain informally why Protocol A satisfies the tamper-proofness property. Formal analysis of Protocol A is presented in Section 5.

We refer to keys that have smaller indices than the current key used by the logger as old keys. The following two properties hold: (1) an attacker cannot learn the old keys and (2) without the old keys, the attacker cannot tamper with the logs generated prior to the attacker gaining root privilege, i.e., modify entries, remove entries, and truncate the log.

Property (1) holds both before and after the attacker gains root privilege. Before the attacker gains root privilege, the memory and disk locations are properly protected. When the attacker gains root privilege, it has access to all memory and disk locations. However, old keys are not present in the machine's memory as the logger erases these keys upon generation of the next key. The sealed key objects of these old keys cannot be used to extract keys, because these sealed key objects are sealed to past values of the NV monotonic counter of the TPM and there is no way to decrement the counter value. In particular, if the adversary deletes the monotonic counter (by means of his root privilege), then any new monotonic counter will start with the maximum value of all counters that ever existed on the TPM. Finally, the keys form a hash chain, and, therefore, there is no way to generate the old keys directly from the current key. (2) follows directly from (1) and the property of HMACs: without the correct key, an attacker cannot generate valid HMACs that pass the verification. Tamper-proofness follows from (1) and (2).

4   Enhanced Protocol (Protocol B)

The basic protocol (Protocol A) has the tamper-proofness property, but is not very practical. Enhanced protocol (Protocol B) uses additional mechanisms to satisfy the following practical requirements. (1) Hard disk space is limited, and, thus, logs need to be periodically truncated. (2) Power failures may not permit the logger's shutdown phase to complete, leading to the loss of the current key. The protocol needs to be able to recover from power failures. (3) For efficient and modular enforcement of several policies, the protocol needs to support verification of an arbitrary subset of the log independently.

4.1 New Mechanisms

Branched Key Chain. The enhanced protocol evolves keys in a branched manner. Keys are divided into epochs. The initial keys of each epoch form a hash chain staring from $key(0)$. The initial key for epoch k is computed as: $key(k) = hash(key(k-1) \mid "epoch")$. There is a fixed maximum number (E) of keys within an epoch. These keys form another hash chain indexed by the epoch number and a sub-epoch number. The ith sub-epoch key in epoch k $(key(k,i))$ is $hash(key(k,i-1) \mid "subepoch")$. Here, $key(k,0) = key(k)$.

Mapping between Keys and Log Entries. To increase the flexibility of the verification and relieve the verifier from the burden of deriving key indices for checking HMACs, we incorporate key index information into the log data. Each log entry now includes the log data, the epoch and sub-epoch indices of the key producing the HMAC, and an HMAC of the log data and the key indices.

4.2 Protocol Description

Logger. The logger in Protocol B cycles through the same phases as in Protocol A. To maintain the branched key chain, the logger starts a new epoch either when the previous epoch is completed or at startup. We first describe the sub-routine that is invoked when a *new epoch* starts. For brevity, we omit the argument of the location of the NV counter from seal and unseal, as this protocol uses only a fixed monotonic counter. The pseudo code is shown in Figure 1.

New epoch. In this sub-routine, the sealed object from location $sKeyLoc$ is unsealed to obtain the current epoch key. Then, the next epoch key is computed and sealed to the next TPM counter value. Finally, the TPM counter is incremented and the epoch and sub-epoch counters are set appropriately.

A power failure that occurs in the middle of the new epoch routine could create a discrepancy between the TPM monotonic counter value and the value that the sealed blob on disk is sealed to. If the power failure occurs right after the instruction that writes the sealed blob to disk and before the TPM counter is incremented, the TPM counter value will be one step behind the value that the sealed blob is sealed to. The startup phase handles this situation.

Startup. Similarly to Protocol A, the logger locks critical locations in memory and on disk (and releases them on a restart). Next, it invokes the new epoch sub-routine. Depending on whether the previous power-off is a clean shutdown or a power failure, the sealed blob stored on the hard disk at startup is sealed to

NewEpoch Sub-routine	Logging Phase
$epochkey \leftarrow unseal$(data in $sKeyLoc$) **if** $unseal\ fails$ **then** $\quad \llcorner$ return $fail;$ $nextepochkey \leftarrow$ $hash(epochkey \mid$ "$epoch$") $n \leftarrow$ read TPM counter $sKeyLoc \leftarrow seal(nextepochkey, n + 1)$ increment TPM counter $key \leftarrow epochkey$ $epoch \leftarrow n;\ subepoch \leftarrow 0$	**while** $no\ shutdown\ notification$ **do** $\quad data \leftarrow$ get log data $\quad logentry \leftarrow (data \mid epoch \mid subepoch,$ $\quad hmac(data \mid epoch \mid subepoch, key))$ $\quad$ increment $subepoch$ $\quad key \leftarrow hash(key \mid$ "$subepoch$") $\quad$ write $logentry$ to disk $\quad$ **if** $subepoch = E$ **then** $\quad\quad \llcorner$ start newepoch phase start shutdown phase

Startup Phase	Shutdown Phase
lock all required memory locations start newepoch phase if failure, increment TPM counter start newepoch phase if successful, notify the OS	wait for log producer to stop **while** $message\ queue\ is\ not\ empty$ **do** $\quad \llcorner$ process data as in logging phase $finaldata \leftarrow hash(key \mid shutdown)$ process $finaldata$ as in logging phase

Fig. 1. Programs for Protocol B, not including the verifier stage

either the current value of the monotonic TPM counter or that value incremented by one. If the new epoch sub-routine fails to unseal the key, then TPM counter is incremented and the new epoch sub-routine is called again.

Logging. The logger computes keys in the branched key chain. It computes a new sub-epoch key for each new log entry until the maximum sub-epoch number is reached. At this point, a new epoch key is computed by invoking the new epoch sub-routine. For each log entry, the logger places the epoch and sub-epoch indices in the log to build an explicit mapping between log entries and keys.

Shutdown. In the shutdown phase, all remaining log entries are processed. Unlike protocol A, the logger does not create a sealed blob for the current key, as this has been done inside each new epoch sub-routine during logging. Instead, it writes a special log entry $hash(key \mid shutdown)$ to disk indicating the completion of a clean shutdown. The absence of such an entry at machine startup is the evidence of a power failure.

Verification. The verification phase of the logger is the same as protocol A, except for the deletion of logs after each successful verification and attestation of the *resetCount* value in TPM. The verifier sends a ticket containing encrypted information about how many epochs have been verified. The logger stores this ticket on disk and sends this ticket back to the verifier along with log entries in response to the next verification request.

Verifier. Differently from protocol A, the verifier starts by asking for the value of *resetCount* to determine if there was a power failure. The verifier additionally generates a ticket attesting to the successful verification up to a check point for

Verification Phase	Verifier Program
attest to *resetCount*.	ask for attestation of *resetCount*
nonce ← recv from verifier	*powfail* ← current *resetCount* $\neq$ old *resetCount*
fhmac ← hmac(*nonce*, *key*)	*nonce*, *r* ← generate nonces
log ← read whole log	send *nonce* to logger
tct ← read ticket	$(fhm, log, enc_V(n|r'))$ ← recv from logger
send (*fhm*, *log*, *tct*) to verifier	check r' is nonce used in last ticket, halt if not
recv. (*st*, *tct*, *del*) from verifier	*epochkey* ← $hash^n(sharedsecret|$"epoch"$)$
if *st* = *1* then	*logavailable* ← true; *idx* ← 0
save *tct* to disk	while *logavailable* do
delete epochs till *del*	*key* ← *epochkey*; $n \leftarrow n + 1$
	for *j*: *0* to *E-1* do
	if *no more log entries* then
	logavailable ← false; break
	verifyhmac($log(idx)_{data}, log(idx)_{mac}, key$)
	if *log entry data is* "shutdown" then
	break
	$idx \leftarrow idx + 1$; *key* ← $hash(key|$"subepoch"$)$
	epochkey ← $hash(epochkey|$"epoch"$)$
	verifyhmac(*nonce*, *fhm*, *key*)
	if *all* verifyhmac *pass and not powfail* then
	send $(1, enc_V(n-1|r), n-1)$ to logger

Fig. 2. Verification stage programs for Protocol B

the logger. The verifier, after verification till epoch k (the last verified epoch), sends a ticket to the logger stating that the verification till epoch k is successful. The ticket is an encryption: $enc_V(k \mid r)$, where k is the last verified epoch, r is a nonce known only to the verifier and V is the public key of the verifier. The ticket is sent to the verifier in the next verification phase along with log entries from epoch $k + 1$. The verifier uses the information from the ticket sent by the logger to jump to the appropriate epoch key to start the verification.

The verifier's pseudo code is shown in Figure 2. The verifier, upon receiving the log and the ticket, decrypts the ticket to obtain the epoch index. If the ticket is valid, the verifier computes the sub-epoch key and begins verification. In the end, the verifier generates a new ticket and sends it to the logger. It is also easy to modify the verifier to verify any subset of the log by making use of the *epoch* and *subepoch* indices contained in each log entry.

4.3   Improvements to the Logging Infrastructure

We highlight how the extensions to the protocol address the practical concerns that we summarized at the beginning of this section.

Rolling Logs. Using the ticket, the logger can delete logs up to a verification check point. Instead of sending the entire log starting from the first log entry, the logger only needs to send the ticket for the first k epochs and the log starting from the $k+1$ epoch. To further lower the requirement of disk space for storing the HMACs of logs, it is possible to store a hash of all HMACs in an epoch after the completion of the epoch, instead of storing each HMAC.

Recovery from Power Failure. A power failure may prevent the logger from completing the shutdown phase and storing the current key to disk. As a result, the logger in Protocol A has no way of deriving the valid key at the next startup without help from a remote server. The branched key chain used in Protocol B offers a means to recover from such a loss. Dividing the keys into epochs allows the logger to periodically store the sealed blob of the next epoch key to disk without sacrificing performance. Upon rebooting after a power failure, the logger simply increments the TPM counter to retrieve the key from disk.

Portions of the log buffered in memory that are not written to disk due to a power failure are lost. However, a power failure can be detected by the verifier by checking the value of TPM's *resetCount* counter.

Modular Log Analysis. With the epoch and sub-epoch indices stored with each log entry, the verifier can request the logger to send portions of the log entries that it wants to verify. One application is enforcing multiple policies on the same system modularly. Each policy analysis can select relevant portions of the log and perform the verification independently; as the verifier can compute the keys based on the *epoch* and *subepoch* information contained in each log entry.

4.4   Design Choices and Limitations

Power Attacks. One limitation of our infrastructure is that we cannot distinguish genuine power failures from adversarial system crashes. An attacker can hide malicious activities before the power failure because log entries buffered in memory are lost. Existing logging schemes that use volatile memory for buffering logs [1] or even work in verifiable computation [12] suffer from the same problem. Our choice of using volatile memory for log buffering is driven by the desire to accommodate high-frequency logging. Accesses to non-volatile memory (hard disk or TPM) are slow; thus, it is not feasible to use them to process each log entry. Additional hardware support could mitigate this problem.

Tradeoffs between Performance and Security Guarantees. Disk write operations are expensive, and, therefore, the bigger the size of the buffered log entry blocks, the more efficient the logger program becomes. However, in case of a power failure, the logger loses the log entries buffered in memory, which may record adversary actions. Consequently, the security guarantee becomes weaker as the block size increases. This problem is mitigated in protocol B by allowing offline recovery from a power failure and detection of the power failure.

Another tradeoff lies in our decision to hash keys in RAM instead of the TPM to accommodate high-frequency log updates. A potential issue is that non-root processes may coerce a root process to write the memory to disk, e.g., by stressing the system memory, and thus leak the keys. Special precaution need to be taken to protect memory regions that store the keys, which we leave for future work.

Suggested Hardware Features to Defend against Power Attacks. One way to prevent power attacks is to rely on hardware support to allow for a clean shutdown in spite of a power failure. One possibility is to provide a "fast" memory interface for NV memory of the TPM with assured write on a power failure. The logger uses the NV memory as a buffer instead of the RAM. The logger always maintains an entry composed of a string "power failure" and its HMAC using the current key. This last log entry is never written to disk, except after recovering from a power failure when the TPM NV memory content is flushed to disk. An attacker cannot generate the last entry on its own, so tampering with entries stored in the TPM NV memory can be detected. This scheme requires the logger to compute an additional HMAC for every log entry. However, software HMAC is very fast and is unlikely to be a performance bottleneck.

5 Verification

We augment the modeling language and program logic from an existing work [13, 14] and formally prove that Protocol A satisfies the tamper-proofness property. Protocol B uses similar techniques to ensure tamper-proofness, so the verification results of Protocol A can be straightforwardly extended to Protocol B.

System Modeling. We assume the system has a set of principals $\mathcal{P}$ and there is a partial order on the principals: we write $\hat{X} \preceq \hat{Y}$ if $\hat{Y}$ is more privileged than $\hat{X}$, i.e., can access all the resources that $\hat{X}$ can. We write $\widehat{root}$ to denote the root and $\widehat{tpm}$ to denote TPM. $(\mathcal{P}, \preceq)$ is an access control lattice, where the maximal elements are $\widehat{root}$ and $\widehat{tpm}$.

The system is modeled as several components, which we call *threads*, running concurrently. Each thread is owned by a principal. Threads share several common data structures, which include storage (RAM and disk) and read and write locks on storage. The logger, verifier, OS, and TPM are encoded using our modeling language. Other threads (including adversary) in the system are modeled as arbitrary programs interacting with the rest of the system. Their behavior is constrained by our adversary model, which is specified by predicates stating a principal's knowledge based on what it has learned so far. For instance, a principal can compute the HMAC of d using key k if it has both the data and the key. This resembles Dolev-Yao's network adversary.

The behavior of the system is captured by the set of traces generated by all possible interleaving executions of the threads. The security property is specified as a first-order logic formula that holds on every trace of the system.

Predicates. We define the predicates used in the verification. Action predicates, summarized below, describe the semantics of actions such as read and write, with @ u denoting the time u when the predicate holds.

Read(i, l, m)@u	: thread i reads m from location l
Write(i, l, m)@u	: thread i writes m to location l
Hmac(i, d, l, m)@u	: thread i produces $m = hmac(d, k)$
	where key k is stored in location l
VerifyHmac(i, m, d, k)@u	: thread i verifies $m = hmac(d, k)$

Other key predicates used in the verification are shown below.

Mem(l, m)@u	: location l has value m
CanRead(i, l)@u	: i can read location l
IsReadLocked(i, l)@u	: thread i holds the read lock of l
HT$(i, \hat{X}, e)$@u	: thread i owned by $\hat{X}$ runs expression e
Has(i, s)@u	: thread i knows s
Owner$(i, \widehat{K})$	: principal $\widehat{K}$ owns thread i
Contains(m, m', S)@u	: m' can be derived from m using S
MayDerive(e, e', S)	: e' can be derived from e using S

The Contains(m, m', S) predicate is true when the term m' can be extracted from m using elements of the set S; for instance, m is an encryption of m' using a key k and S contains the key k. It is defined with respect to an inductively-defined predicate MayDerive. One example rule is that MayDerive$(e, hash(e), S)$ is true without any premises: from a term e, its hash can always be computed. Predicate Has(i, s) is true if thread i has the plain text of s. It is defined using Contains: i has s if there exists a term m that contains s, and thread i receives m or reads m from the storage. These predicates state the assumptions that cryptographic functions are correct and thus capture the adversary's capabilities.

Axioms about Actions. Our proof also uses sound axioms specifying the semantics of actions. We show the axioms for generating and verifying HMACs below.

Axiom A_1 states that on successful verification, it is the case that someone must have produced the HMAC with a key stored in location l. Axiom A_2 states that if a thread j computes a HMAC using a key key based on location l, it must be the case that j can read l. Similar to the Has predicate, these axioms also state assumptions about the correctness of cryptographic functions.

A_1 $\forall i, mac, d, key, u.$ VerifyHmac(i, mac, d, key) @ $u \supset$
$\qquad \exists j, l, u'.(u' < u) \wedge$ Hmac(j, d, l, mac) @ $u' \wedge$ Mem(l, key) @ u'
A_2 $\forall j, mac, d, key, u.$ Hmac(j, d, l, mac) @ $u \supset$ CanRead(j, l) @ u

System Assumptions. System assumptions are specified as axioms as well. We define three axioms for this: one specifies the capability of the forward-integrity adversary, one specifies an assumption about the processes running during the logger's startup phase, and one specifies the effect of the access control lattice. We write u_a to denote the time when the adversary gains root privilege.

The following axiom specifies that before time u_a, processes owned by $\widehat{root}$ are well-behaved and do not interfere with the logger. Predicate RW(i, L)@u is true if thread i reads from or writes to any location in the set L at time u. The axiom states that processes owned by $\widehat{root}$ do not access any of the storage locations owned by the logger (specified as LoggerLoc), and only threads running with the privilege of the OS can access locations shared between the OS and the logger (specified as LoggerOSLoc).

$$A_{adv} \quad = \forall u \leq u_a.\ \mathsf{NoAdv}(u)$$
$$\mathsf{NoAdv}(u) = \forall i.\ \mathsf{Owner}(i, \widehat{root}) @ u \supset (\forall L.\ \mathsf{LoggerLoc}(L) \supset \neg\mathsf{RW}(i, L) @ u)$$
$$\wedge\big(\forall L.\mathsf{LoggerOSLoc}(L) \wedge \mathsf{RW}(i, L) @ u \supset \mathsf{HT}(i, \widehat{root}, \mathsf{OS}) @ u\big)$$

Axiom A_{NR} states that before the machine is compromised, after any reset, no thread reads and unseals the sealed key before the logger increments the TPM counter. Predicate $\mathsf{Early}(u)$ is true if u is a time point between a reset and the logger incrementing the TPM counter and there are no other resets or counter incrementing operations between them.

$$A_{NR} = \forall u, i, m.\ \mathsf{Early}(u) \wedge (u \leq u_a) \wedge \neg\mathsf{HT}(i, \hat{L}, \mathsf{LOGGER}) @ u$$
$$\supset \neg\mathsf{Read}(i, M.disk.sKeyLoc, m) @ u$$

This may seem to be a strong assumption; however, verifying that it holds on a real system is feasible. We discuss this further at the end of this section.

The protection provided by the access-control lattice to guard sensitive operations is captured using axioms similar to the one shown below, which specifies the effects of the lattice on memory read accesses.

$$A_{RDLattice} = \forall i, j, u, l, I, K.\ \mathsf{IsReadLocked}(i, l) @ u \wedge \mathsf{Owner}(i, I) \wedge I \prec K \wedge$$
$$\mathsf{Owner}(j, K) \supset \mathsf{CanRead}(j, l) @ u$$

If a location l is locked by a thread i owned by principal I, then any thread j owned by a principal K higher than I on the access control lattice can read l.

Verification Goal. We define an auxiliary predicate $\mathsf{LastLogIdx}(k, u, u_{end})$ to state that before time u_{end}, the last log entry the logger writes is indexed by k, and written at time u. We write γ to denote the context containing all the axioms introduced so far. The main result of our verification is a derivation of the following judgment:

$$\gamma \vdash \forall k, k', u_b, u_e, u_l, u_r, u_w, i, j, log, n, fhm.\ \mathsf{HT}(i, \hat{V}, \mathsf{VERIFIER}) \text{ on } [u_b, u_e] \wedge$$
$$(u_b < u_c < u_r < u_v < u_e) \wedge \mathsf{Send}(i, VERIFY)@u_b \wedge \mathsf{New}(i, nonce)@u_c \wedge$$
$$\mathsf{Recv}(i, (log[n], n, fhm)) @ u_r \wedge \mathsf{VerifyHmac}(i, fhm, nonce, key(n+1))@u_v \wedge$$
$$((u_r \leq u_a) \supset \mathsf{LastLogIdx}(k, u_l, u_r)) \wedge ((u_r > u_a) \supset \mathsf{LastLogIdx}(k, u_l, u_a)) \wedge$$
$$(1 \leq k' \leq k) \wedge (u_l \geq u_w) \wedge \mathsf{Write}(j, fileloc(k'), v) @ u_w$$
$$\wedge \mathsf{HT}(j, \hat{L}, \mathsf{LOGGER}) @ u_w \supset data(v) = data(log(k'))$$

It says that if the verifier completes successfully then for the log data received by the verifier at time u_r, the received data at index k' is the same as the log data v that was written to disk by the logger at index k', conditional on the assumption that k' was written to disk by the logger before time $\min(u_r, u_a)$. In other words, the log entries written before the adversary took control at time u_a

will not pass verification if they are tampered with. The formula to the right of the ⊢ is the formal definition of the tamper-proofness property.

Derivation Steps. The proof of the tamper-proofness property relies on the following four invariants. Predicate keyOwnerIn(u) states that at time u only the logger, TPM, and verifier have the key. keyMemIn(u) states that at time u the only locations that may have the key reside in the memory owned by the logger, or the memory shared between the logger and the TPM, or the disk location that contains the sealed key object. Predicate oldKeyAdv(u, u_a) states that at time u, no thread other than the logger, TPM, or verifier has an old key (key used before time u_a). Finally, predicate oldKeyNotInMem(u, u_a) states that at time u, no memory location contains an old key (key used before time u_a).

1. $\forall u. u \leq u_a \supset$ keyOwnerIn(u)   3. $\forall u. u > u_a \supset$ oldKeyAdv(u, u_a)

2. $\forall u. u \leq u_a \supset$ keyMemIn(u)   4. $\forall u. u > u_a \supset$ oldKeyNotInMem(u, u_a)

The proofs of these invariants use transfinite induction on time; given the invariants hold before time u, we prove that they hold at u. In particular, we use the program logic to reason about the protocol roles to show that these invariants are maintained when programs belonging to these roles execute in an adversarial environment.

From (1) and (2), we can prove that the adversary does not have access to any valid keys generated before time u_a at any time prior to u_a. (3) and (4) imply that, after u_a, the adversary cannot obtain keys that were generated prior to time u_a. From the above, we can conclude that at no time does the adversary possess keys used by the logger prior to time u_a. Then, it can be shown that the adversary cannot produce valid log entries generated before time u_a, which is the desired tamper-proofness property.

Design Decisions Based on Verification. One important system assumption that the tamper-proofness property depends on is A_{NR}: at any time (before the adversary gets root access) between the machine startup and the logger startup, no process should read the sealed blob on disk. The fact that the logger starts soon after machine startup after a reset makes the number of running threads during that period of time small. The remote attestation feature of the TPM can be used to check that A_{NR} holds by verifying the code that runs on system reset. This assumption leads to important design decisions of the logger. For example, to satisfy this assumption, the logger cannot be implemented as a user-level application. It would be extremely difficult to ensure the tamper-proofness property of such a design, because the logger may not be the first user application to start and other user applications starting before the logger cannot be trusted.

Several axioms (e.g., $A_{RDLattice}$) capture the requirements of access-control lattice. For these axioms to be sound in reality, we need to ensure that the implemented access control mechanisms are correct and cannot be compromised by threads not owned by $\widehat{root}$. For instance, we use process isolation to protect logger-owned memory locations.

Table 1. Time to log 100,000 entries with varying block size

Block size	Total time (ms)	Disk time (ms)
512	5,135	2,513
256	6,675	4,056
128	11,074	8,320
64	15,882	12,997
32	29,148	25,505
16	53,306	49,168

Table 2. Time (in seconds) to verify logs in a serial manner

Log size	#log entries	Verif. time (s)
175MB	1,211,168	27
390MB	2,684,760	61
736MB	5,075,958	116
1.48GB	10,198,014	234

6 Implementation and Evaluation

Implementation. We implement a prototype logger and verifier based on Protocol B. Our logger application is a user-level Windows service that uses the ETW logging framework of Windows 7 to receive events from applications and log them. Our implementation relies on the assumption that services in Windows are trusted (see the discussion in Section 5). However, we need not trust any user-level application because services start before these applications. We use keys and HMACs of 256 bits and use SHA256 to produce keys. A 64-bit NV memory location is designated as the monotonic counter that keys are sealed to.

We used a 2.8GHz quad core machine with 6GB of RAM. We use a TPM 2.0 simulator that opens two network ports to receive binary TPM commands and return appropriate responses after processing those commands. The TPM simulator is built from the TPM 2.0 specs and models all TPM 2.0 functionality. We also use a C# TPM library that offers an easy interface to the TPM.

The most significant challenge that we faced in the implementation was that high-level languages that use garbage collectors do not usually provide language support for secure erasure of memory objects, because the memory manager (garbage collector) moves objects around. Though C# offers pinning of memory that can be used to securely erase memory, the use of C# libraries that do not pin memory makes securely erasing keys extremely difficult. However, the tamper-proofness property requires secure erasure of the memory objects that store the keys. Hence, we implement an intermediate layer in C such that the current key always lives in the memory of the C process. This C process uses the TPM library to interact with the TPM. Also, to avoid unexpected behavior due to compiler optimizations we used SecureZeroMemory, which is a guaranteed way of setting memory in Microsoft's version of C.

Our implementation relies on the process memory isolation provided by the operating system to implement locks on volatile memory to prevent an attacker from gaining access to the key during startup phase. We rely on user privilege access control to implement locks on disk.

The prototype system was stable across clean shutdowns and power failures.

Evaluation. Table 1 shows the logger's log-processing time given different block sizes. As the block size grows, the processing time decreases, and so does the percentage of disk time over the total processing time. This shows that the bigger the block size, the more efficient the logging process. However, the system becomes less secure as block size increases; the attacker has a better chance of hiding its activities in buffered logs that will be discarded after a power failure.

Our storage overhead for HMACs for approximately 32 million log entries is 1 GB. If we store hashes of HMACs in an epoch, then with an E value (sub-epoch number) of 1000, the storage overhead of 32 billion log entries is 1 GB. Thus, the storage overhead of the HMACs is not a bottleneck. Further, with periodic verification, log entries can be removed frequently.

Table 2 shows the evaluation results of the verifier's performance. Verification is reasonably fast, even with simple sequential verification. We expect a huge speed up if the verification process is parallelized using pre-computed keys.

7   Related Work

Secure Logging Schemes. Auditing has been studied extensively; for example, in the context of detecting misconfiguration in access control policies [15, 16], and in the context of holding agents accountable for their actions [17]. Security guarantees provided by these systems are based on the assumption that logs are tamper-proof.

Most closely related to our approach is work by Kelsey and Schneier [1, 18]. They also use a hash chain of keys to ensure the integrity and confidentiality of logs. Our main improvement over theirs is that we support continuous logging across machine restarts, which they do not. Our protocol allows truncation of logs after verification. As we only care about integrity of log entries, our scheme is much simpler than theirs, and therefore allows for faster log appending operations. They additionally study variants of untrusted verifier, which we do not consider. It is straightforward to extend our protocol using the ideas introduced by Kelsey and Schneier to lift the assumption that the verifier is trusted. Follow-up work [19, 20] does not tackle the issues we address in this paper, and instead, focuses on making the encrypted log searchable [19] or implementing the scheme [20]. Recent work addresses the issue of log deletion required by law [6] and uses similar scheme as [1, 18], but does not work across system restarts and lacks formal verification.

Monotonic counters have been used to ensure the tamper-proofness of logs [2, 8, 7]. They use the monotonic counter inside the attestation of each log entry, whereas we use a software-based hash chain of keys to generate attestations for log entries and only use the counter on system startup/shutdown to ensure the continuity and secrecy of the keys. More concretely, we seal the current key to the counter value using the TPM. The sealed blob is unrecoverable after the counter increments. Thus, we create *use and discard* blobs, which is a novel use of the monotonic counter. Because we do not use the TPM in normal logging activities, our log appending operation is much faster than that in prior work. In the best case, our scheme appends approximately 20, 000 log entries per second using a Intel 2.8GHz processor with 6GB RAM (Table 1), much faster than prior similar schemes [3, 2, 20, 1, 8, 7]. The best of these schemes can process 1750 entries per second using Intel Core 2 Duo 2.4GHz CPU with 4GB of RAM [3]. A2M, another work on secure logging that precedes TrInc, stores logs in trusted memory [4]. Due to the limited size of trusted memory, this scheme is not practical to be used to protect logs on the order of gigabytes, which our work aims to support.

There has been much work on designing efficient data structures for storing logs along with auxiliary information (such as a hash tree) to provide guarantees of tamper-proofness [21–23, 3, 5]. For instance, the work by Crossby et al. [3] provides a dynamic history tree data structure to store the log and capture the history of log insertions through commitments. These structures require publishing the updated state of the auxiliary data structure quite frequently; e.g., after each log addition. However, in our scenario, external communication may not be feasible given the high bandwidth requirement of logs generated at high frequency. While these schemes are effectively online schemes, our scheme provides the forward integrity guarantee in an offline manner, even if the verifier does not verify before the adversary takes control. Also, our infrastructure is able to append logs at much faster rate due to the simplicity of our approach.

Other Schemes That Use Trusted Hardware. TPMs have been used extensively to design schemes that guarantee some form of trust in computing devices, in spite of malicious software running on the device [24, 25, 12]. We use the TPM to protect a key by producing a sealed object of the key that can only be unsealed when the TPM's monotonic counter has a specific value. Incrementing the counter makes the object unsealable by this TPM in the future.

Due to practical constraints, such as size, power consumption and cost, the TPM is limited in its functionality, e.g., small non-volatile memory that degrades with about 100,000 writes. An ideal hardware solution for tamper-proof logging is trusted secure hardware that stores the whole log itself, guaranteeing not only detection of tampering but also recovery of the tampered logs. Other hardware like iButtons [26] has been used in secure logging [20] that implements the scheme of Kelsey and Schneier [1]. While they provide many of the guarantees that our scheme can, they do not address the issue of auditing across power cycles, and their implementation is slow in appending log entries ($\sim$1 second for an append).

The challenge of distinguishing power failures from malicious power attacks that we face is also encountered in another work using the TPM for secure code execution [12]. A trusted power source or a fail-safe power failure mechanism is needed to allow TPMs to shutdown cleanly in case of a power failure.

Formal Verification of System Software. Formally verifying the security guarantees of critical system software has become increasingly important. Several projects have demonstrated the value of formal verification (e.g., [27, 14, 28]). The high-level goal of our work is the same. A model of an adversary against forward integrity was proposed by Bellare et al. [9], which is the same adversary model in our formal verification. As far as we know, we are the first to formally specify the two-phase adversary model and the forward integrity property in logic. Another semi-formal model proposed by Crossby et al. focuses on specifying integrity as prefix consistency of a log and its extension [3], which essentially requires online commitment of log entries. Therefore, that model is not relevant to our logging scenarios. Ma et al. provide a cryptographic style definition of the security properties of a hash chain [29, 30], much like Bellare et al. [9] However, unlike our analysis, they cannot verify security properties of logging protocols, as they lack the logic/language framework to reason about protocols.

Our verification technique is based on the compositional reasoning principles developed by Garg et al. [13] We additionally allow dynamic forking of new threads and resetting the machine, which are essential in modeling and reasoning about the behavior of protocols across machine resets and power failures.

8   Conclusion

Our secure logging protocols use new TPM features to guarantee forward integrity of logs in an offline setting and address practical issues such as limited disk space, high-frequency log updates, and unexpected power failures. As future work, we are interested in investigating how to select log block sizes for optimal balance between the strength of the security guarantees and performance. One promising direction is to include an adaptive block size choice module that takes into consideration the costs of security and performance. Another issue we want to explore is the scheduling priority for the logger process, so that other processes are not able to exhaust machine resources with the aim of preventing logging and causing a system crash.

Acknowledgment. This work was supported in part by the AFOSR MURI on Science of Cybersecurity and NSF CNS-1018061. Part of this work was done while Arunesh Sinha was an intern at Microsoft Research, Redmond.

References

1. Schneier, B., Kelsey, J.: Cryptographic support for secure logs on untrusted machines. In: USENIX Security (1998)
2. Levin, D., Douceur, J.R., Lorch, J.R., Moscibroda, T.: Trinc: Small trusted hardware for large distributed systems. In: NSDI (2009)
3. Crosby, S.A., Wallach, D.S.: Efficient data structures for tamper evident logging. In: USENIX Security (2009)
4. Chun, B.-G., Maniatis, P., Shenker, S., Kubiatowicz, J.: Attested append-only memory: Making adversaries stick to their word. ACM SIGOPS Operating Systems Review 41(6), 189–204 (2007)
5. Snodgrass, R.T., Yao, S.S., Collberg, C.: Tamper detection in audit logs. In: VLDB (2004)
6. Von Eye, F., Schmitz, D., Hommel, W.: A framework for secure logging with privacy protection and integrity. In: ICIMP (2014)
7. Sarmenta, L.F.G., van Dijk, M., O'Donnell, C.W., Rhodes, J., Devadas, S.: Virtual monotonic counters and count-limited objects using a TPM without a trusted OS. In: ACM STC (2006)

8. van Dijk, M., Rhodes, J., Sarmenta, L.F.G., Devadas, S.: Offline untrusted storage with immediate detection of forking and replay attacks. In: ACM STC (2007)
9. Bellare, M., Yee, B.: Forward integrity for secure audit logs. Technical report, University of California at San Diego (1997)
10. Sinha, A., Jia, L., England, P., Lorch, J.: Continuous tamper-proof logging using TPM 2.0. Technical Report CMU-CyLab-13-008, Carngie Mellon University (2013)
11. TrustedComputingGroup: TPM library specification,
    http://www.trustedcomputinggroup.org/
    resources/tpm_library_specification
12. Parno, B., Lorch, J.R., Douceur, J.R., Mickens, J.W., McCune, J.M.: Memoir: Practical state continuity for protected modules. In: IEEE S&P (2011)
13. Garg, D., Franklin, J., Kaynar, D.K., Datta, A.: Compositional system security with interface-confined adversaries. In: MFPS (2010)
14. Datta, A., Franklin, J., Garg, D., Kaynar, D.K.: A logic of secure systems and its application to trusted computing. In: IEEE S&P (2009)
15. Vaughan, J.A., Jia, L., Mazurak, K., Zdancewic, S.: Evidence-based audit. In: CSF (2008)
16. Bauer, L., Garriss, S., Reiter, M.K.: Detecting and resolving policy misconfigurations in access-control systems. ACM Transactions on Information and System Security 14(1) (2011)
17. Feigenbaum, J., Jaggard, A.D., Wright, R.N.: Towards a formal model of accountability. In: NSPW (2011)
18. Kelsey, J., Schneier, B.: Minimizing bandwidth for remote access to cryptographically protected audit logs. In: RAID (1999)
19. Waters, B.R., Balfanz, D., Durfee, G., Smetters, D.K.: Building an encrypted and searchable audit log. In: NDSS (2004)
20. Chong, C.N., Peng, Z.: Secure audit logging with tamper-resistant hardware. In: IFIP SEC (2003)
21. Naor, M., Nissim, K.: Certificate revocation and certificate update. In: USENIX Security (1998)
22. Goodrich, M.T., Tamassia, R., Schwerin, A.: Implementation of an authenticated dictionary with skip lists and commutative hashing. In: DISCEX (2001)
23. Martel, C., Nuckolls, G., Devanbu, P., Gertz, M., Kwong, A., Stubblebine, S.G.: A general model for authenticated data structures. Algorithmica 39(1), 21–41 (2004)
24. McCune, J.M., Parno, B.J., Perrig, A., Reiter, M.K., Isozaki, H.: Flicker: An execution infrastructure for TCB minimization. ACM SIGOPS Operating Systems Review 42(4), 315–328 (2008)
25. Parno, B., McCune, J.M., Perrig, A.: Bootstrapping trust in commodity computers. In: IEEE S&P (2010)
26. MaximIntegrated: What is an iButton device?
    http://www.maximintegrated.com/products/ibutton/ibuttons/
27. Jang, D., Tatlock, Z., Lerner, S.: Establishing browser security guarantees through formal shim verification. In: USENIX Security (2012)
28. Klein, G., Elphinstone, K., Heiser, G., Andronick, J., Cock, D., Derrin, P., Elkaduwe, D., Engelhardt, K., Kolanski, R., Norrish, M., Sewell, T., Tuch, H., Winwood, S.: seL4: formal verification of an OS kernel. In: SOSP (2009)
29. Ma, D., Tsudik, G.: Forward-secure sequential aggregate authentication. In: IEEE S&P (2007)
30. Ma, D., Tsudik, G.: A new approach to secure logging. Trans. Storage 5(1), 1–2 (2009)

Affordable Separation on Embedded Platforms

Soft Reboot Enabled Virtualization on a Dual Mode System

Oliver Schwarz, Christian Gehrmann, and Viktor Do

SICS Swedish ICT
{oliver,chrisg,viktordo}@sics.se
http://www.sics.se/groups/security-lab-sec

Abstract. While security has become important in embedded systems, commodity operating systems often fail in effectively separating processes, mainly due to a too large trusted computing base. System virtualization can establish isolation already with a small code base, but many existing embedded CPU architectures have very limited virtualization hardware support, so that the performance impact is often non-negligible. Targeting both security and performance, we investigate an approach in which a few minor hardware additions together with virtualization offer protected execution in embedded systems while still allowing non-virtualized execution when secure services are not needed. Benchmarks of a prototype implementation on an emulated ARM Cortex A8 platform confirm that switching between those two execution forms can be done efficiently.

Keywords: Dual Mode, Separation, Soft Reboot, Virtualization, Hypervisor, Embedded Systems, Security.

1 Introduction

Embedded systems are becoming more powerful, distributed and globally connected. We see a transition from classical single function embedded systems to powerful collaborative special purpose computing devices often controlling sensitive or critical infrastructure functions, so called *cyber-physical systems*. In the past, software attacks were mainly targeting high performance computers such as desktop computers, laptops, and recently also mobile devices. This is about to change rapidly. Security threats against cyber-physical systems have become a severe issue, requiring strong platform security protection techniques such as separation [26] without overly increasing performance or system costs.

The need for separation of security critical data and code on mobile devices motivated ARM to introduce the TrustZone technology [4], available for some (but not all) ARM systems. TrustZone is a System-on-Chip (SoC) isolation technique that establishes a high degree of separation between *trusted* and *non-trusted* execution, while keeping context switches fast. To distinguish between trusted and non-trusted address space, TrustZone adds an additional address bit

T. Holz and S. Ioannidis (Eds.): TRUST 2014, LNCS 8564, pp. 37–54, 2014.

to the bus system. In order to not break isolation, careful SoC adaptations at the design level of application specific integrated circuits (ASIC) are necessary to make memory interfaces, interrupt controllers, Direct Memory Access (DMA) devices etc. aware of that bit.

System virtualization is an alternative way to protect security critical assets [15,16]. However, in tiny embedded systems with limited hardware virtualization support, system virtualization implies a non-negligible performance overhead [12]. On the other hand, security services typically do not run on the system all the time. They can be scheduled on a regular basis to perform monitoring or be called upon demand (e.g., for secret key operations).

In this paper we propose an alternative system virtualization enabled approach for separation, based on dual mode execution, i.e., the ability of choosing between virtualized and non-virtualized execution mode, and switching between the modes through soft reboots. The goal of the solution is to provide separation while keeping both performance overhead and required SoC adaptations to a minimum. Only a few hardware adaptations to an existing architecture are required. In one of the typical use cases, a service for proving the device's identity to its environment wants to keep the authentication key secret from the rest of the system. The system would run non-virtualized in the majority of the time, but activate the trusted service domain only for the actual authentication process. The exchange of required challenge-response-messages throughout that process will happen via remote procedure calls (RPCs).

Different from general purpose hypervisors (also called virtual machine monitors (VMM)) such as Xen [19] and KVM for ARM [12], a hypervisor with the purpose of separation or monitoring has a more focused scope and several optimizations can be made. We have developed a tiny hypervisor for ARM Cortex A8 with focus on separation. It was recently released as open source, and isolation properties of one version of this hypervisor have been formally verified on binary level. Based on this hypervisor, FreeRTOS as main guest, and emulated ARM Cortex A8 hardware enriched by our hardware extensions, we have implemented the suggested approach for dual mode protected execution. Benchmark figures show the feasibility of the concept. The main costs for enabling isolated services consists of their decryption and the integrity check of those services and of the lightweight hypervisor. Returning to non-virtualized execution does not take much longer than the erasure of newly produced confidential data.

Contrary to other approaches, that are for example based on TrustZone or trusted computing enabled late launch [17], the solution presented in this paper does not require any particular CPU architecture or extensions to the CPU, which keeps costs low and makes the concept applicable to a large set of embedded systems. Summarized, our solution offers the following benefits:

1. Trusted domains can be executed with guaranteed separation without causing performance overhead in phases where their services are not required.

2. If desired and the use case allows the resulting latency, the commodity OS can be paused throughout the protected phase, so that trusted domains can execute without the need of paravirtualization[1] of the commodity OS.[2]

3. The proposed protocol includes a secure boot scheme, so that confidentiality and integrity of hypervisor and trusted domains are maintained even in the presence of external accesses to their non-volatile storage.

2   Hardware and Protocol

We consider a concept that relies on minor adaptations on SoC design level to make it possible to run the system in two modes, *protected mode* and *normal mode*. In protected mode a dedicated hypervisor runs in the most privileged level on each CPU in the system and trusted guests (such as secret key services) can run separated by the commodity OS, while in normal mode no hypervisor needs to be present in the system, as depicted in Figure 1 for a single CPU system.[3] Priviliged software can cause transitions between modes by requesting a *soft reboot* (also referred to as *soft reset* or *warm reboot*), which is initiated by the system's reset signal.

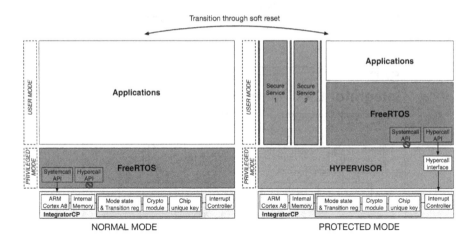

Fig. 1. Dual mode operation

---

[1] Paravirtualization [28, p. 422] describes any modification of guest operating systems, in order to enable their execution on a virtualized environment instead of bare metal, e.g. by making them use software interrupts (*hypercalls*) to perform privileged operations, according to the hypervisor's API.

[2] Depending on the scenario, interrupts would be recorded by the hypervisor or just masked during the pause.

[3] Here, we illustrate a single CPU architecture, but the principle can easily be extended to a multicore architecture, see Section 2.1.

The SoC contains two special purpose *volatile* memory registers: a *mode state register* and a *transition register*. The mode state register states whether the system is currently in protected or normal mode. The transition register is used to state the intention of commodity OS or hypervisor about which mode to enter. The mode state register can *only* be changed in early booting phases. Thereafter it will be locked through a sticky bit so that it can not be modified anymore until a chip reset (and consequently a soft reboot) occurs. The boot code responsible for the hypervisor and OS kernel launch determines which mode to boot into - and consequently the value to set in the mode state register. In a *cold boot* (full hardware reset) the default mode value is given by a boot configuration. In a warm/soft reboot the value is determined by the transition register, as set by the higher level software.

When running in protected mode, the hypervisor controls sensitive applications, I/O devices and data and can protect the system from illegal access to these units. This can be achieved using the normal Memory Management Unit (MMU) or Memory Protection Unit (MPU) present in most systems. If applicable, additional hardware protection support can be utilized, such as an Input/Output MMU (IOMMU). The memory protection mechanisms are also used to make sure that, when running in protected mode, a soft reboot to normal mode can *only* be initiated by the hypervisor or hypervisor protected units, such as a watch dog timer reset function (placed in a protected address space).[4]

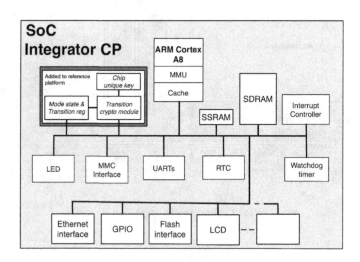

Fig. 2. SoC system view

---

[4] As discussed in Section 5.2, unprivileged software can at most achieve a soft reboot to protected mode or a cold reboot.

Figure 2 shows a SoC design according to the approach and the proof of concept implementation we have done using emulated hardware (see Section 5). In addition to the two special purpose registers, the SoC design includes one or several chip unique secret key(s), stored in non-volatile registers. They are used to decrypt and check the integrity of security critical code/data that is loaded into the chip internal or external RAM. To prevent any usage of the chip unique secrets in normal mode, they are tied to the mode state register and locked to protected mode. In our proof of concept implementation we have optimized performance with a fully functional cryptographic module, the *transition crypto module*. However, cryptographic operations can be performed in software as well, reducing the number of changes to integrated circuits, but at the prize of an increased performance overhead. If not mentioned otherwise, we assume the presence of a transition crypto module in the remainder of the paper.

In order to show how these SoC components are used in the suggested approach, below we describe the details of the cold boot, the transition from protected to normal mode and the transition from normal to protected mode.

Cold Boot. The following steps are performed in a cold boot:

1. After the machine is powered on, a first stage boot code is executed. To prevent security from being compromised, this code needs to be protected from modifications by storing it in write-protected memory such as on-chip-ROM.
2. The first stage boot code loads the integrity protected second stage boot code and boot configurations into on-chip-RAM. The second stage boot code and its configurations are protected with signatures verifiable with a public key stored in write-protected memory, such as ROM, or hardware registers, such as e-fuse registers.
3. The first stage boot code reads the verified boot configurations and writes the default boot mode (normal or protected) into the mode state register, which is then locked.
4. The first stage boot code launches the second stage boot code. Depending on the system and use case, one or several intermediate boot stages are processed until the boot code responsible for hypervisor or operating system launch is reached. We call this boot stage *transition boot stage*.
5. The transition boot stage reads the current value of the mode state register. If the register indicates normal mode, the operating system indicated in the boot configurations is launched. If the register indicates protected mode, the following steps are performed:
   (a) The transition boot code loads hypervisor, trusted guest(s) and data from external memory and verifies the integrity (e.g., by using a transition crypto module). The confidentiality of trusted guests is protected through fast symmetric encryption with a chip unique secret key. If required, confidentiality protection can also be applied to the hypervisor or parts thereof.
   (b) If decryption and integrity verification in the previous step were successful, the transition boot code hands over the execution to the hypervisor.

Otherwise, the transition boot stage code clears all security sensitive data on the system, writes "normal mode" into the transition register and issues a soft reset, so that the system reboots into normal mode. This allows the system to recover even if it could not be started into protected mode.

Transition from Protected to Normal Mode. When the system is in protected mode and secure services are no longer needed on the system, the hypervisor switches the system back to normal mode, as follows:

1. All trusted guests currently running are halted by the hypervisor. If required, persistent data is stored, integrity and confidentiality protected. Subsequently, the memory of trusted guests is cleared.
2. All confidential hypervisor data is cleared from memory.
3. The hypervisor can choose to maintain non-confidential code/data in memory to avoid reloading and reinitializing when returning to protected mode. In that case, *Message Authentication Codes* (MACs) protecting the integrity are recomputed, given that the concerned memory regions have changed.
4. The hypervisor sets the transition register to "normal" and issues a SoC-wide (soft) reset signal. This can be done via the component containing the two special purpose registers. The resulting soft reboot of the system will keep the content of most volatile memories, which allows a rather quick booting process without the need to reload all code and data from non-volatile memories.

At reset, the system will be booted into normal mode (analogous to the previous paragraph) running the OS kernel in the most privileged CPU mode as "usual", i.e., as in a non-virtualized system (see Figure 1). Before handing over execution to the commodity OS, the boot code clears all registers to avoid that confidential data from a protected mode phase is leaked into normal mode.

Transition from Normal to Protected Mode. When the system is in normal mode and one or several security critical services are required, the commodity operating system writes "protected" into the transition register and issues a soft reset signal. It can inform the hypervisor about requested services and their parameters by writing service request values into dedicated transition memory before the reset. Subsequently, the boot is performed in analogy to the cold boot into protected mode, retrieving mode information from the transition register. However, the commodity OS is not loaded again and, if chosen so, the non-confidential parts of the hypervisor (such as code, page tables, constants) are not either. In contrast to that, integrity verification is always performed, possibly even for new memory regions used by, for example, page tables created in the previous hypervisor session. If hypervisor memory has been compromised in normal mode or protected mode has not been active before, a fallback option will (re-)load the entire hypervisor from the storage as done in cold boot. Once the system is rebooted, the hypervisor will check the requested secure service(s) by reading the transition memory and launch them with the given parameters after checking that both services and parameters are valid and sound. Alternatively, this information can be passed via a hypercall from the commodity OS, once it is invoked by the hypervisor.

On a mode transition in either direction the commodity OS is usually aware of the upcoming soft reboot and will pause active processes as well as store their contexts before releasing control. Those processes (kept in memory) can then easily be resumed in the new mode. Before the hypervisor or OS reconfigures the peripherals, it needs to check whether interrupts (masked throughout the soft reboot) have occurred. Depending on the use case, the boot code can also be used to record events in a queue. In typical scenarios, the user will be aware of the inherent latency.

2.1 Implementation Alternatives

Enforced Protected Mode through Watch Dog Timer. An alternative realization of the presented approach connects the watch dog timer of the SoC to the mode state register, so that the timer can *only* be reset if the system is in protected mode. If not kept alive, the watch dog issues a soft reset. At soft reset, the transition boot stage code checks the status of the watch dog timer and if it has reached zero, the transition boot code will boot the system into protected mode, *independently* of the transition register. This *forces* the system into protected mode in some pre-defined time intervals, which can be useful for monitoring or to counteract denial of other trusted services.

Soft Reboot Enabled by TrustZone. The ARM TrustZone technology for ARM11 and ARM Cortex embedded processors [4] offers support for creating two securely isolated virtual cores (or *worlds* as they are termed) on a single real core. Both *secure world* and *normal world* manage an own virtual MMU, as well as an own vector table and thus own exception handlers [13]. System hardware, including memory and peripherals, can be allotted to each world. This is realized by an additional address bit. However, that separation requires that peripheral devices are adapted to the setting. A transition between the worlds is initiated by a hardware interrupt or a *Secure Mode Call* (SMC), both invoking the so called *monitor mode*, which is responsible for context switches. The concept of turning a hypervisor on and off on demand, as described in this paper, can also be implemented based on TrustZone instead of the discussed hardware extensions. Bootloader, hypervisor, trusted guest and the current mode would then be kept stored in the memory of the secure world, which only executes code to realize the soft reboot transitions. The execution of all other software (including the hypervisor and the trusted guest) happens in the normal world. Soft resets would be realized through SMCs. One of the advantages of this variant is that no soft reboot specific hardware extension in form of, e.g., a mode state register is required, something which is especially useful when TrustZone is already present anyway. Furthermore, keeping assets in the secure world reduces the need for crypto operations considerably. However, a secure boot scheme would still be needed to ensure that the hypervisor and the trusted guest(s) are loaded into the secure world memory confidentially and integrity protected. Hardware protected keys are therefore still required. Moreover, peripherals have to be adapted in order to maintain separation between the two worlds. This limitation together with the costs of the TrustZone extension makes a TrustZone driven implementation variant only preferable to the standard one if the soft reboot is to be enabled on an already existing system that (including its peripherals) supports TrustZone from the beginning.

Multicore Systems. The presented solution is also applicable to multicore systems. Since the mode state is a global property to control access to the chip unique keys, all CPUs have to agree on the mode. Consequently, when in protected mode, all CPUs need to be protected by a hypervisor, irrespectively if they are running secure services or not. There would be some *master* hypervisor on the system, which has the responsibility to coordinate, to execute trusted services and to issue soft reboots. In order to switch from protected to normal mode, the master hypervisor would inform its neighbors and wait until it has received acknowledgments from all of them before issuing the actual reset signal. Likewise, when booting into protected mode, the master hypervisor will be booted first on the main CPU and then launch all other hypervisors.

3   Hypervisor

A prototype implementation for the described solution has been established on the basis of a type-1 hypervisor[5], available as open source from [27]. Its focus lies on providing security by MMU-supported separation and its isolation properties have been formally verified on binary level [11]. Following the system virtualization principle, it allows the parallel execution of multiple paravirtualized guests in user mode. Both Linux and FreeRTOS have been ported to the hypervisor. Isolation between guests can intentionally be relaxed by the possibility to communicate with well-defined and parameterizable RPCs via the hypervisor. In addition to inter-guest-separation, the hypervisor offers introspection features such as virtual guest modes that enable intra-guest-separation as well, for example in order to maintain the guest OS' kernel separation even when executing in the processor's non-privileged operation mode. The implementation of the hypervisor comprises 2717 lines of C code and 942 lines of assembly, resulting in a compiled binary of 31 KB. The hypervisor was developed for single-core ARMv5 and ARMv7 architectures and deployed on Beaglebone [9], Beagleboard [7], Beagleboard-xM [8], NovaThor [29] and the Integrator development board [3], as well as on emulated platforms within the OVP framework [24].

---

[5] Hypervisors of type 1, also called native hypervisors, are not running on any host OS, but on bare metal.

4   Software Adaptions

We have implemented a single-core prototype of the solution, based on FreeR-TOS as commodity OS and the inhouse hypervisor for ARMv7 described in Section 3. Both FreeRTOS and the hypervisor had to be modified to support the soft reboot functionality, as described in this section. The trusted domain was easily implemented since it only needs to offer an entry point for receiving RPCs and the awareness about the RPC parameter passing protocol. Three different interrupt vector tables were configured and are mapped according to the mode; while the vector of the boot code is only referred to on reset, the hypervisor vector is active in protected mode and FreeRTOS' vector is either referred to directly (in normal mode) or used to receive control from the hypervisor. Otherwise, memory mapping is static and access rights only change in dependency to the current mode. Binaries are linked/built separately for each entity and, where required, encrypted and/or integrity protected before deployment.

Adaptations to the Commodity OS. The core adaptation in the commodity OS consists of changes that enables it to run both as guest on top of the hypervisor and natively on bare metal with control over the privileged operation ring of the CPU. While in the latter setting, privileged operations are performed directly by the corresponding privileged instructions, hypercalls have to be used in the first setting. We added a dual API layer that selects the required implementation for each functionality in dependency of a mode indicating configuration bit set by the bootloader. Similarly, FreeRTOS was made able to switch between its own kernel separation enforcement and the kernel protection provided by the hypervisor. On startup, the commodity OS either performs its own hardware configurations or it registers itself to the hypervisor, before creating or resuming processes. Finally, we inserted code that makes use of the RPC functionality to communicate with a trusted domain and that actually initiates soft reboots for demonstration and benchmark purposes.

Adaptations to the Hypervisor. The adaptations to the hypervisor were quite limited. Essentially, besides providing configuration information about commodity OS and trusted guest, only a hypercall needed to be added, that realizes the initiation of a soft reboot into normal mode, including the optional write back of the trusted domain and the erasure of all confidential data. The hypervisor makes use of the possibility to be partly kept in memory on soft reboot. In particular, this applies to the sections for code and constants, that both do not change throughout the system's uptime, and the page tables, for which a new MAC is computed after they are generated. Data section, BSS section, heap and stack are treated confidential and cleared before soft reboot. The data section is the only part that needs to be reloaded when coming back to protected mode, given that no memory corruptions have occurred in normal mode. Whether the hypervisor memory is still uncorrupted or had to be reloaded by the bootloader is indicated as argument to the hypervisor, so that page tables can be recomputed if necessary. Note that we migrated the responsibility of loading guests from the hypervisor to the bootloader. Similarly, we decided to invoke trusted services via RPCs by the commodity OS after a soft reboot to protected mode instead of passing parameters about the desired service to the hypervisor. In that way, no decisions are required by the hypervisor upon boot, but control can simply be transfered to the guest's entry point directly.

Bootloader. The implementation of the bootloader was carried out in a straight forward manner according to the protocol in Section 2, using a transition crypto module for cryptographic operations. In our implementation the bootloader is divided into two stages. The first stage boot code checks the transition register, loads and verifies the second stage boot code and is placed into ROM along with its vector table. The second stage boot code loads the commodity OS, the hypervisor and the trusted guest (depended on the mode), carries out needed verification steps and finally calls the commodity OS or hypervisor.

5   Evaluation

The approach can be implemented on many current embedded architectures with minor hardware changes (a few special purpose registers and hardware protected keys), as most of the functionality relies on existing hardware features and functions implemented in software, mainly the boot code and the hypervisor. To demonstrate our solution and in order to obtain benchmarks on its performance, we have implemented the described hardware extensions within the emulation framework OVP [24]. It allows to implement and simulate the behavior of new SoC hardware components with reasonable effort. The additional registers are realized as memory mapped device connected to a SoC (emulation) with an integratorCP platform that includes a single ARM Cortex-A8 CPU. The register extension has been wired to perform system resets when required. Furthermore, a dedicated transition crypto module has been modelled in OVP, allowing us to verify the required encryption/decryption and integrity check tasks. As OVP can not provide exact simulation times, especially with respect to peripherals, MMU and caches, the main purpose has been to test the concept as such and get a good picture of the performance one can expect. Hence, the transition crypto module is simplified with respect to its hardware interface and we allow direct memory read from the transition crypto module over the bus. This allows us to test the different boot cases and the concept, but not to simulate real transition crypto module data transfers from the CPU or via DMA. We believe those simplifications are reasonable since exact time estimates for these access forms can not be obtained in an emulation environment such as OVP anyway.

5.1   Performance

The suggested approach allows running secure services isolated by a hypervisor layer only when needed instead of permanently. Consequently, the secure services can be implemented with a very small performance impact. This comes at the price of soft resets when the secure services are needed. The objective of our benchmarks is thus to estimate the overall costs for a soft reboot.

The evaluation includes three factors:

- the number of bytes copied (or erased) between/from storage devices (NAND flash, RAM),
- the number of bytes fed into the transition crypto module for en-/decryption or integrity value calculation and integrity checks,
- the number of remaining CPU instructions not involved in any such feeding, copying or clearing operations.

These figures together allow us to estimate the overall time for all steps of the suggested approach, making the following assumptions about the platform:

- The CPU is clocked with 720 MHz and nominally executes 200 MIPS, as typical on many Cortex A8 development boards such as BeagleBoard [7].
- We assume a rather conservative RAM copy speed of 150 MB/second, which is a lower estimate from [5].
- The copy speed from NAND flash to RAM is estimated by 6 MB/second [21].
- We assume a transition crypto module supporting SHA-256 HMAC generation and AES-128 en-/decryption with a fair trade off between size and speed, clocked at 174 MHz and with the ability to perform parallel hashing/encryption or hashing/decryption with the speed of 171 MB/second. Since hashing is the dominating work load in such parallelized operations, the feasibility of such a speed can be concluded from, e.g., [10].

Table 1 provides an overview of the results for the single steps required, depending on which transition is been considered. We distinguish between a cold boot into protected mode (cp), a cold boot into normal mode (cn), a (warm/soft) reboot into protected mode (wp) and a (warm/soft) reboot into normal mode (wn). Crosses (X) indicate which step is involved in which transition. A dash (-) indicates that the step in question is optional or does only occur in the first of typically many soft reboots.

The benchmarks are based on a second stage boot code of 2.9 KB, FreeRTOS as commodity operating system with a binary blob of 1 MB, the hypervisor sections for code and constants, together 30 KB, hypervisor data of 1 KB and a trusted domain of 380 KB. Those specifications refer to the initial volumes. However, we allow the trusted domain to grow up to 1 MB for the usage of stacks, data structures etc. The space reserved for the hypervisor's heap, stack and BSS section is 900 KB, while page table memory can be up to 64 KB.

A complete soft reboot cycle including two mode switches is with 19 milliseconds estimated considerably faster than any cold boot, irrespectively of the targeted mode. Avoiding slow accesses to external storage is responsible for the main share of those performance benefits. However, also the number of boot instructions is reduced in warm reboot, in respect to both the hypervisor and the commodity OS. In both cases this optimization is mainly due to the dispensed page table reconfiguration. Preconfigured page tables could reduce the hypervisor's booting phase also in a cold boot, but that would come at the costs of an increased foot print and

Table 1. Execution Costs per Step

step	cp	cn	wp	wn	Bytes accessed in storage	crypto module load in B	other instr.	estimated time in ms
configure registers and mode	X	X	X	X			29	0.0001
clean registers				X			41	0.0002
load + verify 2nd stage code	X	X	X	X	2,987	2,987	26	0.4916
load FreeRTOS	X	X			1,043,288		19	165.8263
load + verify hypervisor code	X				30,500	30,500	24	5.0181
verify hypervisor code			X			30,500	22	0.1940
load + verify hypervisor data	X		X		960	960	22	0.1581
verify hypervisor page tables			X			65,536	21	0.4168
copy encrypted trusted guest	X				389,732		0	61.9562
decrypt + verify trusted guest	X		X			389,732	24	4.9558
boot hypervisor	X						247,940	1.2397
*re*boot hypervisor			X				27,707	0.1385
boot FreeRTOS, normal mode		X					9,146	0.0457
*re*boot FreeRTOS, normal mode				X			140	0.0007
(re-)boot FreeRTOS, protected	X		X				305	0.0015
compute page table MAC				-		65,536	129	0.4173
(write back trusted guest)				-		1,048,576	216	13.3341
erase confidential memory				X	1,964,252		98	12.4889
initiate reset to protected mode			X				41	0.0002
cold boot, protected mode	X						248,389	239.6374
cold boot, normal mode		X					9,220	166.3637
warm reboot, protected mode			X				28,197	6.3566
warm reboot, normal mode				X			334	12.9815

less flexibility. Since we allow the trusted guest to grow to a size of up to 1 MB, writing it back (including MAC computation and encryption) is comparatively expensive, and so is its deletion. In order to optimize write back and clearing, one would need to narrow down the space actually claimed by the trusted guest. However, writing the trusted guest back might not be needed in many cases and is therefore listed as optional. The share of cryptographic operations on the estimated costs of a warm reboot to protected mode is 88%. Clearing confidential data is constituting the main part of the costs when soft rebooting into normal mode. We believe that the soft reboot performance is more than reasonable in settings where a hypervisor is only needed sporadically. Assuming the estimations from above and a hypervisor overhead of at least 2%, an execution phase of 1 second in which secure services are not required is already enough to make a temporarily deactivation of service and hypervisor through a soft reboot profitable. As the soft reset, different from a full reset, keeps all volatile memory content, soft reboots are also considerably faster than cold reboots with full resets. In order to achieve the same functionality of enabling and disabling virtualization on demand with full resets, additional costs to the ones listed above would arise, for example for storing application data before rebooting.

5.2   Security

Attacker Model. We assume that the attacker has full control over the commodity OS. However, the hypervisor is supposed to be free from vulnerabilities, which can be assured by formal verification. Furthermore, we trust CPU, MMU and BIOS. Hardware attacks are out of scope of this paper. Devices are assumed to reset whenever a reset signal is issued.[6] In particular, no previously pending DMA operations will be performed after the reset until DMA controllers are reprogrammed. We furthermore assume that the hypervisor is aware of the specification of all present DMA devices, so it can intercept accordingly, and that the devices' behavior actually follows their (non-hostile) specifications. Alternatively, an IOMMU can be used to protect against DMA attacks.

We assume that the attacker aims at obtaining confidential data about the trusted guest and/or to affect its execution outside of the controlled communication channel provided. Denial of Service (DoS) attacks are out of scope of this paper, since a malicious commodity OS has the ability of shutting down the machine or otherwise introducing delays anyway. However, making the watch dog timer aware of the mode state register as described in Section 2.1 improves the protection against DoS attacks, even though complete protection is not achieved by this enhancement either.

Protection in Different Execution Phases. In the following, we discuss the different aspects of the system's security in detail.

Execution in Normal Mode. When in normal mode, the trusted guest and confidential parts of the hypervisor are stored in encrypted form. Access to the corresponding chip unique key(s) is rejected.

Entering Protected Mode. The system can only enter protected mode along with the execution of a trusted and unmodifiable bootcode. In order to change the mode register, it needs to be unlocked. It is guaranteed by hardware that this unlocking is performed together with a CPU reset. The reset sets the program counter to a fixed address pointing to the bootcode in ROM. On ARM processors, neither this address nor the endianess or the instruction set used after reset can be changed by the commodity OS, even when running in privileged mode, since the values for those system parameters are copied from the System Control Register (SCTLR) register of coprocessor 15 which in turn is set back to default values first on reset [2, pp. B1-1202, B1-1203]. In particular, the MMU is disabled [2, p. B3-1308], so that the used entrance point of the exception vector table can not be translated to a different address. Standard interrupts are masked by the reset and not unmasked before control has been transferred to the hypervisor. Fast interrupts are disabled by the boot code, even though there are no devices tied to fast interrupts in our setting. The remaining bits of the Current Processor

---

[6] For functionality, the operating system or hypervisor respectively needs to wait until devices have finished pending tasks before issuing a reset signal. However, the specific time of a reset has no effect on the security.

State Register (CPSR) are set to default values by the boot code. If the integrity verification of either hypervisor or trusted guest fails, the memory is cleared and a reset to normal mode is enforced, so that compromised software will never be executed.

Execution in Protected Mode. The hypervisor is the first software invoked by the boot code. It configures the system's memory protection in such a way that the hypervisor code and data, the trusted domain, the transition crypto module, chip unique keys and register extensions are inaccessible to guests. All exceptions are mapped to handlers under the control of the hypervisor.

Leaving Protected Mode. In order for the commodity OS to (re-)gain privileged rights, a reset has to be issued, since the hypervisor is maintaining control over the system in all other cases. From a functional perspective, this is ideally done through the hypervisor by sending an unlock request to the mode register. However, from a security point of view we have to assume that the attacker can establish a reset signal at any arbitrary time. In case this happens when the transition register is (still) set to protected, the system will either get back to a state where the hypervisor is in charge or (if integrity verification fails) all data will be erased and the mode changed to normal before booting the commodity OS. Even achieving one or several more reset signals during the soft reboot process will not be of any benefit to the attacker since she has no possibility to set the transition register to normal during that phase. In the other case that the transition register is set to normal before reset, the system has either been in normal mode anyway (and confidential data is not present) or the hypervisor has already erased all confidential data (as required by the protocol before setting the transition register back to normal). The MMU is preventing unprivileged access to the transition register. Multiple randomized overwriting of confidential memory regions can be used instead of single overwriting, if deleted information must to not be retrievable in hardware forensics. Before handing over execution to the commodity OS, the boot code clears all registers to avoid that confidential data from a protected mode phase is leaked to normal mode.

Further Aspects

DMA Devices. In normal mode, devices do not have any more privileges than the commodity OS. In protected mode, the hypervisor is able to intercept all attempts to program DMA devices or can configure an IOMMU to protect security critical parts of the memory. On soft reboot, pending DMA tasks are canceled. In particular, the only DMA operations performed during the booting phase are those executed with respect to the (trusted) transition crypto module.

Proof of Mode. A design assumption of our solution was that the fact that the system is running in protected mode will be proven to the user by functionality. For many common applications (e.g., for secret key services such as signing) it is impossible for the attacker to make the user believe the trusted application was active if it was actually not. However, alternative embodiments are possible where a secret is displayed to the user or a LED is tied to the mode register.

6   Related Work

In [18] IBM describes a method for directing the system's reset signal to a specific partition in a virtualized setting. The method is therefore another suggestion on how to make use of reset functionality in virtualized environments, but does not address virtualization overhead.

Instead of disabling virtualization completely when it is not needed, a natural first step is to reduce its costs to a minimum. For example, in specific I/O operations hypervisors can be bypassed [20]. However, this requires hardware support and applies only to a subset of all (I/O) operations. Naughton et al. [23] discuss approaches to extend the Xen hypervisor dynamically by loading additional modules on runtime. In that way, the usage of space and other resources can be optimized. Still, a basic instance of Xen would always be active, something we avoid in our solution.

How to turn off a hypervisor while keeping other software running has been demonstrated for a machine with a dedicated processor mode for virtualization [14]. However, in many embedded architectures - for example on the common ARMv7-processor - the additional requirement of lifting the operating system to the privileged ring needs to be accomplished as well. Furthermore, the soft reboot approach described in the present paper allows turning on the hypervisor (again), guaranteeing the integrity protection of both the booted hypervisor and additional guests while the hypervisor is off.

The separation facilities provided by TrustZone (see Section 2.1) can be used to execute trusted services isolated without suffering from the performance overhead introduced by virtualization and without the need of paravirtualizing the commodity OS. At the same time, other CPUs on the system stay unaffected, which can be seen as additional advantage over the soft reboot approach, which requires all CPUs to agree on the mode. However, even if considering a system with a CPU already supporting TrustZone (which is not given for many embedded processors, such as CPUs with ARMv5 architecture), using TrustZone to execute software isolated requires from the SoC that peripherals are adapted in order to respect the extended address format and thus maintain separation between the two worlds. In contrast, the solution presented in this paper requires only minor additions to the SoC. If the execution of several isolated services or a symmetric protection between service(s) and commodity OS is required in a TrustZone solution, the secure world will need to run a separation kernel, as used in the proposed soft reboot solution as well. Note that TrustZone based approaches still need to make sure that trusted services are kept confidential before being loaded from external storage to the secure world. To achieve this, further hardware extensions are required in order to provide a secure boot scheme.

An alternative way to securely invoke a hypervisor at an arbitrary point of time is provided by *trusted computing* technology [30]. Similar to our solution, trusted guests (and hypervisor) would be kept encrypted and integrity protected until a cryptographic hardware module (in that case the *Trusted Platform Module* (TPM)) decrypts and verifies them. However, in this method called *sealed storage*, the collaboration of the decrypting module does not depend on a mode, but on binaries loaded to the system. Applying the *late launch* technology, as available for modern Intel and AMD processors, this check ignores already loaded software and instead ensures that a dedicated secure load block (SLB) is executed. Only a loaded and unmodifed SLB will enable the decryption of the sealed data [17,1,22]. This principle is comparable to the entanglement of the mode register's unlocking and the reset that enforces the execution of the first stage boot code in our approach. However, not only is the technology not available for embedded systems, it has also been demonstrated that late launch can be circumvented and hypervisors can be modified by malicious code injected to the system before the late launch [31,25]. Even if this attack cannot be applied to all architectures and the vulnerability might be fixed in the future, it gives reason to doubt that TPM-based solutions provide a holistic principle covering the entire system. Furthermore, TPM-operations are comparatively expensive, due to a slow bus connection and relatively slow asymmetric decryption algorithms. A proper (and still simple) mode aware cryptographic module (with DMA support), which we suggest for our approach, is more efficient and cost-effective and does not require any modifications to the CPU.

Making use of the same enablers (sealed storage and late launch), the Flicker environment [22] focuses on the isolated execution of single trusted applications instead of the delayed activation of a hypervisor. This decision against virtualization certainly decreases the trusted computing base even more, but comes with the drawback that the commodity operating system has to be paused while the trusted application is being executed and that only one trusted service can be active at a time. A similar functionality to the one of Flicker can be achieved with the hardware extensions that we propose. However, the feature of remote attestation is naturally reserved to platforms with trusted computing support. Furthermore, [22] admittedly provides a stronger protection against replay attacks even without further hardware extension.

SICE [6] makes use of x86's System Management Mode (SMM) to provide an asymmetric isolation between commodity OS and isolated software, based on a TCB including only the hardware, the BIOS and the SMM with a software foundation of 300 LoC (excluding cryptographic libraries). However, isolated software can not access peripherals directly and - as the authors point out themselves - since the SMM was not designed with security in mind and several attacks on it are already known, careful security reviews are necessary before deployment. While still seeming to be a promising approach for asymmetric isolation on x86 systems, SICE's principle is not applicable to embedded systems.

7   Conclusion

We have presented a dual mode approach to turn the system's hypervisor on and off on demand. Integrity and privacy of trusted guests are maintained at all times: while virtualization is active (in *protected mode*), while it is not (in *normal mode*), and while the machine is powered off. The solution requires only minor additions to an existing SoC design, namely two new registers and hardware protected keys. Hardware support for the cryptographic operations guarantees efficiency. No extensions to the CPU or adaption of other devices are needed. The performance measurements of a prototype implementation in emulated hardware show that soft reboots can provide benefits in several scenarios for embedded systems. In particular, the efficiency is higher than when performing a cold reboot or maintaining virtualization while not needed. The main costs for enabling isolated services consists of their decryption and the integrity check of those services and of the lightweight hypervisor. Returning to non-virtualized execution does not take much longer than the erasure of newly produced confidential data. Furthermore, paravirtualization is not necessary in settings where the commodity OS can be paused while in protected mode. We leave the formal verification of our approach as possible future work.

Acknowledgements. Work supported by framework grant "IT 2010" from the Swedish Foundation for Strategic Research.

References

1. AMD: AMD64 virtualization: Secure virtualization: Secure virtual machine architecture reference manual. AMD Publication number 33047, revision 3.01 (2005)
2. ARM: ARMv7-A architecture reference manual, issue C,
   http://infocenter.arm.com/help/index.jsp?topic=/com.arm.doc.ddi0406c
3. ARM: Integrator baseboards, http://infocenter.arm.com/help/topic/
   com.arm.doc.subset.boards.integratorbaseboards
4. ARM: TrustZone Technology, http://www.arm.com/products/processors/
   technologies/trustzone.php/
5. ARM Technical Support Knowledge Articles: What is the fastest way to copy memory on a Cortex-A8? (2011), http://infocenter.arm.com/help/
   index.jsp?topic=/com.arm.doc.faqs/ka13544.html
6. Azab, A.M., Ning, P., Zhang, X.: SICE: a hardware-level strongly isolated computing environment for x86 multi-core platforms. In: Proceedings of the 18th ACM Conference on Computer and Communications Security, pp. 375–388 (2011)
7. BeagleBoard.org Foundation: BeagleBoard product page,
   http://beagleboard.org/Products/BeagleBoard
8. BeagleBoard.org Foundation: BeagleBoard-xM product page,
   http://beagleboard.org/Products/BeagleBoard-xM
9. BeagleBoard.org Foundation: BeagleBone product page,
   http://beagleboard.org/Products/BeagleBone
10. Chaves, R., Kuzmanov, G., Sousa, L., Vassiliadis, S.: Improving SHA-2 hardware implementations. In: Goubin, L., Matsui, M. (eds.) CHES 2006. LNCS, vol. 4249, pp. 298–310. Springer, Heidelberg (2006)
11. Dam, M., Guanciale, R., Khakpour, N., Nemati, H., Schwarz, O.: Formal verification of information flow security for a simple ARM-based separation kernel. In: Proceedings of the 2013 ACM SIGSAC Conference on Computer and Communications Security, CCS 2013 (2013)
12. Ding, J.H., Lin, C.J., Chang, P.H., Tsang, C.H., Hsu, W.C., Chung, Y.C.: ARMvisor: System virtualization for ARM. In: Linux Symposium (2012)

13. Douglas, H., Gehrmann, C.: Secure virtualization and multicore platforms state-of-the-art report. Tech. Report (2009), http://soda.swedish-ict.se/3800/
14. Gábriš, F.: Turning off hypervisor and resuming OS in 100 instructions. Presentation at FASM CON 2009, Myjava, Slovak Republic (2009),
    http://fdbg.x86asm.net/
    Turning_off_hypervisor_and_resuming_OS_in_100_instructions.ppt
15. Goldberg, R.P.: Architectural principles of virtual machines. Ph.D. thesis, Harvard University (1972)
16. Goldberg, R.P.: Survey of virtual machine research. IEEE Comp. Magazine (1974)
17. Grawrock, D.: The Intel safer computing initiative: Building blocks for trusted computing (2006)
18. Harrington, B.R., Mehta, C., Milton, D.M.I., Perez, M.A., Randall, D.L., Willoughby, D.R.: System and method for selectively executing a reboot request after a reset to power on state for a particular partition in a logically partitioned system. US patent US 7146515 B2, http://www.google.com/patents/US7146515
19. Hwang, J.Y., Suh, S.B., Heo, S.K., Park, C.J., Ryu, J.M., Park, S.Y., Kim, C.R.: Xen on ARM: System virtualization using Xen hypervisor for ARM-based secure mobile phones. In: CCNC (2008)
20. Liu, J., Huang, W., Abali, B., Panda, D.K.: High performance VMM-bypass I/O in virtual machines. In: Proceedings of the annual conference on USENIX 2006 Annual Technical Conference, ATEC 2006, p. 3. USENIX Association, Berkeley (2006)
21. Make Linux Software: Super fast boot of embedded Linux,
    http://www.makelinux.com/emb/fastboot/omap
22. McCune, J.M., Parno, B.J., Perrig, A., Reiter, M.K., Isozaki, H.: Flicker: an execution infrastructure for TCB minimization. SIGOPS Oper. Syst. Rev. 42, 315–328 (2008)
23. Naughton, T., Vallee, G., Scott, S.: Dynamic adaptation using Xen. In: System-level Virtualization for High Performance Computing, HPCVirt (2007)
24. Open Virtual Platforms: OVP website, http://www.ovpworld.org/
25. Schellekens, D.: Design and Analysis of Trusted Computing Platforms. Ph.D. thesis, Katholieke Universiteit Leuven (2012)
26. Shafi, Q.: Cyber physical systems security: A brief survey. In: Computational Science and Its Applications (ICCSA), pp. 146–150 (2012)
27. SICS: SICS Thin Hypervisor (STH) source, https://bitbucket.org/sicssec/sth
28. Smith, J.E., Nair, R.: Virtual Machines: Versatile Platforms for Systems and Processes. Morgan Kaufmann Publishers, USA (2005)
29. Sony Mobile: NovaThor U8500 product page,
    http://developer.sonymobile.com/
    knowledge-base/technologies/novethor-u8500/
30. Trusted Computing Group: PC client specific TPM interface specification. Version 1.2, Revision 1.0 (2005)
31. Wojtczuk, R., Rutkowska, J.: Attacking Intel trusted execution technology. Black Hat DC (2009)

Owner-Centric Protection of Unstructured Data on Smartphones

Yajin Zhou[1,*], Kapil Singh[2], and Xuxian Jiang[1]

[1] North Carolina State University
yajin_zhou@ncsu.edu, jiang@cs.ncsu.edu
[2] IBM T.J. Watson Research Center
kapil@us.ibm.com

Abstract. Modern smartphone apps tend to contain and use vast amounts of data that can be broadly classified as *structured* and *unstructured*. Structured data, such as an user's geolocation, has predefined semantics that can be retrieved by well-defined platform APIs. Unstructured data, on the other hand, relies on the context of the apps to reflect its meaning and value, and is typically provided by the user directly into an app's interface. Recent research has shown that third-party apps are leaking highly-sensitive unstructured data, including user's banking credentials. Unfortunately, none of the current solutions focus on the protection of unstructured data.

In this paper, we propose an owner-centric solution to protect unstructured data on smartphones. Our approach allows the data owners to specify security policies when providing their *untrusted* data to third-party apps. It tracks the flow of information to enforce the owner's policies at strategic exit points. Based on this approach, we design and implement a system, called `DataChest`. We develop several mechanisms to reduce user burden and keep interruption to the minimum, while at the same time preventing the malicious apps from tricking the user. We evaluate our system against a set of real-world malicious apps and a series of synthetic attacks to show that it can successfully prevent the leakage of unstructured data while incurring reasonable performance overhead.

Keywords: unstructured data, information flow tracking, DataChest.

1 Introduction

Smartphone apps tend to contain vast amounts of sensitive data. In many cases, such data items have predefined structure and consistent access semantics across different apps. These data items, such as user's location or contact information, are often regulated by the mobile platform that provides apps access to these items via well-defined platform APIs. For example, apps can retrieve user's geolocation from phone's GPS sensor and subsequently provide location-aware features to users. We classify such data as *structured* data. With the need to protect

---

* Part of the work was done when the first author was an intern at IBM T.J. Watson Research Center.

T. Holz and S. Ioannidis (Eds.): TRUST 2014, LNCS 8564, pp. 55–73, 2014.
© Springer International Publishing Switzerland 2014

sensitive information in structured data, a wide variety of security mechanisms have been developed by the platform developers as well as the research community [19][24][27][30].

At the same time, the apps also alternatively consume data collected directly from the users using the application-controlled visual interfaces (i.e., the users act as *data owners* in this environment). The underlying platform renders minimum to no control in the collection of such data. This type of data, classified as *unstructured* data, relies on the *context* of the app to reflect its meaning and values. One such example is the data collected using an user input box that can have different semantics in different apps. For instance, user can provide his bank credentials in the user input box of one app while he can type the hobbies in another app.

In recent years, there have been several known real-world instances in which apps have leaked unstructured data both *intentionally* and *unintentionally*. In January 2010, several fake banking apps that aim to collect banking credentials were identified [4] in official Android Market. Later in the same year, a fake version of the Netflix app was found to leak user's Netflix credentials to adversary's servers [6]. Besides intentional leaks by these fake (and malicious) apps, genuine apps with vulnerabilities can be exploited to unintentionally leak unstructured data. Recent studies have revealed several instances of benign apps leaking sensitive information, such as user's email login identifier and password [28]. While privacy threat to users is always a major concern, certain information when leaked, can result in serious financial losses.

Unfortunately, all the previous efforts [19][27][30] were focusing on securing structured data. The protection of unstructured data has been largely ignored and left at the mercy of third-party apps. As a result, the owners of unstructured data, i.e., users of third-party apps, have to *blindly* trust these apps and provide security-sensitive data to them. However, the growing number of real-world threats and the sensitive nature of the data that have been leaked emphasize the urgent need for a system-driven solution to protect such unstructured data.

In this work, we are concerned with protecting unstructured data in the presence of *untrusted* third-party apps. To this end, we propose an *owner-centric* approach in which the data owners can determine the security policies for their contributed data. Our solution is based on the insight that data owners could best understand the semantics and sensitivity of their data and hence are best suited to determine who can have access to the data.

Accordingly, we design and implement a system, called `DataChest`, that enables data owners to associate security policies to their data being fed to the untrusted third-party apps. Our system subsequently tracks the flow of the data and applies data owners' policies at strategic exit points in the system. Any policy violation will result in immediate halting of the data transmission.

To encourage real-world acceptability of `DataChest`, we develop several mechanisms to reduce user efforts in specifying policies for user-provided data. In particular, `DataChest` provides persistent policies for *statically* generated input data elements. For *dynamically* generated elements, our system automatically applies the policies based on user's intent. Furthermore, our system provides semantic-aware tag (or policy) suggestions. All these mechanisms reduce user burden and interruption as much as possible, while at the same time guaranteeing that the user's data security is never compromised.

Many of our design choices to reduce user burden have been derived from techniques that have been well proven to be usable in other work streams. For example, the semantic-aware tag suggestion feature based on user's input value (Section 3.4) has been extensively used in search engines, albeit for suggesting related search topics. Other choices are self-intuitive, e.g. if the GUI shown to the user does not change, it is safe to apply previously-specified tags (Section 3.3 and Section 3.5). Usability can be further improved by leveraging additional knowledge, e.g. policies can be pre-specified by trusted authorities such as corporate administrators, and reputation of external entities can be automatically applied using blacklisting databases.

We demonstrate the effectiveness of `DataChest` in tracking unstructured data by analyzing it against popular benign apps from multiple categories. We further evaluate our system against real-world malicious apps and synthetic attacks to show that our system can successfully prevent the unstructured data from being leaked to both (malicious) remote servers and unintended third-party apps. With a CPU-bound benchmark, the results also show that our system has a relative low runtime overhead of 14% with respect to the unmodified Android system. Moreover, the extra time needed to initialize the GUI interface is around 40 ms for a representative real-world scenario, which is a negligible latency that users can actually perceive.

In summary, the paper makes the following contributions:

- To the best our knowledge, we are the first to address the challenge of protecting unstructured data on smartphones. Our system takes an owner-centric approach and engages the data owners to explicitly specify the security policies for their data that are subsequently enforced by our system.
- To minimize user burden, we develop mechanisms to address the challenges of distinguishing both statically- and dynamically-generated input elements, so that they can be effectively tagged with minimum to no user intervention.
- We develop a proof-of-concept system, called `DataChest`, and evaluate its protection capabilities against real-world, malicious mobile apps as well as some synthetically-generated attacks. Our results illustrate that `DataChest` can successfully prevent all such attacks. Our performance results further demonstrate that `DataChest`'s protection mechanism incurs reasonable performance overhead with negligible perceived latency for the end users.

2   Motivating Examples

In contrast to structured data that has well-defined semantics, the semantics of unstructured data can vary substantially in different app contexts. One example of unstructured data is the data entered into input boxes. The exact type of data that users would enter into the boxes cannot be determined without knowing

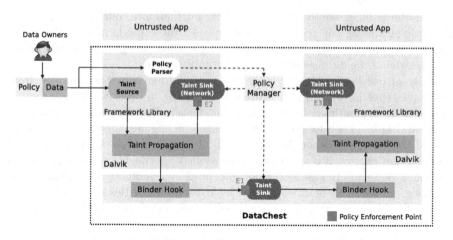

Fig. 1. High-level system architecture of DataChest

the context of apps. The APIs (`EditText.getText()` in Android platform) used
to retrieve the values in these input boxes cannot be directly leveraged to understand their semantic meanings. In fact, these values could range anywhere from
security-sensitive data such as user's password or SSN to less sensitive data such
as user's hobbies.

Since the context of an app is unknown to the underlying Android framework,
it does not understand the semantics of any unstructured data entered into the
app. As a result, the framework cannot enforce any access control policies (or
permissions) that correspond to unstructured data. This further implies that an
app can freely access and leak unstructured data without any constraints from
the framework. For example, a malicious app can launch phishing attacks by
masquerading itself as a banking app [4] and consequently steal users' banking
credentials potentially leading to financial loss for the users.

Our work is motivated by real-world threats and aims to provide protection
to user-provided unstructured data by means of an owner-centric approach.

3   Design

Figure 1 shows the high-level architecture of our DataChest system. When data
owners (i.e., the users) provide data to third-party apps, they also include policies
that specify how their data can be used and shared with other apps and remote
servers. DataChest subsequently retrieves these policies and tracks the flow of
unstructured data at runtime. Our system will enforce corresponding policies
when such data is shared with other apps (E1 in Figure 1) or remote servers
(E2 and E3 in Figure 1). In the following, we will describe the associated design
challenges and how these challenges are addressed in our system.

3.1 Design Challenges

With an owner-centric approach, our system requires additional efforts from data owners to specify policies. In order to make the system more user friendly and thereby enhance its acceptability, we need to reduce the burden and interruption for users as much as possible, while at the same time, we also need to make sure malicious apps cannot trick users and compromise the security of their data.

Our system leverages TaintDroid [13] to track the information flow of unstructured data. However, TaintDroid only supports limited number of taints (32), which is not sufficient for our system. In our system, we need to track user-provided data for each individual input element. Since these items can significantly vary in number based on the app, we need to support a large number of taints.

3.2 In-Context User Policies

Users can specify their security policies in the context of apps, i.e., users specify policies at the time when they actually type their data in the input boxes of a particular app. Since users are entering the data based on their own perception of the app's visual interface, they know the semantics and values of the data they are providing and hence are the best suited to specify the policies based on the context of user inputs. However, the major challenge here is that users need to *explicitly* identify the external entities[1] *before* data items are actually sent out. Users may have no idea of the remote server(s) that are used in the apps and which one should be allowed in advance.

In DataChest, we address this challenge by allowing users to specify policies in the context of users' inputs *without* explicitly providing external entities. Specifically, when typing content into user input boxes that may contain sensitive data, users can *tag* the content with meaningful, user-specific, *labels*. This can help users maintain the context of particular user inputs. For example, user can tag the input box that accepts his Paypal password as *Paypal.password*. The flow of tagged information entered into the user input boxes is tracked in the system. When such data is being sent out to remote servers, our system alerts users with the destination and data labels. By showing users the data labels, they can know the types of user inputs that are currently being sent out. Subsequently, users can specify their policies by allowing or disallowing such data transmission temporarily or permanently. For example, they can allow the data with particular label *Paypal.password* to transmit to paypal.com permanently while disallowing such data transmission to evil.com.

3.3 Persistent User Policies

In order to make our system more user-friendly, we want to reduce user's burden and interruption as much as possible. Note that visual elements, such as user

---

[1] External entity in our system means remote servers or apps with the different developer's signature.

input boxes, can either be statically defined by XML layout files [2] or dynamically generated by apps at runtime in Android. In this section, we will discuss our approach to handle the static user input boxes and leave the dynamically generated ones for Section 3.5.

For static user inputs, we provide persistent tags and policy settings so that users need to tag input boxes and specify the policies only once. Subsequently, for each user input box that has been tagged with labels and associated with policies, the same labels and policies will be applied to this input box automatically every time it is instantiated in the system. A malicious developer might attempt to trick our system by first making the users to enter low-sensitive data into an input box and subsequently tricking the user into entering high-sensitive data into the same input box. However, our system is resistant against such attacks as it compares visual layouts of Android apps (Section 3.5) in order to determine if the input box in question is a mere instance of a previously-tagged box and only applies persistent tags if the visual layout remains same. The malicious developer would need to modify the visual screen shown to the user to make the user enter a different value for the same input box and in such a case, persistent tags would not be applied thus preventing the attack.

One design consideration is to decide whether we need to maintain the old policies associated with an app when the app is upgraded. From a user-friendly design perspective, we should keep the policies so that users do not need to specify policies again for the app. However, apps are untrusted in our system and *blindly* applying old policies opens up potential avenues for a malicious app to trick the user into giving away sensitive information. For instance, the malicious app can replace an input box with less restricted policies in the older version with an input box that can accept more sensitive data in the new version, thereby enabling the app to leak this sensitive data. In DataChest, we take a more restrictive approach and preserve old policies for newly installed app if and only if it has same package name *and* same hash as the older one. We understand that it limits usability in case only minor changes are made between two versions of the app and the semantics of user input boxes are the same. However, it is a trade-off that we made between security and usability. Moreover, the semantic-aware tag suggestion feature described in the next section can make the policy specification for the new app version much easier.

3.4   Semantic-Aware Tag Suggestion

We further reduce user burden by providing semantic-aware tag suggestions, i.e., suggestions based on the value of the data being entered. Note that when users tag an input box, they actually correlate the content of their input with the particular label (and its corresponding policies). Therefore, it is possible to infer a user's choice of label for an input box based on the current content of the box. For instance, if the user has tagged an input box with label SSN and entered a value of 111-22-3333, we can suggest the same label to the user when he is entering same value into another input box (in the same app). The suggestion is displayed at the bottom of the input box. The user can accept this suggestion by

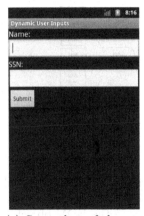
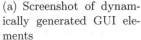
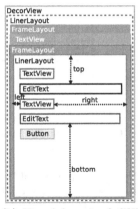

(a) Screenshot of dynamically generated GUI elements

(b) Visual layout of GUI elements

Fig. 2. Screenshot of an activity and its visual layout

simply clicking on it and consequently this label (and its corresponding policies) will be automatically applied to the input box.

This feature is particularly useful for the case of upgraded version of an app. In previous section, we discussed that the old policies and tags would be discarded after app upgrading. Users can benefit from this feature while using the new version of the app since our system can provide accurate tag suggestions to them based on the content they have provided in the old version.

3.5   Dynamic User Input Elements

Dynamic input elements, such as the input boxes, are created at app runtime and are not predefined in the XML layout file of the app. We cannot assign unique IDs to such dynamically-generated input boxes and consequently have no way to uniquely distinguish them. Therefore, it is not possible to provide persistent tags and policies to such elements. However, requiring users to explicitly tag the user input boxes and specify corresponding policies every time they use the app is a major usability limitation and might not be acceptable. We need to find a better solution to address this challenge.

An effective solution would be to apply tags and policy settings to user input boxes based on their *visual layouts* that are presented to the users, and not solely based on their IDs. For statically-generated user input boxes, their visual layouts are predefined and fixed, hence the IDs of the input boxes effectively reflect their visual layouts. However, it is not the case for dynamically-generated input boxes. If we find a way to compare two visual GUI layouts in one app in different runs, we can automatically apply the same tag settings to them if they are *visually* same.

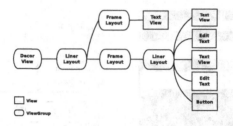

Fig. 3. View tree of the GUI elements in Figure 2

However, effective comparison of two visual layouts of GUI is challenging and requires an understanding of how GUI elements are created, instanced and how their visual positions are determined. Similar to the DOM objects in browsers, the GUI elements in Android are organized as a tree. All the nodes in this tree are View or ViewGroup objects [5]. The difference between View and ViewGroup objects is that ViewGroup is the container that can embody other View or ViewGroup objects. Therefore, all the leaf nodes in this tree are View objects while inner nodes are ViewGroup objects.

Figure 2 shows the screenshot of an activity with dynamically-generated GUI elements and its visual layout. The corresponding view tree is shown in Figure 3. The root node of the view tree is a special component DecorView, which is an internal framework class and represents the top window. It contains a single LinerLayout (subclass of ViewGroup) object, which has two FrameLayout (subclass of ViewGroup) children. One of them holds the title of current activity while the other holds the main content of the current activity (another LinerLayout object). This LinerLayout object contains two TextView objects which hold the text "Name:" and "SSN:", two EditText objects which can receive user inputs and another Button object. For each node in the tree, it knows the *relative* offset to its parent. For example, in Figure 2(b), we can get the *relative* left, right, top and bottom potion of UI elements to its parent (LinerLayout object) in dotted lines.

When being initialized, all the objects in the view tree are drawn from the root node to the last leaf node. All the GUI elements are subsequently laid out and positioned on the screen. For each View and ViewGroup object, it maintains the *relative* position in four dimensions, i.e., left, right, top and bottom, to its parent. Since the view tree represents the visual layout of an activity, we can compare the view trees of two activities to check whether the visual layouts of them are identical. To this end, for each view tree, we generate the corresponding signature. If the signatures of two view trees are same, then the visual layouts rendered by these two trees are identical. The algorithm to generated the signature of a view tree is summarized in Algorithm 1. It recursively generates the signature for each sub-tree (inner node) and leaf node and concatenates the generated signature as a string.

One challenge here is how to generate the signature for the leaf nodes, which are the actual UI elements such as TextView, EditText and Button. In our system,

---

Algorithm 1. Signature generation for a view tree

```
1: procedure GENTREESIGNATURE(viewTree)
2:     for all child in viewTree do
3:         genNodeSignature(child)
4:         if (child is inner node) then
5:             genTreeSignature(child)
6:         end if
7:     end for
8: end procedure
```

---

we include the properties of a `View` object that can impact its visual layout to generate its signature. For example, we use the actual text values and the four dimensional *relative* positions to its parents to generate the signature for `TextView` object.

When users specify policies for dynamically generated user inputs in an activity at first time, our system generates and saves the signature of current view tree along with the specified policies. After that if there is a match between the signature of a new view tree with a saved one, our system will automatically apply the saved policies to the dynamic user inputs in the new view tree.

Our technique to generate and compare view tree signatures ensures that if two view trees are same, their corresponding visual layouts are identical. However, there are instances in which visual layouts could be same even when the view trees are not identical. For example, two `TextView` objects with text value "Na" and "me" placed next to each other on the screen may have same visual layout as that of one `TextView` with text value "Name". In such scenarios, we cannot automatically apply the tag settings even the visual layouts of two activities are same. Our approach is conservative in such cases as we err on the side of security by not allowing malicious apps to trick the users. At the same time, we can still reduce user burden when using benign apps.

4   Implementation

We have implemented a working prototype of `DataChest` by extending Taint-Droid [13] (based on Android 2.3.4[2]) and Android framework in several significant ways. In this section, we illustrate the details of our system implementation.

4.1   User-Provided Unstructured Data

As discussed in Section 3.2, users associate security policies with user inputs within the app context by first tagging user input boxes with custom, user-defined labels that reflect the semantics of the input boxes. In our current implementation, we supplement the default user input method (i.e. the on-screen

---

[2] The latest version of TaintDroid is based on Android 4.3. We leave the porting of our prototype to this version of TaintDroid as our future work.

keyboard) with a special *tag* button to allow users to provide labels to the input boxes. We believe that it is a convenient approach for the users as they can enter values and their corresponding labels from a single UI (input method). However, the default UI cannot be leveraged for providing labels if the app uses its own custom input method. In such a case, our system provides an alternate way to enter labels using a UI that is triggered when a user keeps his finger focused on the input box for a relatively longer period.

To support semantic-aware tag suggestions for reducing user burden, we save the mapping between the data label and the hash value of the content entered by the user into the input box. Note that we do not save the user's input as plaintext for privacy concerns. To this end, we monitor the content of the *tagged* user input boxes by hooking `onTextChanged()` method and update the hash value accordingly. For the *untagged* user input boxes, we also hook the `onTextChanged()` method to compare the hash value of currently typed content with the saved ones. If there is a match, we display the corresponding saved data label under the current input box as a suggestion to users.

For dynamically-generated user inputs in one app, we automatically apply the tag settings if their visual layouts do not change in different runs. When users tag the dynamic user inputs, we save the current view tree and the tag settings, i.e., data labels for this view tree. The saved data labels will be automatically applied to a new activity (in the same app) if its view tree is identical to a saved one. For this purpose, we generate the signature for the view trees by recursively generating the signatures of both *inner* nodes and *leaf* nodes in the view tree. In the Android platform, function `ViewGroup.performTraversals()` is called when current GUI is drawn or redrawn. We hook into this function to generate the signature for the whole view tree.

4.2   System-Wide Information Tracking

4.2.1   Taint Tag Format

Our system needs to track the flow of user-provided data. For this purpose, we extend TaintDroid [13] in our system. Note that our system design is not restricted to only TaintDroid and we can readily leverage other information tracking systems if such systems are available in the future. In the following we leverage TaintDroid as an example to describe information flow tracking in our system.

As previously stated, one major challenge of using TaintDroid to track information flow is that it only supports a limited number of taints. Specifically, it encodes the taints into a 32-bit tag, in which each bit denotes a taint. However, in our system, any user input box represents a different taint and needs to be tracked independently. That is because during program execution, the data from different sources (different user input boxes from different apps for example) can be combined together and we need to know the exact source of the data (e.g., from which user input box in which app) and check the policies when combined user inputs are being sent out.

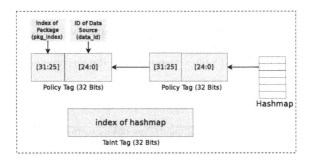

Fig. 4. The taint tag structure in DataChest

In `DataChest`, we extend the format of TaintDroid's original taint tag to support large number of taints. Figure 4 shows the format of taint tag used in our system. Instead of directly using the 32-bit taint tag to place taints, we use a linked list to store the actual taint tags. To distinguish from the original taint tags, we call the actual taint tag as *policy tag* in our system. For each policy tag, we need to store the source information of data that our system is tracking. Such source information is denoted as the identification of data source, such as the ID of a user input box, and this identification is directly encoded into the policy tag (`data_id` field).

4.2.2   Taint Propagation

During program execution, the taints will be propagated through the whole system. This makes sure that even the tainted data is converted to other format, it is still being tracked. TaintDroid propagates taints by extending the Dalvik virtual machine and applying taint propagation rules.

Because of the differences between the format of taint tags, the original rules used to propagate taints need to be changed accordingly. Specifically, for the operation of `result := data`$_1$` + data`$_2$, TaintDroid can directly combine two tags together using `or` operation (`tag(result) = or(tag(data`$_1$`), tag(data`$_2$`))`). However, in our system, we have to merge two linked lists of policy tags together and place the address of new linked list into the hash map. Finally, the index of new linked list in hash map is encoded into the taint tag.

We also extended TaintDroid to add other features that were required for our implementation. One such example scenario is that TaintDroid propagates taints in native methods of system libraries. In particular, TaintDroid uses a method profile (a list of (from, to) pairs) to indicate information flow between variables, which may be method parameters, class variables, or return values in the *same* native method. However, this method profile may miss the information flow that crosses *different* native methods *without* any use of a variable. On such example is the `Md5MessageDigest` class in which the taint should propagate from the parameters of a void function `void update(byte[] input)` to the return value of `byte[] digest()` that has no parameters. The original method profile cannot handle this. We extend the method profile that can propagate taints across *different* methods *without* using variables.

4.2.3   Taint Sources and Sinks

For user-provided unstructured data, when one input box is tagged with a particular label, our system treats this input box as a taint source and creates corresponding taint tags (and policy tags) for the data retrieved from this input box.

Table 1. List of apps that leak user-provided unstructured data

App/Malware Name	Malware?	Type of Unstructured Data
FakeNetflix	Y	Netflix Login Identification and Password
Repackaged Paypal	Y	Paypal Username and Password
Youdao Dictionary	N	Netease Username and Password

When the data with taint tags is reaching certain exit points, our system checks and enforces the corresponding policies. In our system, we treat such exit points as taint sinks. Similar to TaintDroid, the network interface is one taint sink in our system. If no policy has been specified, we block the current network operation (using Linux pipe) and display a popup window (through a management system app) to let users make decision. Besides network interface, there is another new taint sink in our system. That is the point where one app is sharing the data with another app through the binder interface. By checking and enforcing policies (see E1, E2 and E3 in Figure 1) at taint sinks, our system can prevent the app from sharing (tainted) unstructured data with unauthorized external entities.

5   Evaluation

In this section, we present our evaluation of the effectiveness and performance overhead of DataChest.

5.1   Effectiveness

To demonstrate the effectiveness of DataChest, we downloaded 50 popular benign apps from Google Play and subsequently selected 23 apps that collect sensitive user-provided unstructured data, such as login credentials. We use these apps to evaluate the effectiveness of our system in tracking the information flow of sensitive user-provided unstructured data.

Our evaluation shows that all of the user-provided unstructured data to these apps can be successfully tracked by our system. Note that even in cases where the app does not use the default EditText class to accept user inputs, our system still can successfully track the unstructured data provided by users. One such example is the search input box in Amazon Mobile app that implements its own class (SearchEditText) to accept user inputs. This class extends the default EditText class (which is a subclass of the base GUI class View) to include

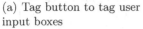

(a) Tag button to tag user input boxes

(b) Popup to let users make runtime access decision

Fig. 5. Our system prevents data leakage from a repackaged Paypal app

some app-specific features. Our system mainly hooks the functions in the base framework GUI class (`View`) and all other classes that extend from this class automatically inherit these hooked functions. If these hooked functions in `View` class are overwritten in subclasses and not called from the subclasses, the GUI will not be successfully initialized.

To demonstrate the capability that our system can prevent user-provided sensitive unstructured data from being leaked by malicious apps, we evaluated it against two malware samples that leak sensitive data to remote servers. The first app is the `FakeNetflix` [6] malware that was discovered in October 2011. It disguises itself as the real Netflix app and leaks the user's Netflix credentials to a remote server. This malware only masquerades the UI of the Netflix app and does not provide any real functionality of video streaming. Another app is a repackaged Paypal app that we developed in-house for our evaluation. In contrast to the previous app, this repackaged Paypal app is more stealthy since it has the same functionalities as the real Paypal app. However, in the background, it leaks the user's Paypal username and password to a remote server.

Moreover, besides intentional leakage of unstructured data by malicious apps, some benign apps have been found to be vulnerable and can be exploited to leak unstructured data. We also use one such app, `Youdao Dictionary` [7], for our evaluation. This app has an open content provider that stores the username and password of a Netease account in plain text [28]. Any malicious app on the phone can access the stored account information through the open content provider. The apps and the corresponding types of unstructured data that could be leaked are shown in Table 1.

Our experiments show that `DataChest` can successfully prevent data leaks by these malicious and vulnerable apps. In particular, when using these apps, we tag

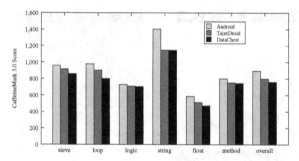

Fig. 6. Evaluation results from the Caffeine benchmark

the input boxes that accept user's credential with specific labels (`paypal.password` for example). Figure 5(a) shows our enhancements to the default on-screen keyboard to include a special tag button to tag user input boxes for the repackaged Paypal app. The flow of data from these tagged user inputs will be tracked in the whole system. As a result, when such tagged user inputs are being leaked to remote servers, the user would be notified using a pop up notification. This prompt includes the destination of this data transmission and the data label that provides the semantics of the data. Users can make decisions to allow or block this data transmission temporally or permanently. Figure 5(b) shows this pop up window. Note that users only need to tag input boxes and make their decision only once since all the tagged user inputs (with their data labels) and users' decisions (or policies) will be saved (see Section 3.3).

5.2 Performance Overhead

In this section, we study `DataChest`'s performance overhead. All the evaluations are performed on Google Nexus S running Android 2.3.4 that is modified for `DataChest`.

5.2.1 Dalvik Microbenchmark

`DataChest` extends TaintDroid's internal taint tag format and taint propagation logic in Dalvik virtual machine. Therefore, we want to study the performance overhead introduced by this extension. To this end, we used an Android port of the standard CaffeineMark 3.0 [1] benchmark and reported the scores of this benchmark running on original Android, TaintDroid and our system in Figure 6. The x-axis shows the different operations performed by this benchmark and y-axis shows the corresponding score of each operation. These scores are useful for relative comparisons.

The benchmark results are consistent with the results reported in TaintDroid. The String operations of both TaintDroid and DataChest have higher performance overhead than arithmetic and logic operations due to the additional memory comparisons [13]. The overall score of Android is 893 while it is 798 and 760 for TaintDroid and DataChest, respectively. It basically implies that

Table 2. The evaluation results of GUI Microbenchmark (time is in milliseconds)

	#1	#2	#3	#4	#5	average
Signature generation (Our testing app)	99	93	76	133	139	108
Signature generation (Paypal payment library)	63	65	29	13	32	40
Signature comparison	0	0	0	0	0	0
Policy retrieval	2	3	3	1	2	2
Policy insertion	4	9	5	6	7	6

DataChest has a 14% overhead with respect to the unmodified Android system and 5% overhead with respect to TaintDroid.

5.2.2   GUI Microbenchmark

To reduce the user burden in DataChest, we generate the signature of a view tree and use this signature for visual layout comparison (see section 4.1). In this section, we evaluate the performance overhead due to this signature generation and comparison. For this purpose, we developed a testing app which dynamically creates 40 TextView objects and 40 EditText objects in an activity. Additionally, we used a real library (Paypal mobile payment Library [3]) which dynamically generates its UI. We calculate the time used to generate the signature for the view tree and the time to compare two view trees. For each evaluation, we measure 5 times and report the results in Table 2. We find that the time used to generate signature of a view tree is around 100 ms for our testing app and 40 ms for Paypal payment library. Note that our testing app has 80 dynamic GUI elements that is considerably more than the number of GUI elements of a typical app. Surprisingly, the time used to compare two signatures is nearly zero. This is because the comparison is merely a string comparison. Moreover, in exiting points, our system needs to retrieve the policies from another separate app which is responsible for maintaining policies. We also evaluate the time latency that was introduced by this operation. The experiments show that the time used to retrieve and insert a policy is 2 ms and 6 ms, respectively. We believe that the time latency introduced by our system is negligible that users can actually perceive and is within the acceptable range of 50–150ms [25].

6   Discussion

In this section, we discuss the current limitations of our system and propose possible solutions.

Although the system is effective in preventing data leaks, it might be limited against certain advanced attacks. One possible attack would be the side-channel attack. For example, instead of getting the contents of user input boxes and then sending them to the remote server, the attackers continuously take a screenshot of the current activity and send these screenshots to the remote server. The current solution cannot handle such side-channel leaks. Another possible attack is the man-in-middle attack to steal data if the data is being sent out without any encryption. In our work, we do not consider such attack and trust the network infrastructure.

The current policies in our system use the host name as an identifier for external entity, which may be ineffective for a proxied network connection. In this case, all the connections will go to this proxy first, not the real remote servers. In the presence of a proxy, users have no idea of the real destination of the data transmission and hence cannot make an informed decision. Users may have similar situation in the case of remote servers without meaningful domain names. Nevertheless, users can still protect their data by blocking all transmissions of the tagged user inputs, though this may break the legitimate functionalities of some benign apps.

For user-provided data, our system requires users to specify the policies. However there are some potential ways to reduce user's burden when specifying policies. For instance, one user's policies of one app could be shared online with other users so that other users do not need to specify the policies for that app again. In the scenario of BYOD, all the policies could be specified and pushed by enterprise device management platform, instead of users. From the perspective of usability, our system provides several ways to reduce user burden (Section 3.3, Section 3.4 and Section 3.5). We believe that there is still potential room for improvement by better understanding the system's usability (e.g. via user studies) and we plan to explore this as part of our future work.

Since we extend TaintDroid to track the flow of unstructured data, our system is also limited by some of TaintDroid's inherent limitations. First of all, TaintDroid only tracks data flows (i.e., explicit flows) and does not track control flows (i.e., implicit flows) as demonstrated in ScrubDroid [23]. As a result, it is possible that malicious app may use implicit flow to leak unstructured data to remote servers. To solve this problem, static analysis may be deployed to analyze the apps. Secondly, the taint propagation between different apps and files is still coarse-grained. For example, the whole IPC message between different apps shares one taint tag, which may cause data to be over tainted. Thirdly, TaintDroid does not support native code in third-party apps. To prevent malicious apps from using native code to leak unstructured data, we do not execute the third-party apps with native libs and thus may cause compatibility issues. Fortunately, the number of apps with native code is only around 5% [29]. We leave the work of extending TaintDroid to provide information flow tracking in native code as our future work. As mentioned before, our system design is not bound to TaintDroid and we can leverage advanced information tracking system on Android if such system is available in the future.

7   Related Work

Smartphone privacy issues have attracted a lot of interest in recent times. Previous research works reveal that third-party apps [12, 13] along with in-app advertisement libraries [15] are actively leaking user's private information. To deal with this problem, researchers propose solutions to provide fine-grained control of private information on smartphones. Such solutions include TISSA [30], Apex [21], Aurasium [27], AdDroid [22] and AdSplit [24]. Our work has a different focus from these works since their main focus is to protect structured data while our work is dedicated to the protection of unstructured data.

At the same time, the classic confused-deputy [18] problem or capability leaks are identified on Android. Examples include ComDroid [10], CHEX [20] and Woodpecker [16]. They employ static analysis to identify such problems in third-party apps and pre-loaded apps. Accordingly, possible solutions [8][11][14] are proposed to mitigate such threats. Our work does not intend to detect such problems. But our system can be used to prevent the unintentional data leak by the apps with this problem.

Among the most related ones, AppFence [19] leverages TaintDroid to track information flow and protects private data from being leaked. However, AppFence's focus is on structured data, while our system is protecting unstructured data. TaintEraser [31] shares a similar design to prevent unwanted information exposure, including user inputs. Our system provides more fine-grained polices to let data owners specify the external entities that the data can be shared with. D2Taint [17] expands TaintDroid to track the information coming from Internet sources. Our system tracks and protects unstructured data coming from users.

A recent system called DataSafe [9] allows data owners to specify particular policies to protect their data. Our system has several key differences from DataSafe. First, the target platforms are different. Our system is concerned with the protection of unstructured data on smartphones while DataSafe aims to protect sensitive data on desktop or cloud computing servers. Second, our system addresses the challenge of user-friendly policy specification and provides several mechanisms to reduce user burden, which is critical for smartphone platforms, while DataSafe does not address this challenge. Third, DataSafe is based on hardware-assisted information flow tracking while ours is software-based tracking. The requirement of custom hardware is a challenge for deployment. Another system CleanOS [26] evicts the sensitive data such as user-provided password, from the phone and keeps a clean environment all the time. Our system instead ensures that such sensitive data cannot be obtained by unintended (and potentially malicious) external entities.

8   Conclusions

We presented the design of a system, called `DataChest`, that offers protection of unstructured data in the presence of untrusted third-party apps. Our system develops an owner-centric approach in which data owners (i.e., users) can determine the security policies of their contributed data. We enhance the usability of the system by developing several mechanisms to reduce user burden, while ensuring the security of the system is never compromised. Our evaluation shows `DataChest` is effective in preventing leakage of unstructured data against a variety of attacks and incurs reasonable performance overhead.

Acknowledgements. The authors would like to thank the anonymous reviewers for their insightful comments that helped improve the presentation of this paper. This work was supported in part by the US National Science Foundation (NSF) under Grants 0855036 and 0952640. Any opinions, findings, and conclusions or recommendations expressed in this material are those of the authors and do not necessarily reflect the views of the NSF.

References

[1] CaffeineMark 3.0, http://www.benchmarkhq.ru/cm30/
[2] Layouts, http://developer.android.com/
    guide/topics/ui/declaring-layout.html
[3] Mobile Payment Libraries, https://www.x.com/developers/paypal/products/
    mobile-payment-libraries
[4] Rogue phishing app smuggled onto Android Marketplace,
    http://www.theregister.co.uk/2010/01/11/android_phishing_app/
[5] UI Overview, http://developer.android.com/
    guide/topics/ui/overview.html
[6] Will Your Next TV Manual Ask You to Run a Scan Instead of Adjusting the Antenna? http://www.symantec.com/connect/blogs/
    will-your-next-tv-manual-ask-you-run-scan-instead-adjusting-antenna
[7] YouDao Dictionary, https://play.google.com/store/
    apps/details?id=com.youdao.dict
[8] Bugiel, S., Davi, L., Dmitrienko, A., Fischer, T., Sadeghi, A.-R., Shastry, B.: Towards Taming Privilege-Escalation Attacks on Android. In: NDSS (2012)
[9] Chen, Y.-Y., Jamkhedkar, P.A., Lee, R.B.: A Software-Hardware Architecture for Self-Protecting Data. In: CCS (2012)
[10] Chin, E., Felt, A.P., Greenwood, K., Wagner, D.: Analyzing Inter-Application Communication in Android. In: MobiSys (2011)
[11] Dietz, M., Shekhar, S., Pisetsky, Y., Shu, A., Wallach, D.S.: QUIRE: Lightweight Provenance for Smart Phone Operating Systems. In: USENIX Security Symposium (2011)
[12] Egele, M., Kruegel, C., Kirda, E., Vigna, G.: PiOS: Detecting Privacy Leaks in iOS Applications. In: NDSS (2011)
[13] Enck, W., Gilbert, P., gon Chun, B., Cox L.P., Jung, J., McDaniel, P., Sheth, A.N.: TaintDroid: An Information-Flow Tracking System for Realtime Privacy Monitoring on Smartphones. In: USENIX Symposium on OSDI (2010)
[14] Felt, A.P., Wang, H.J., Moshchuk, A., Hanna, S., Chin, E.: Permission Re-Delegation: Attacks and Defenses. In: USENIX Security Symposium (2011)
[15] Grace, M., Zhou, W., Jiang, X., Sadeghi, A.-R.: Unsafe Exposure Analysis of Mobile In-App Advertisements. In: ACM WiSec (2012)
[16] Grace, M., Zhou, Y., Wang, Z., Jiang, X.: Systematic Detection of Capability Leaks in Stock Android Smartphones. In: NDSS (2012)
[17] Gu, B., Li, X., Li, G., Champion, A.C., Chen, Z., Qin, F., Xuan, D.: D2Taint: Differentiated and Dynamic Information Flow Tracking on Smartphones for Numerous Data Sources. In: INFOCOM (2013)
[18] Hardy, N.: The Confused Deputy (or why capabilities might have been invented). ACM SIGOPS Operating Systems Review, 22 (October 1998)

[19] Hornyack, P., Han, S., Jung, J., Schechter, S., Wetherall, D.: These Aren't the Droids You're Looking For": Retrofitting Android to Protect Data from Imperious Applications. In: ACM CCS (2011)

[20] Lu, L., Li, Z., Wu, Z., Lee, W., Jiang, G.: CHEX: Statically Vetting Android Apps for Component Hijacking Vulnerabilities. In: CCS (2012)

[21] Nauman, M., Khan, S., Zhang, X.: Apex: Extending Android Permission Model and Enforcement with User-Defined Runtime Constraints. In: ASIACCS (2010)

[22] Pearce, P., Felt, A.P., Nunez, G., Wagner, D.: AdDroid: Privilege Separation for Applications and Advertisers in Android. In: ASIACCS (2012)

[23] Sarwar, G., Mehani, O., Boreli, R., Kaafarn, M.A.: On the Effectiveness of Dynamic Taint Analysis for Protecting Against Private Information Leaks on Android-based Devices. In: SECRYPT (2013)

[24] Shekhar, S., Dietz, M., Wallach, D.S.: AdSplit: Separating smartphone advertising from applications. In: USENIX Security Symposium (2012)

[25] Shneiderman, B.: Designing the User Interface: Strategies for Effective Human-Computer Interaction, 3rd edn. Addison-Wesley (1998)

[26] Tang, Y., Ames, P., Bhamidipati, S., Bijlani, A., Geambasu, R., Sarda, N.: CleanOS: Limiting Mobile Data Exposure with Idle Eviction. In: USENIX Symposium on OSDI (2012)

[27] Xu, R., Saidi, H., Anderson, R.: Aurasium: Practical Policy Enforcement for Android Applications. In: USENIX Security Symposium (2012)

[28] Zhou, Y., Jian, X.: Detecting Passive Content Leaks and Pollution in Android Applications. In: NDSS (2013)

[29] Zhou, Y., Wang, Z., Zhou, W., Jiang, X.: Hey, You, Get off of My Market: Detecting Malicious Apps in Official and Alternative Android Markets. In: NDSS (2012)

[30] Zhou, Y., Zhang, X., Jiang, X., Freeh, V.W.: Taming Information-Stealing Smartphone Applications (on Android). In: McCune, J.M., Balacheff, B., Perrig, A., Sadeghi, A.-R., Sasse, A., Beres, Y. (eds.) Trust 2011. LNCS, vol. 6740, pp. 93–107. Springer, Heidelberg (2011)

[31] Zhu, D.Y., Jung, J., Song, D., Kohno, T., Wetherall, D.: TaintEraser: Protecting Sensitive Data Leaks Using Application-Level Taint Tracking. In: ACM Operating Systems Review (2011)

On Usable Location Privacy for Android
with Crowd-Recommendations

Benjamin Henne[1], Christian Kater[1], and Matthew Smith[2]

[1] Distributed Computing & Security Group,
Leibniz Universität Hannover, Hannover, Germany
`henne@dcsec.uni-hannover.de`
[2] Usable Security and Privacy Group, Universität Bonn, Bonn, Germany
`smith@cs.uni-bonn.de`

Abstract. The boom of smart devices with location capabilities has also led to a boom of apps that use location data for many different purposes. While there are of course apps that require users' precise locations, such as navigation apps, many apps would work equally well with less precision. Currently, apps that request location information are granted access to location data with maximum precision or not at all. In this work we present a location obfuscation approach for Android devices, which focuses on the usability aspects. Based on results of focus group discussions (n = 19) we designed and implemented a solution that can be used by even unskilled users. When an app requests for location data the first time, the user configures accuracy of location data that is to be revealed to the app by selecting one of five precision levels. Unskilled users are supported by crowd-based recommendations.

Keywords: mobile, usable security and privacy, location, crowd-sourcing.

1 Introduction

In May 2012 the Pew Internet & American Life Project reported[1] that 74 % of US smartphone owners use their device to get real-time location-based information and that 18 % of them use geo-social services to check into locations or share their locations with friends. Many different kinds of apps implement location-based features today. These range from classical apps for navigation, location sharing, geo-tagging or location-based information retrieval to apps for fitness training, location-aware games and apps that serve location-based advertisement. To get an idea of the scale of how many Android apps request access to the location data we crawled the Google Play Store in June 2013. We found that 17 % of the paid apps and 34 % of the free apps required location permissions. In total, 27.2 % of the 20,681 most popular Android apps requested access to location data. While some apps like navigation naturally require exact locations to work, there are apps that would work equally or similarly well with a more rough positioning,

---

[1] `http://pewinternet.org/Reports/2012/Location-based-services.aspx`

T. Holz and S. Ioannidis (Eds.): TRUST 2014, LNCS 8564, pp. 74–82, 2014.

such as geo-tagging status updates in social network services or location-based advertisement. In these cases it would be possible to improve users' privacy by reducing accuracy without loss of functionality.

Location obfuscation has been a topic of privacy research for several years, but none of the proposed systems has seen any significant level of adoption. We argue that one of the main reasons for this is the complexity of the algorithms, which need to be understood and configured by the users; these need to be tailored to both, the users' desired privacy/functionality trade-off as well as to the application in question. However, obfuscation is an important topic, since it is preferable to reduce data details before disclosure, but not disclosing it in full detail and trying to solve privacy issues by complex access control rules afterwards as done in other works [2]. In this paper, we present a usable location privacy approach for Android that allows users to restrict the accuracy of location data given to apps in an easy-to-understand manner. Based on findings from focus group discussions we implemented a solution that allows users to select location obfuscation on a per-app basis. Users are presented with a dialog in which they can state their privacy wish when the app first tries to access the location service. To further aid unskilled users our system offers crowd-based recommendations for privacy settings. We also address participants' requests for transparency of location usage by giving insights into apps' location access frequencies.

2   Background and Related Work

The two major mobile platforms Android and iOS deal with location permissions in different ways: Android only allows its users to enable or disable location services entirely. While apps must declare that they require access to the location service, users cannot install an app without granting that permission. Users can however specify which source Android uses to determine the location (Wi-Fi or GPS), which gives some control about the accuracy. However, this setting is also global. In iOS users can also activate or deactivate location services entirely, but they can also do so on a per-app basis. When an app requests location the first time, a pop-up dialog asks the users whether they want to allow location access or not. Within this dialog developers can support user decisions with a purpose description, which however is rarely used today. Since Android is an open system, there are different tweaks to improve privacy. *Cyanogenmod 10* for instance implements *Privacy Guard* that can block access to private data like location information on a per-app basis. Similar functionality is implemented by the apps *LBE Privacy Guard* or *PDroid 2.0*. *App Ops* introduced similar to Android 4.3, but recently was removed again. Likewise, different research works [3,7] aimed at prohibiting the disclosure of private data. All these approaches have in common that they allow an app to access the location service with full precision or deny access entirely; or always return a single fixed position—which from a functional perspective is worse than disallowing access. Our solution offers a more fine-grained approach, which allows users to benefit from location-based services without having to give apps access to their most precise location.

Fisher et al. [5] studied the behavior of 273 iPhone users concerning which apps they allowed access to location services. Their results indicate that there is a high variance both between apps and users. For instance while 98 % of Foursquare users granted permission to the app, only about half did so for Shazam.

Brush et al. [4] studied with which parties users would share location traces. They equipped 32 people with GPS loggers and tracked their movements for two months. They then presented tracks to the participants applying different obfuscation methods. They explained them the methods used for removing track details and showed that users can be included in the decisions on obfuscation.

Tang et al. [9] compared sharing location based on an all-or-nothing approach with having the choice from four location abstractions with varying granularities, such as an address or a name of a city. In their study ($n = 30$) they showed that the more abstract descriptions could lead to more open location sharing. They also showed that participants reported a higher perceived comfort level when they had a wider choice of different granularities.

All these studies show that users are interested in restricting the use and accuracy of location services. However, currently no mobile operating system allows users to use location-based services while at the same time restricting the level of detail given to apps or services. While the above works indicate that there is a desire for reducing the level of detail in location data offered to apps, there is no related work examining what levels of trade-off users want in the context of apps. More importantly, there is no work on how users could interact with such a privacy protecting service. In the next section we present the results from a focus group study we did to answer these questions as a basis for the privacy service we implemented.

3   Focus Group Study

For a qualitative study on users' needs concerning location privacy on mobile devices, we conducted three focus group sessions on this topic. We chose this method to identify users' experiences, requirements, worries and wishes towards location privacy and existing implementations as base for our work. We initially sent invitations to 1,510 people from our university study mailing list, advertising a group discussion on "daily use of mobile apps" to avoid bias caused by mentioning privacy. 98 invitees answered the initial screening survey in which we collected demographics, technical expertise, experience with mobile devices, and Westin's privacy segmentation. Based on these values we compiled 3 balanced focus groups with 19 participants in sum: 11 female and 8 male; aged 24±4 years; from 14 fields of study; 12 Android users and 7 iOS users; diverging technical expertise; 9 privacy fundamentalist and 10 pragmatists. Each session took about 90 minutes. Participants were paid € 20 as compensation.

3.1   Usage Habits of Location-Aware Apps

Most of the participants reported in the screening survey that they use different apps with location integration like public transport timetables, traffic news, navigation, maps, and weather reports on a daily to weekly basis. While most of them stated that they post content in social network services, only 6 of them stated to occasionally share their location online. When talking about using location services on their smartphones, most of them stated that they use them selectively. The iPhone owners utilized per-app configuration. Since Android does not enable this, some Android users resorted to turning location services on and off prior to using specific apps. Two female participants actually used location features for live tracking with their partners for security reasons when going out late. Only four of our participants stated that they never use location services. Three of them did not want to be observed by "others" or apps, while one iPhone user completely turned off location use, because he dislikes being asked for location permissions for every single app. Battery drain was a major factor for selective use of location services besides the objection of being observed. A major factor for using location although feeling being observed that participants often referred to was convenience.

3.2   Participants' Experiences and Requests

When we discussed current location features, most iOS users stated to be fairly satisfied. One of them requested to know last location usage of each app. While such feature already exists in iOS, it only provides rough information if an app used location "recently" or within the last 24 hours. One iOS user requested that apps should explain why they request location data to allow an informed decision about giving location permissions. Others of that group disagreed, since they would not trust developers' purpose specifications. Android users generally had a wish for transparency of information usage. They stated, that even if they might not regularly use it, they would like to be able to review last location usage and usage frequencies to get a better feeling about privacy. Besides, such feature "should make developers use location more prudently". After having discussed with the iOS users, over half of our Android users requested per-app location settings. They also liked the direct feedback of the iOS permission pop-up dialog, since Android's Settings app was felt to be very complex.

Inaccuracy of Locations. When discussing possible improvement for privacy control, one participant introduced the aspect of location accuracy: She stated that a public transport app justifiably needs her exact location to determine the nearest station, however when "looking for local shopping coupons her current city would be entirely sufficient". Thus, two levels of detail, i.e. precise and imprecise as the city would be enough. While only one participants worried about complex settings, the others of that group appreciated the "imprecise" option. Participants stated they would prefer to select an imprecise level where possible. However, there were different opinions—for instance when looking for a restaurant, or geo-tagging a Facebook post—on what would be a good level of imprecision: city, district, 1 kilometer, and so on. In another group participants appreciated the idea of imprecision, but strictly argued against manually configuring what imprecision means to them.

Obfuscation Methods. At the end of the focus group sessions we tried to introduce participants to a set of obfuscation methods by visually outlining their effects and giving basic explanations. Participants did not think that using fixed self-determined locations was a good option, but for "tricking other concerning their whereabouts'", since using a location-based service needs at least few information about their real location. This emphasizes that prior work, which addressed the prevention of location disclosure or faking location data [1,3,7], does not fit users' needs when using location-based services. Random shifting of location was criticized by our participants, because results were random and the resulting location could be in an absolutely unrelated place or even in an inadequate place like when randomly been mapped to an adult shop. This criticism also applies to rounding or cutting coordinates' decimal places [1]. They stated that even if obfuscation is used, obfuscated locations should be somehow related to real locations. For this reason participants liked the idea of mapping their real location to geographic object, i. e. to the center of the street they currently were on, or the center of the urban district or city where they stay. While the participants of one focus group clearly stated that they would accept that one service (like Google Maps), which assists them in the obfuscation process, knows their real location, the participants from one of the other groups expressed that they did not want that their locations are disclosed to any external (privacy) service. When talking about basic k-anonymity, participants were interested in the general approach of non-distinguishability out of k people, but they disliked the fact that obfuscation results were dependent on other users. This is particularly relevant since k-anonymity is quite popular in privacy research.

In conclusion, participants wanted to be able to control the precision of location revealed to apps. Locations should be inaccurate, but the inaccuracy should be predictable and understandable to them.

Uncertainty about Trust. We could not identify recurring opinions on trust towards apps or service providers in focus group discussions, since participants' opinions were very diverse and obviously biased by latest NSA mass surveillance disclosures. Interestingly, when asking participants how they decide if allowing an app location usage, one participant stated that she mainly bases her decision on "how important an app is to herself, and how well-known the app developer is", while others reported to base on gut feelings. Such users could benefit from recommendations as provided by our solution. Android users' opinions concerning Google ranged from "Google is the only one I trust" to "they know everything about me including my location even if I try to disallowed access to them".

4   Usable Location Obfuscation for Android

Based on the findings from the focus groups discussions we designed our usable location privacy extension for the Android system. It was built on top of our previous framework [6], which allows for modifying location data before handing it to a requesting app by extending the operating system's location services.

Our extension introduces location permissions on a per-app basis, whereat the user can deny location access for an app, allow access to exact location data, or set up location obfuscation with different pre-determined levels of detail. Transparency of location usage is created by access statistics. Users are supported in decision making by integrated crowd-based recommendations.

4.1   Obfuscation

Backed by the results of the group discussions, we chose to implement two obfuscation methods. The *geodata-based mapping* was perceived as mostly intuitive and easy to grasp by our participants. Based on the actual location of the user and a pre-selected type of geographic object like *city*, it maps the location to the coordinates of the center of the nearest geo-object of the selected type like the center of the city the user is staying at. The mapping is achieved by reverse geocoding current coordinates to an address, removing unwanted details like the street name, and finally geocoding the modified address back to coordinates. In our implementation geocoding relies in the corresponding API of the Android system leveraging data from Google Maps. However, other map services such as the free ones of Bing, Yahoo, or MapQuest/OpenStreetMap could be used as well. Unlike many other obfuscation algorithms the geodata-based mapping does not require users to configure any parameters besides the level of detail. Related to the group discussions the obfuscation levels *city*, *district* and *street* were chosen, whereat district is equivalent to the next village in rural areas. Another benefit of this mapping is that it dynamically adapts the actual changes to coordinates corresponding to the users' whereabouts depending on if a user is in a metropolis or in a provincial town.

While some of our participants agreed on sharing their location with a single known service in order to obfuscate their location, others objected to share their location with any online service. For this reason we implemented an offline alternative that never requires revealing real location data. To keep the overall extension simple from the user perspective, the offline obfuscation was designed to approximate the service-based mapping. However, due to geodata size and the complexity of data and queries it was impossible to run and utilize geodata services directly on mobile devices. Since it was no option to reduce obfuscation to city-level only, which most likely could be implemented on the devices, we chose *random shifting* for the offline mode. In this case the real location is shifted in a random direction by a random distance limited by a lower and an upper bound. Since participants argued against handling numeric parameters, metaphors were an easy-to-understand replacement, for instance allowing for choosing one's location to be "as imprecise as being somewhere in a city block". However, there are no basic metaphors that are valid across city or even country boundaries. For instance the area of city blocks in the US cities Houston and Manhattan differs by factor 3, or the size of playing fields differ between sports and sport associations. For this reason, we opted to re-use the same levels of detail as for the first obfuscation method. In this case users have to manually enter static values for *street*, *district*, and *city* once, or alternatively use a configuration wizard that we included. Using the wizard, a user first selects a minimum distance between real and obfuscated locations and a "representative" city, which determines the dimension of distances. Then the user is asked to pick three specific locations on a map of the selected city, which are used to calculate rough sizes of the city, a district and a street that are used for upper bounds of the different levels.

4.2   User Interface

Since most of our participants were either satisfied with the UI features of iOS, or desired a similar interface for Android, we implemented location obfuscation in the style of iOS. When an app requests location data the first time, a pop-up dialog opens and asks the user for location privacy setup of that app. As shown in Figure 1, the user can select one of the five levels of location precision from *exact* to *none*. If a user cancels the pop-up without a selection, the unset privacy setting is handled like denying location access. Notifications remind the user to configure privacy setting later in this case. If a recommendation service is used, recommendations are shown at the bottom of the dialog, either as text or alternatively visualized as rating stars. In the Settings app users can view or modify location privacy settings of all apps that already requested locations as shown in Figure 2. Clicking an app allows to change its configuration. In advanced settings users can switch between online and offline obfuscation, setup values for the offline mode, enable or disable the use of recommendations as well as the publication of their settings if using a social recommendation service.

Transparency. To address participants' wish for transparency, we added usage statistics. The statistics overview shows for each app that requested location data the date and time of its last location data access. Additionally, details can be viewed for each app as shown in Figure 3: The mean deviation of obfuscated and real locations, a plot of location access count per hour for the last 24 hours and access counts per day for the last four weeks. The access frequencies allow the users insights into how they are tracked by apps or services.

4.3   Supporting Decision Making with Recommendations

Most of our participants stated that they feel able to judge which apps need which location accuracy for most apps. However, some apps were considered tricky to judge, such as the Facebook app having diverse functionality. All our participants stated that they would not allow anyone else making privacy decisions on their behalf, but stated that they would consult others for advice. We discussed profile-based recommendation systems (profiles like privacy fundamentalists or unconcerned), which would make recommendations to users due to different profiles. Though creating different profiles would be inapplicable for such a small set of different obfuscation levels as discussed and used by our solution. Building app categories was also proposed for reducing configuration efforts, but it would be hard to reduce apps to distinct non-overlapping groups.

  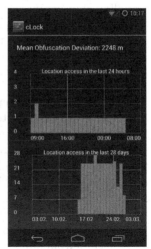

Fig. 1. Pop-up asking for obfuscation level of an app

Fig. 2. Privacy Settings: app obfuscation overview

Fig. 3. Detailed location usage of lock clock widget

We finally discussed the possibility of an online community as a supporting entity for decisions. While some participants expressed mistrust, since such a service might be manipulated "like Amazon ratings or Wikipedia articles", others would look to such a source for help. About half of the participants stated that they would provide data for recommendations, while others stated to be only consumers. Some participants stated that they would feel confident following the recommendation made by public non-profit organization. For instance, consumer advice centers, consumer reports, or even IT security associations could provide recommendation services. However, the only way to keep data of such listings up-to-date is the restriction to some kind of top 1000 list, which excludes less popular apps that might be even harder to configure for many users. Interestingly, our participants indicated willingness to pay up to €2 per year for such a service.

For our solution we decided to create a crowd-based social service for location privacy setting recommendations. We leverage the crowd to inform users about what others chose as their personal privacy/functionality trade-off. We do not catch their perceptions or expectations about apps' behavior for improving users' trust decisions [8]. Since the mass and diversity of apps in the Android markets is immense, we think that such a crowd-based service is most adaptive to the changing landscape of apps and our focus groups indicated that there would be demand and support for this kind of service. We implemented anonymous sharing of obfuscation settings, whereat authentication provided by the Google Play services is used to differentiate users and secure the service. Users that contribute data send an app's location privacy setting to the service after it was configured. When another user is asked for location privacy configuration, the service is queried for recommendation, which is then displayed to the user.

For offline obfuscation the crowd-service additionally stores the numeric values allocated to users' selections, which are mapped to requesting users' own levels to fit recommendations to their personal settings.

5   Conclusion

The participants of our focus groups were interested in location obfuscation for mobile devices. They rejected complex and (for them) unpredictable algorithms like k-anonymity, preferring simple and predictable location obfuscation that keeps locations somewhat related to their real positions. Based on these findings we built an implementation for Android that offers such simple location obfuscation on a per-app basis. Besides basic obfuscation, we implemented different features to support location usage transparency and support unskilled users with crowd-based recommendations. We argue that crowd-based recommendation can provide suitable support for privacy decisions of unskilled users.

The results from our focus groups suggest our service should be well received and field tests are planed as the next step. Furthermore, we currently do not differentiate between types of users in our service. However, it must be kept in mind that the quality of recommendations in a crowd-based service depends on participants' expertise. In future work we will extend the crowd-service by introducing quality controls. We plan to introduce a skill-based and pattern-based classification of users and weight recommendations based on this.

References

1. Beede, R., Warbritton, D., Han, R.: Myshield: Protecting mobile device data via security circles. Tech. Rep. CU-CS-1091-12, Univ. of Colorado Boulder (2012)
2. Benisch, M., Kelley, P.G., Sadeh, N., Cranor, L.F.: Capturing location-privacy preferences: quantifying accuracy and user-burden tradeoffs. Personal and Ubiquitous Computing 15(7), 679–694 (2011)
3. Beresford, A.R., Rice, A., Skehin, N., Sohan, R.: Mockdroid: Trading privacy for application functionality on smartphones. In: Proc. HotMobile 2011, pp. 49–54. ACM (2011)
4. Brush, A.B., Krumm, J., Scott, J.: Exploring end user preferences for location obfuscation, location-based services, and the value of location. In: Proc. UbiComp 2010, pp. 95–104. ACM (2010)
5. Fisher, D., Dorner, L., Wagner, D.: Location Privacy: User Behavior In The Field. In: Proc. SPSM 2012, pp. 51–56. ACM (2012)
6. Henne, B., Kater, C., Brenner, M., Smith, M.: Selective cloaking: Need-to-know for location-based apps. In: Proc. PST 2013. IEEE (2013)
7. Hornyack, P., Han, S., Jung, J., Schechter, S., Wetherall, D.: These aren't the droids you're looking for: retrofitting android to protect data from imperious applications. In: Proc. CCS 2011, pp. 639–652. ACM (2011)
8. Lin, J., Amini, S., Hong, J.I., Sadeh, N., Lindqvist, J., Zhang, J.: Expectation and purpose: Understanding users' mental models of mobile app privacy through crowdsourcing. In: Proc. UbiComp 2012, pp. 501–510. ACM (2012)
9. Tang, K., Hong, J., Siewiorek, D.: The implications of offering more disclosure choices for social location sharing. In: Proc. CHI 2012, pp. 391–394. ACM (2012)

Lightweight Anti-counterfeiting Solution for Low-End Commodity Hardware Using Inherent PUFs

André Schaller[1], Tolga Arul[2], Vincent van der Leest[3], and Stefan Katzenbeisser[1]

[1] TU Darmstadt, Security Engineering Group
lastname@seceng.informatik.tu-darmstadt.de
http://www.seceng.de/
[2] CASED, Mornewegstrasse 32, 64293 Darmstadt,
tolga.arul@cased.de
[3] Intrinsic-ID, Eindhoven, The Netherlands
vincent.van.der.leest@intrinsic-id.com
http://www.intrinsic-id.com

Abstract. This paper presents a lightweight anti-counterfeiting solution using intrinsic Physically Unclonable Functions (PUFs), which are already embedded in most commodity hardware platforms. The presented solution is particularly suitable for low-end computing devices without on-board security features. Our anti-counterfeiting approach is based on extracting a unique fingerprint for individual devices exploiting inherent PUF characteristics from the on-chip static random-access memory (SRAM), which in turn allows to bind software to a particular hardware platform. Our solution does not require additional hardware, making it flexible as well as cost efficient. In a first step, we statistically analyze the characteristics of the intrinsic PUF instances found in two device types, both based on a widely used ARM Cortex-M microcontroller. We show that the quality of the PUF characteristics is almost ideal. Subsequently, we propose a security architecture to protect the platform's firmware by using a modified boot loader. In a proof of concept, we embed our solution on a state-of-the-art commodity system-on-a-chip platform equipped with an MCU similar to the ones previously analyzed.

1 Introduction

With the proliferation of mobile computing the influence of low-end devices on our every day communication steadily grows. As their computational power increases, such devices are embedded into many objects we are interacting with on a daily basis. Besides their implementation in smart phones and tablets, low-end devices are employed in Car2X communication [16] where microcontrollers (MCUs) are used in modern cars to improve road safety, traffic efficiency or to act as an infotainment platform [10]. Additional use cases arise with the growing importance of sensor nodes with applications in the fields of health care, military

T. Holz and S. Ioannidis (Eds.): TRUST 2014, LNCS 8564, pp. 83–100, 2014.
© Springer International Publishing Switzerland 2014

and environmental monitoring [18]. Furthermore, objects in our everyday-life (e.g. fridges, televisions, smart-metering, etc.) are increasingly equipped with computing capabilities, which will eventually yield the Internet-Of-Things [4,12].

A high proportion of such low-end devices are not equipped with special on-board security mechanisms such as secure memory or trusted execution environments. Devices without security features range from lightweight MCUs to more complex system-on-a-chip (SoC) platforms. Lightweight devices are designed for microcontroller use (e.g. ARM Cortex-M processor family). They do not implement security features due to hardware constraints and economic considerations. For example, ARM's Cortex-M series does not support ARM TrustZone technology[1]. More heavyweight SoC platforms can be found in smart phones and tablets. Many SoCs omit hardware security mechanisms due to increased costs and to allow for product evolution. Nevertheless, low-end devices are often used to process sensitive data. Thus, they are a worthwhile target of cyber-criminals. Malicious parties are gaining interest in attacking such devices to extract intellectual property.

To overcome this issue, we propose a lightweight anti-counterfeiting solution to bind a given firmware instance to a particular hardware platform providing a strict hardware-software binding for low-end commodity hardware. Our scheme relies on a hardware-based anchor of trust in terms of a PUF instance. It uses intrinsic Physical Unclonable Functions (PUFs) of the on-board SRAM to extract a fingerprint, which is unique for individual devices. The fingerprint is further processed to generate an ephemeral cryptographic key during an early boot stage and to subsequently decrypt the firmware. Our scheme establishes trust in the on-chip-hardware and in the firmware executed on the device by linking both instances. We achieve protection against IP extraction or modification on embedded devices without dedicated security mechanisms.

1.1   Contributions

We first analyze the quality of PUF instances extracted from two widely used low-end devices to demonstrate the feasibility of device-dependent cryptographic keys. The ARM Cortex-M3 is a popular example of a lightweight microcontroller, whilst the TI OMAP 4 exemplifies more complex SoC platforms. After statistically assessing the stability and uniqueness of the derived device fingerprints we propose a lightweight security architecture to bind a given firmware to a specific device. Subsequently, we implement the proposed architecture on a SoC platform and demonstrate the compatibility of our solution with off-the-shelf commodity hardware.

1.2   Structure

In Section 2 we discuss current approaches to Physically Unclonable Functions and in particular SRAM PUFs. The analysis of the PUF characteristics of two

---

[1] ARM TrustZone security extension is part of most ARM Cortex-A application processors [1].

popular devices is given in Section 3. We describe the attacker model, present the proposed security architecture and explain the course of usage in Section 4. In Section 5 we describe details related to the implementation of the proof-of-concept. Lastly, in Section 6 we conclude our work.

2   Related Work

A Physically Unclonable Function (PUF) is a complex physical structure that generates a value y in response to a stimulus x. The response y depends on the challenge x as well as on the micro- or nanoscale physical structure of the PUF itself. It is assumed that the PUF is unclonable such that it can not be reproduced, not even by the manufacturer. The challenge-response behavior of the physical system is complex enough such that the response to a randomly selected challenge can not be predicted. Furthermore, due to minuscule manufacturing variations during the production process, embedded PUFs can be used to robustly identify a silicon chip.

Silicon-based PUFs include delay-based or memory-based PUFs. For an exhaustive overview of PUFs and details on their taxonomy we refer to [15]. It has been shown that selected static random-access memory (SRAM) shows PUF-like behavior [11]. Further research in this area support the applicability of SRAM as a Physical Unclonable Function [13,17]. Using SRAM as PUFs exploits manufacturing variations, which manifest themselves in a bias of memory cells inside of SRAM modules. During the power-up phase these cells initialize to either the value of zero or one. Most cells show a stable start-up behavior, which in total creates a start-up pattern we will exploit to generate a fingerprint for the device.

Since not all of the SRAM bytes show a stable behavior in such sense that they are always initialized to a fixed value, the SRAM start-up values include a small amount of unstable bits, so-called noise. Since the goal is to reconstruct a reliable cryptographic key from several noisy measurements, the noise is eliminated by employing a Fuzzy Extractor [9], which extracts the stable part of the PUF response and transforms it to a uniformly distributed value.

3   Finding PUFs in Commodity Hardware

To get a first impression on the feasibility to extract a PUF instance from commodity hardware we evaluated a popular lightweight MCU. We chose ARM's Cortex-M3 as it is a widely distributed low-end processor specially developed for embedded devices. With 212 licenses it is the most popular version among the Cortex processor family. 30% of ARM chips shipped in 2013 were Cortex-M processors [3]. They are integrated into virtually every smart phone.

Secondly, we analyzed commodity hardware from the class of SoC platforms to explore the feasibility to robustly extract a unique fingerprint from more complex devices. Our main interest was to analyze whether active components adjacent to the SRAM influence the stability of key extraction. We chose the PandaBoard [2] and its successor the PandaBoard ES, based on an OMAP4430 platform, respectively on an OMAP4460. They comprise two ARM Cortex-A9 and two Cortex-M3 processors. We selected the PandaBoard as it is available as a general-purpose (GP) edition, which lacks the support for ARM's TrustZone extension. Furthermore, the OMAP 4 is integrated into many mobile phones and tablets from vendors like Nokia, Motorola, Samsung and more. Thus, the PandaBoard as a general-purpose device reflects the security and multimedia configuration of popular smart phones like the Samsung Galaxy SI and SII, Motorola Droid and Milestone series and several devices from LG.

In the following we briefly describe common characteristics for PUFs and later analyze both devices using these measures.

3.1   Common Characteristics for SRAM PUFs

In general, SRAM PUF instances should show properties that mitigate the prediction of correct start-up values (Hamming weight), enable a robust repeated identification of single devices (Within-class Hamming distance) and lastly generate a unique pattern among a pool of similar devices (Between-class Hamming distance).

The *fractional Hamming Weight* $HW(x)$ of individual measurements from the same device indicates whether the start-up values are biased to either zero or one. This measure gives a first impression on the randomness present in the start-up values. The ideal measure is a Gaussian distribution with a mean value of $HW(x) = 50\%$, representing no bias of the start-up values towards zero or one and thus the same amount of both values.

The *fractional Within-class Hamming distance* gives an indication whether the PUF results for a single device are stable when queried repeatedly. It is a normalized count of bits that differ between two PUF measurements and thus is a rational number between 0 and 1. The robustness of the start-up values is required to reliably identify a given device and subsequently reconstruct the corresponding cryptographic key. An optimal value for the within-class Hamming distance is close to zero. However, all start-up values show a certain amount of noise, which originates from SRAM cells that flip their initialization value across multiple trials.

The *fractional Between-class Hamming distance* test expresses whether the start-up values of different devices for the same challenge are independent. This measure states whether start-up values can be used for identification without enabling adversaries to predict a measurement for a second device on the basis of a given device with known start-up values. The optimal value for between-class Hamming distance is a Gaussian distribution with a mean value of 50%, which refers to a pair of independent start-up values from two different devices. Devices with an optimal value exhibit a maximum distinguishability regarding their PUF responses given the same challenge.

3.2   Analysis of the Cortex-M

We evaluated the PUF behavior of an STMicroelectronics STM32F100RB development board that integrates an ARM Cortex-M3, 8 KiB on-chip SRAM and 128 KiB flash memory. To read the PUF measurement we modified the start-up code to display the raw start-up values via UART before the RAM gets initialized. The start-up code is essential to every microcontroller as it initializes the hardware as well as the stack and interrupt vectors and calls the main function.

To assess the PUF quality of the on-chip SRAM we tested 14 devices by extracting the 8 KiB SRAM start-up values 1000 times per device[2]. The devices were triggered using a controller board to repetitively turn the devices on, query the intrinsic PUF instance from on-chip SRAM and turn it off. In between these queries a break of 15 seconds was introduced to give the SRAM the chance to discharge. The summarized results in Table 1 show a decent PUF behavior that is suitable to robustly extract a unique fingerprint. Figure 2a shows the bitmap of an example measurement of one device.

The SRAM start-up values have a worst-case *Hamming Weight* of $HW(x) = 49.18\%$. This value is close to the ideal of 50%. The STM32F100RB start-up values contain almost the same proportion of zeros and ones as depicted in Figure 1a. The worst-case bias is negligible. The number for the *Within-class Hamming distance* in the worst-case is 9.61%, see Figure 1b. The existing proportion of noise can easily be correct by standard error correction algorithms. The minimum *Between-class Hamming distance* is 46.48%, see Figure 1c. The number shows that there is some correlation between the measurements of different devices. This has a negative impact on the size of SRAM bytes needed to reconstruct the device-dependent key. However, this measure is much higher then the noise retrieved for the individual devices. Hence, the start-up values can be used to uniquely identify devices if they are pre-processed by error correction algorithms.

The boxplots shown below can be interpreted as follows. The red line across the central region of each box marks the data median. The blue bottom/top indicates the $25^{th}/75^{th}$ percentile for the data set. The height of the box corresponds to the inter quartile range (IQR) of the data set. The ends of the whiskers mark the lowest and highest values of the data set that are within 1.5 times the IQR of the box edges. The plus signs represent single values that are outside the range of the whiskers.

---

[2] Due to the fragile nature of the test setup, some measurements produced on-chip SRAM values of incorrect length. We removed these obvious measurement errors from the data set. In total 27 out of 14.000 measurements have been removed.

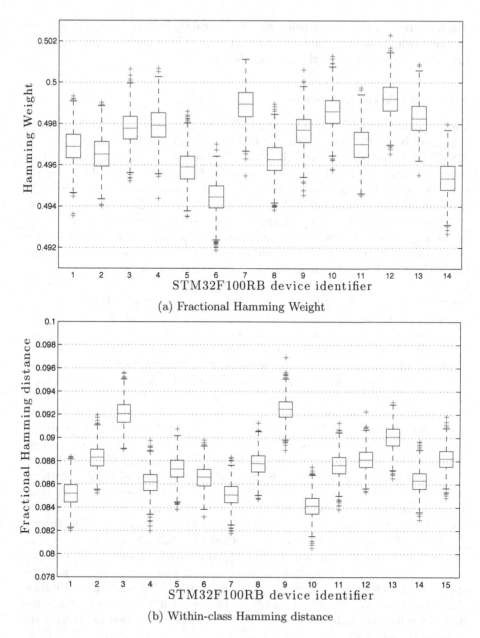

(a) Fractional Hamming Weight

(b) Within-class Hamming distance

Fig. 1. Detailed PUF characteristics for STM32F100RB devices: (a) Fractional Hamming Weights of SRAM start-up values. (b) Within-class fractional Hamming distance of SRAM start-up values. (c) Between-class fractional Hamming distance histogram.

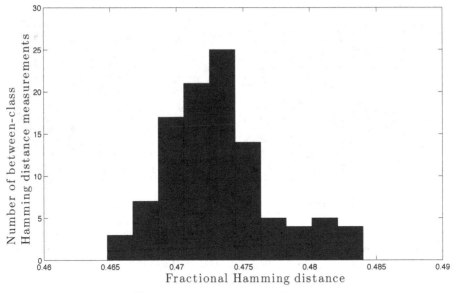

(c) Between-class Hamming distance

Fig. 1. (*Continued.*)

3.3 Analysis of the OMAP

The PandaBoard's OMAP 4 SoC contains two Cortex-M3 processors and thus PUF characteristics are expected, which are similar to those of the Cortex-M3. However, an extensive analysis is necessary because of highly-integrated active components (multimedia hardware accelerator, programmable DSP, integrated graphics processor), which could interfere with the SRAM start-up values. The SRAM is implemented as several instances of on-chip memory (OCM) featuring (i) OCM Save-and-Restore ROM (4 KiB) (ii) OCM Save-and-Restore RAM (8KiB) and (iii) Level-3 RAM (56 KiB).

Analysis of the OCM modules revealed that only a specific part exhibit PUF-like behavior. In particular, the Level-3 on-chip RAM (L3 OCM RAM) can be partially used to extract a fingerprint. The memory is shared among different sub-modules including the Cortex-M3 subsystem. Figure 2b shows the bitmap of the L3 OCM RAM from a PandaBoard shortly after the device gets out of reset.

The bitmap indicates that there are repeating structures in the middle and high address regions. As no other hardware is initialized at this early phase of the boot process we assume that these patterns represent structures used by the on-board ROM code shipped with every PandaBoard. The repeating structures could be caused by the ROM code's API interfaces. Furthermore, we assume that the L3 OCM RAM is used in a similar way as a stack as only higher addresses

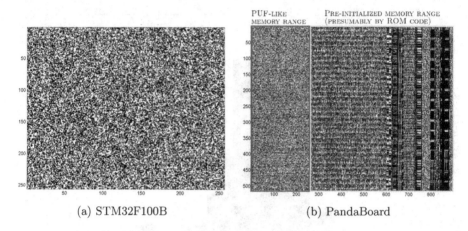

(a) STM32F100B   (b) PandaBoard

Fig. 2. (a) Bitmap of a measurement for STM32F100RB a device. (b) Bitmap of a PUF measurement of a PandaBoard L3 OCM RAM (56 KiB). The red area (12 KiB) is used for fingerprint extraction. The yellow area contains initialized values and does not show PUF characteristics.

exhibit such patterns. However, in the area of the first 12 KiB (0x40300000 – 0x40303000) an apparently random distribution of zeros and ones can be seen. This memory range refers to the part of the L3 OCM RAM we selected for further analysis regarding its PUF behavior.

We performed measurements on a set of 5 PandaBoard instances. The test set included two versions of the platform – an early version of the PandaBoard equipped with an OMAP4430 and an advanced version, PandaBoard ES, based on an OMAP4460. We were using the same experimental setup as for the STM32-F100RB to conduct 1000 measurements per board.

The SRAM start-up values have a worst-case *Hamming Weight* of $HW(x) =$ 48.53%, which is close to the ideal value of 50%. The measurement contains almost the same amount of zeros and ones, see Figure 3a, with a negligible bias towards 0. The OMAP SoC performs identical to the STM32F100 regarding this characteristic. The numbers for the *Within-class Hamming distance* are depicted in Figure 3b. They show a maximum within-class Hamming distance of 4.67%. This value is well below a bit error rate of 15%. In literature, an average bit error rate of 15% can be regarded as a reference value for SRAM PUF noise [13,14]. Compared to the STM32F100RB, the OMAP SoC exhibits less noise which leads to a decreased false rejection rate during the key reconstruction process. The minimum *Between-class Hamming distance* is 49.66%, see Figure 3c. Compared to the STM32F100RB the results for the OMAP 4 are even better, guaranteeing to provide a unique fingerprint for individual devices among a pool of similar platforms. However, it should be noted that the values for this measures are not as statistical significant as one might like. This is because we could only gather values from five distinct devices as it was not possible for us to get sufficient devices to provide as statistical significant results as desired for cost reasons. Table 1 shows the summarized results.

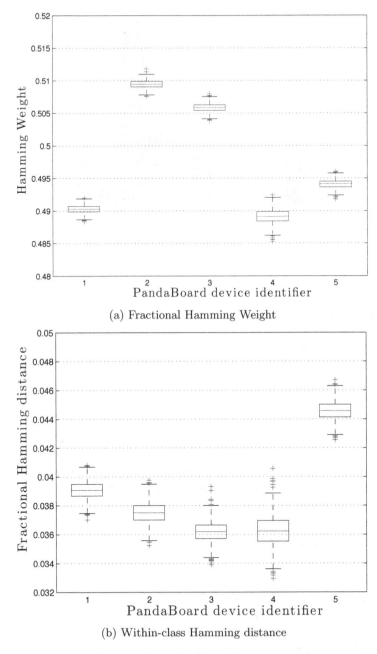

(a) Fractional Hamming Weight

(b) Within-class Hamming distance

Fig. 3. Detailed PUF characteristics for PandaBoards devices: (a) Fractional Hamming Weights of SRAM start-up values. (b) Within-class fractional Hamming distance of SRAM start-up values. (c) Between-class fractional Hamming distance histogram.

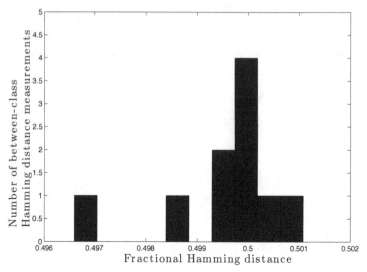

(c) Between-class Hamming distance

Fig. 3. (*Continued.*)

Table 1. PUF characteristics of the STM32F100RB and the OMAP 4 SoC

Characteristic	STM32	OMAP 4
Maximum within-class Hamming distance	9.61%	4.67%
Minimum between-class Hamming distance	46.48%	49.66%
Minimum Hamming weight	49.19%	48.53%
Maximum Hamming weight	50.23%	51.18%

4 PUF-Based Anti-counterfeiting Architecture

In this section we first introduce the capabilities of the attacker. Second, we introduce our proposed anti-counterfeiting architecture with respect to the attacker model. Finally, we show in detail how PUF enrollment and reconstruction works.

4.1 Attacker Model

A malicious party has several motives to attack deployed low-end devices. The attacker might want to extract intellectual property (IP) stored on the device in the form of software or secrets. After successful IP extraction the attacker would be able to use the IP on counterfeit devices or even sell self-made counterfeit solutions for less money than the original product. In another scenario the attacker might want to circumvent the vendor's licensing model by manipulating the firmware. To evade licensing restrictions the attacker could try either to modify the firmware to unlock features reserved for higher valued product versions or he attempts to downgrade to a previous firmware version, to exploit design flaws and consequently escalate privileges on the system. Another motivation to alter the firmware is to capture valuable user data like passwords, credentials and usage data. Furthermore, the attacker might be able to actively alter output data, as for example in the case of smart metering, to report fake consumption data.

For the attacker to achieve one of the mentioned goals we consider him to have the following abilities. The attacker has physical access to the device due to the device's ubiquitous availability or because the attacker possesses the device as a legitimate user. The attacker can read out the contents of the external memory (DDR or flash memory) as it is highly exposed to external accesses. Thus, we imply that the attacker can read out and change the firmware that is stored on external memory. Additionally, the attacker is able to inspect and modify on-chip memory values with software of his choice after the boot process.

Besides these capabilities we assure that the attacker can not perform one of the following actions. The attacker is not able to change the code of the boot loader. We assume that the boot loader is stored in a masked read-only memory (ROM), which is under control of the manufacturer. Furthermore, we consider an attacker to not be able to replace the ROM chip with a second one of his choice, containing boot code under his control. Especially in the case of system-on-a-chip platforms on-chip memory is highly integrated and a replacement of a memory module is beyond the means of the average-skilled attacker. Lastly, the attacker is not able to read out the start-up values of the on-chip SRAM during start-up. The start-up values are protected by the boot loader and are erased shortly after the device gets out of reset. As soon as the device is powered the boot loader reads the start-up values, immediately overwrites them and erases any their instances before the firmware is called. The boot loader is assumed to be trusted and cannot be replaced. Hence, the first possibility for the attacker to execute code of his choice is after the boot loader finished execution.

We are aware of the fact that a physical attacker in possession of sufficient resources in terms of time and money can circumvent virtually any security mechanism. Nevertheless, if the attacker would succeed to extract the SRAM start-up values, i.e. the cryptographic key, he would only able to attack this individual device and has to perform the same attack for any other device.

4.2   General Architecture

The proposed anti-counterfeiting solution is designed for implementation on a variety of commodity hardware without on-board security facilities ranging from lightweight devices to more complex SoC platforms. Our solution requires hardware components, which are already present in virtually any computing device. In particular, we require the devices to be equipped with a masked ROM to hold the modified boot loader, the processor containing the MCU itself, on-board RAM (which is the source of the PUF instance) and external memory to store the encrypted firmware and so-called Helper Data. Helper Data is needed to reliably reconstruct the key using the Fuzzy Extractor; its use will be explained in Section 4. Furthermore, we assume that the manufacturer can modify the boot loader to implement the key extraction and decryption functionality.

The structures of lightweight MCUs and more complex SoCs differ and require different approaches with respect to the architecture of our proposed solution. The general architecture of lightweight devices comprise the boot loader and the firmware. The entire boot loader needs to be stored irreversibly in masked ROM as it protects the SRAM start-up values and implements the functionality to derive the cryptographic key. The key is used to decrypt the firmware that is stored in external memory. In the case of more complex SoCs, usually a multi-staged boot loader is used consisting of a smaller part (1st-stage boot loader) that fits into on-chip SRAM and a larger part (2nd-stage boot loader) stored on external memory. Such platforms operate with a rich embedded operating system instead of a more basic firmware. Here, the 1st-stage boot loader will be modified to perform key extraction and decryption routines and must be stored in masked ROM. The derived key will be used to decrypt the 2nd-stage boot loader instead of the firmware in the MCU scenario. Figure 4 illustrates the two cases.

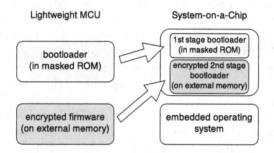

Fig. 4. Architecture of lightweight devices and more complex SoCs

The following paragraph explains the architecture for the SoC case in more detail as we used an SoC for our prototype implementation. In this scenario the 1st-stage bootloader is wired programmed in a masked ROM and is executed as the first binary after the device start-up[3]. It queries the SRAM PUF, deriving the device-dependent key K. The key exists in on-chip memory only for the period of the following two steps. K is used to decrypt the 2nd-stage boot loader, stored on non-volatile memory (e.g. flash memory). After successful decryption the 2nd-stage boot loader derives a second key K' by hashing the concatenation of K and a salt value N: $K' = H(K|N)$. Key K' is subsequently used to decrypt the compressed kernel file that also resides in non-volatile memory (NVM). The second key K' is derived to impede the reconstruction of the initial key K in case an attacker captures K'. If the attacker captured K' then a new version of the

---

[3] More precisely, on our implementation board the first code executed is vendor-specific initialization code, which cannot be disabled and leads to a pre-initialized part of the L3 OCM RAM.

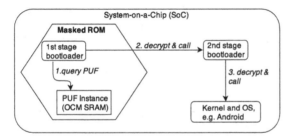

Fig. 5. Schematic view on the general architecture for SoC platforms

2nd-stage boot loader including a new salt must be deployed which will generate a different K'_{new}. Furthermore, a new version of the firmware, encrypted under a new key K'_{new} must be distributed to regain a secure state. This design assures that only a 2nd-stage boot loader can be executed that was encrypted by the correct device-depended cryptographic key K. Since the second key K' is derived from K also only such firmware can be properly loaded and executed, which was encrypted by the correct key as well. Thus, the operating system will only boot properly, if the correct combination of hardware and software is in place. The overall architecture is depicted in Figure 5.

4.3   Process of Usage

The usage of the proposed anti-counterfeiting architecture involves the enrollment of the used PUF (performed by the manufacturer) and the reconstruction phase (conducted every time the user boots the device).

Enrollment. The enrollment process is carried out by the manufacturer and is performed once for each device. It serves two main purposes: the derivation of key K and the generation of Helper Data W. The cryptographic key K is derived from a randomly chosen secret S by hashing it with a hash function H: $K = H(S)$. The secret S is predefined by the manufacturer and must be unique for every device. Since the start-up values always contain a certain amount of noise the raw start-up values need to be further processed to derive a stable output. This is done by applying a Fuzzy Extractor algorithm, to generate so-called Helper Data W. The Helper Data is constructed by XORing the output of the concatenated Fuzzy Extractor with the SRAM reference measurement R (the raw SRAM start-up values).

Helper Data will be used later during the reconstruction phase to reconstruct the secret S and to derive the key K given a noisy SRAM measurement R'. W is stored in external memory as it does not leak information about S. To protect the helper data from tampering several methods can be applied, such as the approach described by Boyen [6]. The enrollment process is shown in the upper part of Figure 6.

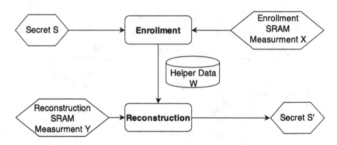

Fig. 6. Illustration of the enrollment and reconstruction of the Fuzzy Extractor

Reconstruction. The reconstruction process is performed at user's side and is executed every time the user boots the corresponding device. After the device gets out of reset, the 1st-stage boot loader reads and stores the noisy SRAM start-up values R' and immediately overwrites the start-up values to make them inaccessible to a physical attacker. In a second step the boot loader reads the Helper Data W from external memory. The Fuzzy Extractor XORs R' with W and decodes the output using the concatenated decoders to construct the secret S'. The generated secret S' will only be equal to the correct secret S if the Helper Data corresponds to the respective device having SRAM start-up values R' that are similar to the enrollment measurement: $d(R, R') < \epsilon$. Next, the key K is derived by hashing secret S', which in turn is used to decrypt the firmware or the 2nd-stage boot loader, depending on the scenario. The schematic composition of the reconstruction processes is depicted in the lower part of Figure 6.

5   Proof of Concept

We implemented the proposed anti-counterfeiting architecture on a SoC platform. We chose an SoC platform for the following reasons. Primarily, we wanted to prove the feasibility to robustly extract a unique fingerprint also from more complex platforms. Furthermore, the boot process is more complicated compared to lightweight devices. Our intention was to show that the proposed solution can be implemented into existing boot loaders. Lastly, the size of the memory available on the SoC for implementing the Fuzzy Extractor logic is comparable to the STM32F100 and similar low-end devices as shown in Section 3. Hence, the requirements regarding memory footprint are equal to those of low-end devices. A successful implementation for the SoC proves the feasibility to implement the architecture for lightweight devices as well.

We used u-boot [8,7], one of the most widely deployed boot loaders. It integrates a 1st-stage boot loader (Memory Locator — MLO), which is small enough to fit into on-chip memory and a larger 2nd-stage boot loader (u-boot.img). The MLO performs minor hardware initialization as well as the setup of external DDR memory. Afterwards it calls u-boot.img that is copied to DDR memory. It initializes further hardware components and eventually calls the operating system kernel.

Enrollment. According to Section 4, the Helper Data W is derived from a randomly chosen secret S and a reference measurement R using a Fuzzy Extractor during the enrollment phase. The Fuzzy Extractor design is based on the construction presented by Bösch et. al [5] and will be explained in more detail in Section 5.1. We also adapted the size for the secret S (22 Byte) from Bösch's design. During the enrollment also the key K is generated by hashing the secret S with the SHA-1 hash function to a 128 bit key such that it can be used as input for the AES cryptosystem in the next step. Having a secret that is larger then the generated key ensures sufficient entropy. K is used to encrypt the u-boot.img using the AES-128 block cipher. The second key K' is used to encrypt the kernel image file (uImage). The generated Helper Data is 675 bytes in total. Eventually, the Helper Data, as well as the encrypted files are stored in non-volatile memory (e.g. the flash card).

Reconstruction. The main part of the reconstruction logic is implemented in the MLO, being one of the first pieces of code to be executed. As described in Section 4 the MLO extracts the on-chip memory chip's fingerprint R' and processes it using a Fuzzy Extractor to derive the device-dependent key K. The Fuzzy extractor requires 675 bytes of L3 OCM RAM SRAM start-up values as well as W from the external memory to reconstruct K. Subsequently, K is used to decrypt u-boot.img. In particular, one after another 16 bytes of the decrypted u-boot.img are read in on-chip memory, get decrypted and are written back to external memory. Subsequently u-boot.img is called and in case of successful decryption it is executed. If the false key K was generated a fault handler routine is called, displays a warning message and cancels the boot process. A detailed scheme of the reconstruction process is depicted in Figure 7.

5.1 Fuzzy Extractor Design

To reproduce the secret key S from various noisy measurements error-correction is required. Following the suggestions of [5] we decided to implement a concatenated code comprising of two linear codes – a Golay code and a repetition code – to reconstruct the 22 byte secret. In particular, we are using a binary Golay-(23,12,7) code in combination with a repetition code with 15 repetitions. The false rejection rate (FRR) of the concatenated code P_e(total) can be calculated by equation (3). It is derived from the FRR probabilities of the linear repetition code – equation (1) – and the Golay code – equation (2).

$$P_e(\text{Repetition}) = \sum_{i=\lceil s/2 \rceil}^{s} \epsilon^i (1-\epsilon)^{s-i} \binom{s}{i} \qquad (1)$$

$$P_e(\text{Golay}) = \sum_{i=4}^{23} P_e(\text{Repetition})^i (1 - P_e(\text{Repetition}))^{23-i} \binom{23}{i} \qquad (2)$$

$$P_e(\text{total}) = 1 - (1 - P_e(\text{Golay}))^g \qquad (3)$$

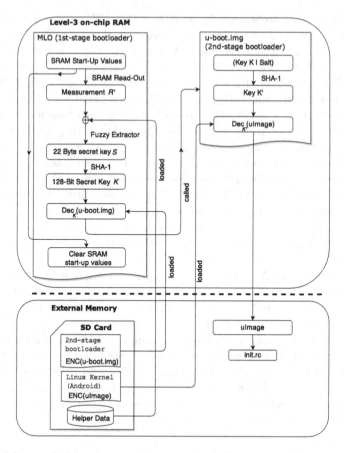

Fig. 7. Scheme of the reconstruction process of the ephemeral key inside the anti-counterfeiting architecture

Here, s is the number of repetitions, ϵ is the average bit error rate (BER) and g is the number of Golay code words needed (g = secret length/12). With this construction we can achieve a false rejection rate of 10^{-8} given an average BER of 15% as commonly used in literature [5]. The false rejection rate of the OMAP devices will be even lower since the measured BER is well below the reference value of 15% used in the calculations. Thus, the Fuzzy Extractor Design is suitable to reliably reconstruct a cryptographic key given several noisy SRAM PUF measurements for individual devices. The implemented Fuzzy Extractor requires 675 bytes of SRAM data to reconstruct a 22 Byte secret. The implementation requires only 0,05% of the available on-chip SRAM memory.

6   Conclusion

In this paper we proposed an anti-counterfeiting architecture and implementation for low-end devices by using intrinsic Physically Unclonable Functions found in commodity hardware. Our approach does not require additional hardware and can be implemented the on-chip memory as a PUF and modifying the boot loader to extract a device-specific cryptographic key to decrypt the firmware with the device-specific key. We showed that low-end devices – including lightweight devices as well as System-on-a-Chip platforms – contain PUF instances that can be used to robustly identify the device. The analysis of the extracted on-board PUF instance showed almost optimal characteristics. Thus, our proposed solution is suitable to strengthen the security of low-end devices without on-board security mechanisms, keeping the costs at a minimum while significantly raising the efforts for attackers trying to extract or modify the firmware stored on such devices.

References

1. ARM TrustZone, http://www.arm.com/products/processors/technologies/trustzone/index.php (last accessed on January 17, 2014)
2. PandaBoard Platform, http://pandaboard.org/content/platform (last accessed on January 17, 2014)
3. ARM. ARM Holdings PLC Reports Results For The Fourth Quarter and Full Year (2013), http://www.arm.com/about/newsroom/arm-holdings-plc-reports-results-for-the-fourth-quarter-and-full-year-2013.php (last accessed on March 7, 2014)
4. Atzori, L., Iera, A., Morabito, G.: The Internet of Things: A Survey. Computer Networks: The International Journal of Computer and Telecommunications Networking, 2787–2805 (2010)
5. Bösch, C., Guajardo, J., Sadeghi, A.-R., Shokrollahi, J., Tuyls, P.: Efficient Helper Data Key Extractor on FPGAs. In: Oswald, E., Rohatgi, P. (eds.) CHES 2008. LNCS, vol. 5154, pp. 181–197. Springer, Heidelberg (2008)
6. Boyen, X.: Reusable Cryptographic Fuzzy Extractors. In: ACM Conference on Computer and Communications Security, pp. 82–91 (2004)
7. Denk, W.: Das U-Boot – the Universal Boot Loader, http://www.denx.de/wiki/U-Boot (last accessed on July 9, 2013)
8. Ding, X., Liao, Y., Fu, J., Huang, H., Liu, W.: Analysis of Bootloader and Transplantation of U-Boot Based on S5PC100 Processor. In: Proceedings of the 2011 Third International Conference on Intelligent Human-Machine Systems and Cybernetics - Volume 01, IHMSC 2011, pp. 61–64 (2011)
9. Dodis, Y., Reyzin, L., Smith, A.: Fuzzy Extractors: How to Generate Strong Keys from Biometrics and Other Noisy Data. In: Cachin, C., Camenisch, J.L. (eds.) EUROCRYPT 2004. LNCS, vol. 3027, pp. 523–540. Springer, Heidelberg (2004)
10. Feiri, M., Petit, J., Kargl, F.: Efficient and Secure Storage of Private Keys for Pseudonymous Vehicular Communication. In: Proceedings of the 2013 ACM Workshop on Security, Privacy & Dependability for Cyber Vehicles, CyCAR 2013, pp. 9–18 (2013)
11. Guajardo, J., Kumar, S.S., Schrijen, G.-J., Tuyls, P.: FPGA Intrinsic PUFs and Their Use for IP Protection. In: Paillier, P., Verbauwhede, I. (eds.) CHES 2007. LNCS, vol. 4727, pp. 63–80. Springer, Heidelberg (2007)
12. Kortuem, G., Kawsar, F., Sundramoorthy, V., Fitton, D.: Smart Objects As Building Blocks for the Internet of Things. IEEE Internet Computing, 44–51 (2010)

13. Maes, R., Tuyls, P., Verbauwhede, I.: Low-Overhead Implementation of a Soft Decision Helper Data Algorithm for SRAM PUFs. In: Clavier, C., Gaj, K. (eds.) CHES 2009. LNCS, vol. 5747, pp. 332–347. Springer, Heidelberg (2009)
14. Maes, R., Tuyls, P., Verbauwhede, I.: Soft Decision Helper Data Algorithm for SRAM PUFs. In: Proceedings of the 2009 IEEE International Conference on Symposium on Information Theory - Volume 3, ISIT 2009, Coex, Seoul, Korea, pp. 2101–2105 (2009)
15. Maes, R., Verbauwhede, I.: Physically Unclonable Functions: A Study on the State of the Art and Future Research Directions. In: Towards Hardware-Intrinsic Security, Information Security and Cryptography, pp. 3–37 (2010)
16. Papadimitratos, P., De La Fortelle, A., Evenssen, K., Brignolo, R., Cosenza, S.: Vehicular Communication Systems: Enabling Technologies, Applications, and Future Outlook on Intelligent Transportation. IEEE Communications Magazine, 84–95 (2009)
17. Schrijen, G.J., van der Leest, V.: Comparative analysis of SRAM memories used as PUF primitives. In: DATE, pp. 1319–1324 (2012)
18. Yick, J., Mukherjee, B., Ghosal, D.: Computer Networks: The International Journal of Computer and Telecommunications Networking. Comput. Netw., 2292–2330 (2008)

Evaluation of Bistable Ring PUFs
Using Single Layer Neural Networks

Dieter Schuster and Robert Hesselbarth

Fraunhofer Institute for Applied and Integrated Security (AISEC), Munich, Germany
{firstname.lastname}@aisec.fraunhofer.de

Abstract. This paper presents an analysis of a bistable ring physical unclonable function (BR-PUF) implemented on a field-programmable gate array (FPGA) using a single layer artificial neural network (ANN). The BR-PUF was proposed as a promising circuit-based strong PUF candidate, given that a simple model for its behaviour is unknown by now and hence modeling-based attacks would be hard. In contrast to this, we were able to find a strongly linear influence in the mapping of challenges to responses in this architecture. Further, we show how an alternative implementation of a bistable ring, the twisted bistable ring PUF (TBR-PUF), leads to an improved response behaviour. The effectiveness and a possible explaination of the improvements is demonstrated using our machine learning analysis approach.

Keywords: bistable ring, twisted bistable ring, PUF, FPGA, machine learning, artificial neural network.

1 Introduction

Physical unclonable functions (PUFs) are physical structures, which exhibit a device-specific challenge-response behaviour. These structures are meant to be hard or impossible to reproduce and their measurement mechanism can for example be optical, magnetic, or electric. In this paper, we focus on so called *strong PUFs* [8,4], which are designed to achieve complex challenge-response behaviour for a large set of possible challenges in relation to the size of their design.

A possible realisation of PUFs can be achieved based on silicon integrated-circuits, where the device-specific behaviour is caused by uncontrollable variations in the manufacturing process. Examples of silicon PUFs, which yield an exponential number of CRPs related to their size, e. g. number of gates, and hence can be considered as strong PUFs, are the arbiter PUF [5] together with its variants and the bistable ring PUF (BR-PUF) [2,3].

Strong PUFs are especially useful for authentication, for which the standard procedure works as follows. First, a trusted third party or the manufacturer of the device reads out a large number of challenge-response pairs (CRPs) from the PUF and saves them to a database. Afterwards, a verifier sends challenges to the device with the PUF and compares the responses to the ones stored in the database of the trusted third party. This can be repeated to compensate for

T. Holz and S. Ioannidis (Eds.): TRUST 2014, LNCS 8564, pp. 101–109, 2014.

inherent measurement errors of the PUF until a certain level of confidence has been reached.

Although PUFs are designed so that every instance provides a unique behaviour, there is the possible attack vector of creating another hardware or software that behaves the same way as the PUF instance and thus is able to predict the output of the PUF for a given challenge. The security of the PUF primitive in this scenario lies in the large amount of possible CRPs and the time an attacker would need for a complete readout. Having gathered a complete list of CRPs, an attacker is then able to impersonate the PUF device, because she can answer every challenge with the response the PUF would return.

An attacker can reduce the amount of CRPs she needs to read out from the PUF by applying machine learning techniques. The idea is to train a machine learning model with a subset of possible CRPs to approximate the behaviour of a PUF instance. Since the CRP behaviour of PUFs is noisy, the trained model is indistinguishable from the PUF instance, if the learning error approaches its noise level.

Based on the additive delay model of the arbiter PUF, Lim et al. [7] were able to successfully model implementations on FPGAs and ASICs with a linear support vector machine (SVM). Later, Rührmair et al. [10] analysed a set of popular silicon PUFs based on CRPs generated by a software implementation of the PUF model. Using logistic regression and evolutional strategies, they concluded that those architectures where vulnerable to machine learning attacks. Hospodar et al. confirmed those findings for actual implementations of arbiter PUFs on 65nm ASICs [6], using a single layer artificial neural network (ANN). The results of these work is that the behaviour of those PUF instances could be learned with a linear machine learning model.

In this paper, we use a single layer ANN to analyse CRP data obtained from an FPGA implementation of a BR-PUF, and a recently proposed variant called twisted bistable ring PUF (TBR-PUF) to demonstrate the shortcomings of BR-PUFs in a strong PUF scenario. The analysis is performed on the basic PUF design without any special hardening against machine learning techniques, like pre-processing of challenges or post-processing of responses [4]. Our first result is the evaluation and comparison of the quality of this PUF design. In contrast to previous work, we use ANNs to evaluate the behaviour of measured CRP data without assuming a model of the PUF. This avoids that the evaluation is biased by some model assumption based on the design. Finally, we want to suggest machine learning techniques not only as an attack or benchmark on PUFs, but also as a tool for improving the design and implementation of PUFs.

2   Bistable Ring and Twisted Bistable Ring PUF

The BR-PUF, as proposed by Chen et al. [2], consists of either two NAND gates or two NOR gates per stage. The challenge bit for each stage decides which gate will be connected to the inverter ring and thus which gate delay will be introduced to the ring. This is achieved by a multiplexer (MUX) after each stage

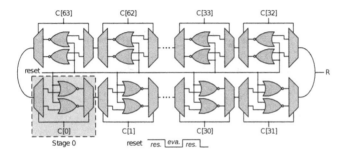

Fig. 1. 64-bit BR-PUF taken from [2,3]

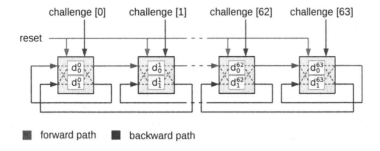

Fig. 2. Concept of a 64-bit TBR-PUF

and a demultiplexer (DEMUX) before each stage. Figure 1 shows an example for a 64-bit BR-PUF, where 2^{64} different ring configurations can be created by applying different challenges. The created bistable ring will be released into an oscillating state, which will finally settle in one of two possible stable states, resulting in a single response bit. The BR-PUF is based on an oscillating system and its behaviour is expected to be non-linear [2] and hence more complex than that of constructions like the arbiter PUF. Also a simple modelling technique has not been found [3]. However, we show that the behaviour of a BR-PUF implemented in FPGAs can be approximated linearly by a large part.

An alternative PUF implementation, the twisted bistable ring PUF (TBR-PUF), was proposed recently [1]. In comparison to the BR-PUF, the challenge bits do not influence which inverters of each stage will be included in the ring. Instead, every inverter is always included, and the challenge influences the positions of the inverters (at even or odd stages) in the ring. Figure 2 illustrates this concept.

3 Methodology of Evaluation

Generation of CRPs. For generating the CRPs we used 20 different Digilent NEXYS FPGA boards with Xilinx Spartan-6 FPGAs that were all configured with the identical design in form of the same bitstream. Each board represents

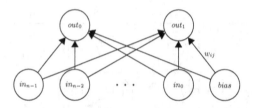

Fig. 3. A visualisation of our single layer ANN

an *instance* of the PUF design. We then once generated 50000 randomly chosen challenges in order to use the same set of challenges for each instance. Because PUF responses are inherently noisy, we measured an odd number of 11 *iterations* for each challenge, and performed a simple error correction by majority voting to compensate the PUF noise.

Analysis of CRP data. Assuming that the majority value for each challenge is the desired value, the *noise* per challenge can be determined by dividing the number of deviating responses by the number of iterations. Then, the noise of the PUF instance is the average over the noise of all measured challenges. The *bias* of an instance is the average of the responses of all challenges and all iterations. Ideally, a PUF instance should show a balanced behaviour with an average response of 0.5. Since we are interested only in the deviation from the ideal value 0.5, we use the absolute value of the difference between 0.5 and the average response value as *bias deviation*.

Approximation of the BR-PUF behaviour using a linear approximation. Usually, when trying to approximate data in machine learning, it is considered beneficial to integrate as much as possible prior knowledge into the machine learning model. This is especially true for those work mentioned in Section 1, where evolutional strategies where used, because a theoretical model has to be postulated beforehand. Also, when using evolutional strategies in case of the BR-PUF, a mathematical model of the behaviour of bistable rings has to be established.

Because there is no known model for the BR-PUF yet [2], we use a rather simple linear model for approximating the BR-PUF. Since other PUF constructions like the arbiter PUF were also approximated with linear models, the results for the BR-PUF using such a model enables a comparison regarding the complexity of the behaviour of these designs in future work. In addition, we want to employ an estimator that is not biased with our knowledge about the implementation of the PUF. The rationale is to find relations in data from real devices, which are not obvious for an analyst knowing the design of the PUF. Finding relations like this might help in improving PUF designs. Further, we want to analyse to which degree the challenge-response behaviour of BR-PUFs can be approximated by a linear machine learning model.

We decided to use a single layer artificial neural network (ANN) as machine learning model, which can approximate any linear function while being unbiased about the linear function to be approximated. Figure 3 shows our chosen neural network, which consists of n input neurons, where n is the number of bits of the challenges, plus one bias neuron, which is constantly set to 1. The input layer is fully connected to the output layer with weights w, where weight w_{ij} is the weight connecting input neuron i to output neuron j. Having a seperate set of weights for each possible outcome makes it possible to analyse the impact of certain challenge bits c_k for each possible result bit. As the problem at hand is a classification problem of whether the response is 0 or 1, our network has two output neurons. This represents a one-hot encoding, where depending on the response bit one of the output neurons should be ideally 1 and the other 0 respectively. The output function of the network is softmax, which in our case is

$$softmax(out_j) = \frac{\exp(out_j)}{\exp(out_0) + \exp(out_1)}; \quad out_j = w_{bias,j} + \sum_{k=0}^{n-1} c_k * w_{kj}$$

with j being the index of the output neuron and n being the number of output neurons, so that the network yields two normalised probabilties for the two possible outcomes. The loss used for validation of the network is a zero-one loss function that sums up the samples which were not correctly predicted[1].

Since challenge bits are zeroes and ones, one would not be able to learn the impact of both inputs, as the output layer would only be influenced by the challenge bits, which are set to 1. To equally allow bits set to 0 to influence the output bits, we apply a preprocessing in which we replace zeroes in the input data with -1 similar to previous work [10]. As optimisation algorithm we employ Rprop [9] which some of the related work [10,6] showed to be the best option for learning CRPs for many PUF architectures.

For the learning process itself, we applied 5-fold cross-validation on error corrected CRP data.

Analysis of the trained neural network. We finally search for patterns among the weights of the trained ANN in order to better understand the challenge-response behaviour of the PUF.

4   Analysis of the Measured CRP Data

Using the data from the FPGA implementation of BR-PUF and TBR-PUF, we analysed the noise of the responses, the bias deviation of the PUF instances, and the error of fitting our ANN against them.

Bias deviation and noise. The values for bias deviation and noise of the PUF are valuable to estimate the quality of the PUF regarding modelling attacks independent of our learned ANN. The noise level is important, since it suffices for an attacker to guess correctly often enough so that a verifier cannot distinguish

---

[1] Negative cross entropy is used for training as zero-one loss is not differentiable.

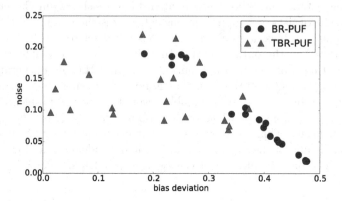

Fig. 4. Relation of bias deviation and noise for 20 instances of both PUF types

between responses from a real PUF and from the guesses of an attacker. When considering both, bias deviation and noise combined, it becomes apparent that it is beneficial for an attacker when the bias deviation and high noise level is high.

Figure 4 shows our results. When looking at the noise of the CRPs of the BR-PUF, some of the instances have a rather low noise level below 10%. However, the same instances also show a rather high bias deviation. The low noise can hence be based upon the fact that those instances return the same response in over 90% of all challenges and their iterations. This relation can be seen in Figure 4, where an ideal PUF instance would be plottet at the origin. The TBR-PUF instances show more noise in the CRP data compared to the ones of the BR-PUF, although the highest noise level is still under 23%. However, there is a much lower bias deviation for the majority of TBR-PUF instances.

Linear approximation. This strongly biased behaviour in the BR-PUF CRPs should also simplify fitting our ANN to the data. Figure 5 visualises the learning error a potential attacker using a single layer ANN would be able to achieve. The lower the error, the better she can reproduce the behaviour. We can see in Figure 5a that the majority of BR-PUF instances were linearily approximated with an error below 10%.

Comparing these results to the learning error distribution for the TBR-PUF data in Figure 5b, a positive correlation can be observed between lower bias and higher learning error. From this, we hypothesise that the TBR-PUF might be more resilient to attacks that are based on a linear model. Here, the majority of instances could only be approximated by an error of at least 10%.

Analysis of the trained neural network. When analysing the influence that the weights of the trained ANN have on each of the output neurons, we noticed no emerging patterns except for the weights of the bias neuron. In the case of a heavily biased PUF, these two weights were the only significant ones.

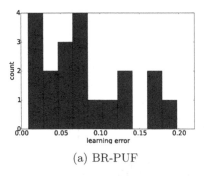

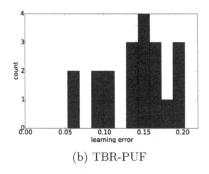

(a) BR-PUF (b) TBR-PUF

Fig. 5. Distribution of the learning errors among all instances

This shows that, in these cases, our ANN primarily matches a naive attacker, who simply makes use of the strongly biased response behaviour, without taking the challenge into account. Since the softmax function in our binary classification problem can be simplified to the decision of which output neuron gets the higher activation, we analysed the difference between the weights for the output neuron responsible for the response 0 and the weights for the output neuron responsible for the response 1:

$$w_i^{comb} = w_{i0} - w_{i1}$$

The result of the combined weight vector is shown in Figure 6. There, it is apparent that the bias weight has a major influence over all measured BR-PUF instances. However, there is also an emerging pattern in the weights that model the influence of the challenges. The weights for the challenge bits are rather close to 0 and their sign is alternating. From observation of the weight distribution the formula of the learned decision function can be given as

$$d = w_{bias}^{comb} + \sum_{i=0}^{63} (-1)^i * w_i^{comb} * c_i; \qquad response = \begin{cases} 0 : d \geq 0 \\ 1 : d < 0 \end{cases}$$

where c_i are the bits of the challenge.

Figure 7 shows the weights after fitting our neural network to the TBR-PUF CRPs, combined in the same way we used above. Here, it can be observed that, compared to the BR-PUF results, the combined weight of the bias neurons has less impact and that the challenge bits thus are more influential towards the response. However, it is still possible to recognise an alternating pattern in some of the weights of the challenge bits. This is an indicator that this alternating pattern might be a common feature of linear behaviour in bistable ring based constructs, which emerges depending on the actual implementation of the ring.

The decision function d, which expresses the alternating pattern in the weights, can be interpreted as grouping the bistable ring stages that are influenced by the challenge bits at even respectively odd positions. Subtracting their gate delay values will decide with high probability what the response will be. If both

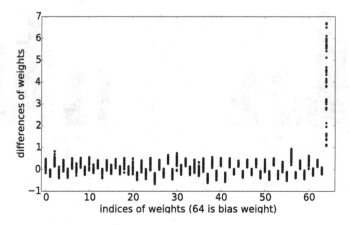

Fig. 6. Combined weights for all instances of BR-PUF

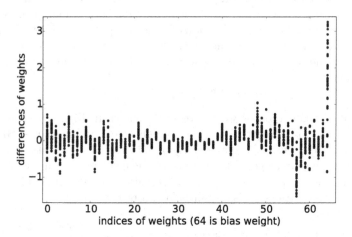

Fig. 7. Combined weights for all instances of TBR-PUF

inverters in one stage have a similar gate delay relatively to the others, then the
bit for this stage will not be influential. This seemed to be the case for some of
our *instances*. However, as can be seen in Section 1, in the case of the TBR-PUF,
the challenge bit influences which gate delays are at even and odd positions in
the stages of the ring. This appears to be the reason, why the TBR-PUF shows
a better behaviour regarding the bias and is harder to approximate by a linear
machine learning model.

5   Conclusion

In this paper, we show that the challenge-response behaviour of a bistable ring
PUF implemented on FPGAs shows weaknesses. The weaknesses are related to

the noise, bias, and linearity of the PUF. We found those weaknesses without a known mathematical model of the BR-PUF, but only by training a single layer artificial neural network with CRP data obtained from real devices.

Further, we demonstrate how machine learning not only can be used to to attack strong PUFs, but also how it can contribute to improvements of PUFs by finding weak spots in the design. The analysis of trained models helps discovering and understanding previously unknown relations between challenges and responses. Those insights can then be used to improve the PUF design. Notably, an example of such an unexpected behaviour was the linear relation found in the BR-PUF data as well as, in extenuated form, in the data for the TBR-PUF. This was surprising, because one would expect that a mathematical model with higher complexity would be necessary to explain the data generated by such an oscillating system reasonably well [2].

We show that the twisted bistable ring PUF is an improvement to the BR-PUF regarding bias and resistance against linear approximation and explain this improvement with the afore mentioned machine learning analysis techniques.

References

1. Modelling and improving bistable ring pufs (under submission)
2. Chen, Q., Csaba, G., Lugli, P., Schlichtmann, U., Rührmair, U.: The bistable ring puf: A new architecture for strong physical unclonable functions. In: HOST, pp. 134–141. IEEE Computer Society (2011)
3. Chen, Q., Csaba, G., Lugli, P., Schlichtmann, U., Rührmair, U.: Characterization of the bistable ring puf. In: Rosenstiel, W., Thiele, L. (eds.) DATE, pp. 1459–1462. IEEE (2012)
4. Gassend, B., Clarke, D.E., van Dijk, M., Devadas, S.: Silicon physical random functions. In: Atluri, V. (ed.) ACM Conference on Computer and Communications Security, pp. 148–160. ACM (2002)
5. Gassend, B., Lim, D., Clarke, D.E., van Dijk, M., Devadas, S.: Identification and authentication of integrated circuits. Concurrency - Practice and Experience 16(11), 1077–1098 (2004)
6. Hospodar, G., Maes, R., Verbauwhede, I.: Machine learning attacks on 65nm arbiter pufs: Accurate modeling poses strict bounds on usability. In: WIFS, pp. 37–42. IEEE (2012)
7. Lim, D., Lee, J.W., Gassend, B., Suh, G.E., van Dijk, M., Devadas, S.: Extracting secret keys from integrated circuits. IEEE Trans. VLSI Syst. 13(10), 1200–1205 (2005)
8. Pappu, R., Recht, B., Taylor, J., Gershenfeld, N.: Physical one-way functions. Science 297(5589), 2026–2030 (2002)
9. Riedmiller, M., Braun, H.: A direct adaptive method for faster backpropagation learning: The rprop algorithm. In: IEEE International Conference on Neural Networks (1993)
10. Rührmair, U., Sehnke, F., Sölter, J., Dror, G., Devadas, S., Schmidhuber, J.: Modeling attacks on physical unclonable functions. In: Proceedings of the 17th ACM Conference on Computer and Communications Security, CCS 2010, pp. 237–249. ACM, New York (2010)

Large-Scale Security Analysis of the Web: Challenges and Findings

Tom van Goethem, Ping Chen, Nick Nikiforakis,
Lieven Desmet, and Wouter Joosen

iMinds-DistriNet, KU Leuven
3001 Leuven, Belgium
{firstname.lastname}@cs.kuleuven.be

Abstract. As the web expands in size and adoption, so does the interest of attackers who seek to exploit web applications and exfiltrate user data. While there is a steady stream of news regarding major breaches and millions of user credentials compromised, it is logical to assume that, over time, the applications of the bigger players of the web are becoming more secure. However, as these applications become resistant to most prevalent attacks, adversaries may be tempted to move to easier, unprotected targets which still hold sensitive user data.

In this paper, we report on the state of security for more than 22,000 websites that originate in 28 EU countries. We first explore the adoption of countermeasures that can be used to defend against common attacks and serve as indicators of "security consciousness". Moreover, we search for the presence of common vulnerabilities and weaknesses and, together with the adoption of defense mechanisms, use our findings to estimate the overall security of these websites. Among other results, we show how a website's popularity relates to the adoption of security defenses and we report on the discovery of three, previously unreported, attack variations that attackers could have used to attack millions of users.

1 Introduction

Over the last decade, the web has become extremely popular. Businesses heavily depend on the web for their day-to-day operations, and billions of users interact on social networking websites on a daily basis. As a consequence of this enormous growth in popularity, the web has also drawn increased attention from attackers. A whole range of web attacks exists in the wild, ranging from Cross-Site Scripting (XSS), Cross-Site Request Forgery (CSRF), and SQL injection, to the exploitation of broken authorization and session management. Moreover, as the technologies that support the web increase in numbers and complexity, new opportunities for exploitable vulnerabilities increase with them.

To assess a website's security, website owners typically choose security consulting firms for internal penetration testing, and code reviewing. It is difficult, however, for outsiders like government and supervisory organizations to assess a website's security externally, especially when the assessment needs to be done

T. Holz and S. Ioannidis (Eds.): TRUST 2014, LNCS 8564, pp. 110–126, 2014.

at a larger scale, e.g., involving a large number of websites belonging to a country, or a specific industry sector. Such an assessment may be desirable since the citizens of each country depend more and more on certain web applications for their daily lives. An example of a real-world equivalent is the mandatory assessment of the structural safety of buildings in order to protect people from future disasters that could have been straightforwardly avoided.

In this paper, we investigate the feasibility of external security evaluations through a large-scale security analysis of the web. In particular, we evaluate the security stance of popular websites in the European Union (EU), and investigate the differences among countries.

To evaluate a website's security, existing approaches typically focus on the discovery of vulnerabilities in websites. For example, WhiteHat publishes yearly reports on website security statistics [31], highlighting the ten most common vulnerabilities, and discussing new attack vectors. Contrastingly, our approach not only accounts for common vulnerabilities and weaknesses, but also measures the presence of security mechanisms deployed on the investigated websites. These mechanisms have been developed by the security community as a response to web application attacks, making their adoption a crucial step towards a more secure web. The presence or absence of each of these mechanisms can be passively detected and can be used as an indicator of the "security consciousness" of each individual site.

In addition, in order to be able to compare websites by their security posture, we also propose a security scoring system for assessing a website's security level, and based on the scoring system, we present a comparative security analysis of European websites. Finally, because of the breadth of our analysis, we report on the discovery of novel variations of existing web application attacks. In one of the discovered cases, an attacker can register an expired Google Code project and serve malicious JavaScript to millions of users of sites that once trusted that specific project for remote code.

Our findings allow the community to assess the adoption of security mechanisms by websites at a large scale, and also prioritize corrective action, based on the severity of the discovered issues. Moreover, we list the challenges that we faced in our experiment, and provide possible directions towards future research in the area.

2   Data Collection

2.1   Dataset

For our experiment, we selected popular websites from the EU as the targets, to evaluate website security, and investigate the presence of potential differences between countries. The 28 member states in the EU represent a diverse set of communities, each with their own demographic characteristics. For each EU country, we selected the top 1,000 websites ending with a country code top-level domain (ccTLD) from Alexa's list of the top 1 million sites. For example, 1,000 websites ending with the Belgian ccTLD '.be' are extracted to represent the

Belgian web. Note that several small EU countries (such as Luxembourg and Malta) do not have 1,000 websites in Alexa's top 1 million list, so we end up with a few countries having less than 1,000 websites in our dataset. We then obtained up to 200 webpage URLs for each website by querying the Bing search engine [1] for the popular webpages of each website. In total, we analyzed more than 3 million webpages for 22,851 EU websites with an average of 141 webpages per website.

2.2   Crawler Setup

After the webpage URLs are obtained, PhantomJS [5], a headless browser, is used to visit the URLs and retrieve data from webpages. By loading every webpage within PhantomJS, we mimicked the behavior of a regular visitor using a Chrome browser. In order to crawl a large number of webpages in reasonable time, we run the experiment in a distributed fashion using 60 networked machines. As a result, our crawling experiment took approximately five days.

3   Security Scoring System

In order to compare the security level among different websites, and among different EU countries (represented by the websites of each country), we developed a security scoring system that gives quantitative security scores for each website. The security scores for a website consist of two parts: a positive score to represent the defense mechanisms adopted by the website (such as the X-Frame-Options and Content-Security-Policy headers), and a negative score for vulnerabilities or weaknesses (such as vulnerable remote JavaScript inclusions and insecure SSL implementations) found on it. For each defense mechanism and vulnerability/weakness, the security scoring system assigns a weighted positive and negative score. The overall positive and negative score for a website, is obtained by summing up each weighted positive and negative score respectively.

Due to our ethically-guided choice of conducting passive analysis for the majority of our tests, our search was limited to eight defense mechanisms, and ten vulnerabilities/weaknesses for each website. In principle, however, the security scoring system is scalable to more measurements. In the following sections, we briefly describe these defense mechanisms and vulnerabilities/weaknesses and elaborate on the scoring system we adopted.

3.1   Defense Mechanisms

In our security assessment for defense mechanisms, we searched whether each website had adopted one or more of the following eight mechanisms:

- **HTTP Strict-Transport-Security (HSTS):** HSTS is a web security policy mechanism where a web server can force complying browsers to interact with it using only HTTPS connections [15]. By sending out the HSTS policy via an HTTP response header named `Strict-Transport-Security`, a web server specifies a period of time during which the user's browser is instructed that all requests to that website need to be sent over HTTPS, regardless of what a user requests. As a result, HSTS can effectively thwart SSL-striping attacks and other Man-in-the-Middle (MitM) attacks [19,22].

- **Secure Cookies:** Website operators can make use of the `Secure` flag when sending out `Set-Cookie` headers. By doing so, the scope of a cookie is limited to only secure channels [10], which makes the cookie less likely to be stolen via eavesdropping.
- **Content Security Policy (CSP):** To mitigate a wide range of injection vulnerabilities, such as Cross-Site Scripting (XSS), a website operator can make use of the CSP mechanism. CSP provides a standard HTTP header that allows website owners to declare approved sources of content that browsers should be allowed to load on any given webpage [27]. Whenever a requested resource originates from a source that is not defined in the policy, it will not be loaded [28]. Hence, if the policy does not allow in-line JavaScript, then even if an attacker is able to inject malicious JavaScript in the webpage, the code will not be executed.
- **HttpOnly Cookies:** By default, cookies are accessible to JavaScript code, which allows attackers to steal a user's cookies in an XSS attack. To protect against the theft of cookies, a website operator can use the `HttpOnly` flag on cookies. An `HttpOnly` cookie will be used only when transmitting HTTP/HTTPS requests, making them unavailable to client-side JavaScript.
- **X-Frame-Options (XFO):** When an attacker is able to load a website, or part of a website in a `frame` or `iframe` element, the website might be vulnerable to ClickJacking attacks. More precisely, by redressing the user interface, an attacker can trick the user into clicking on the framed page while the click is intended for the bottom-level page [18]. To avoid ClickJacking attacks, the XFO HTTP response header [24] can be used to instruct a user's browser whether a certain page is allowed to be embedded in a frame.
- **Iframe sandboxing:** The `sandbox` attribute for the `iframe` element, introduced in HTML5, enables a set of extra restrictions on any content loaded in a frame. By specifying the `sandbox` value, a website operator can instruct the browser to load a specific frame's content in a low-privilege environment, allowing only a limited subset of capabilities to be made available to that frame [30].
- **CSRF Tokens:** The most popular defense for Cross-Site Request Forgery (CSRF) attacks is the inclusion of a secret token with each request and validation of that token at the server side [11]. This secret token, often referred to as a "nonce", should be pseudo-random and of a certain length so it cannot be guessed or brute-forced by an attacker. To check for nonces, we searched for forms that contained a hidden form element that was most likely used as a nonce. More specifically, form elements were marked as nonces when their name contained the keywords "token", "nonce", or "csrf", and when their value was a long alpha-numerical string. These form elements were then manually verified in order to filter out any false positives.

- **X-Content-Type-Options:** Internet Explorer has a MIME-sniffing feature that will attempt to determine the content type for each downloaded resource. This feature, however, can lead to security problems for servers hosting untrusted content. To prevent Internet Explorer from MIME-sniffing, thus reducing exposure to attacks, a web server can send the X-Content-Type-Options response header with the nosniff value .

Apart from the sandboxing of frames and CSRF tokens, all the above defense mechanisms are communicated to the browser via HTTP response headers, and hence can be discovered straightforwardly by parsing a server's response headers. For the sandboxing of frames and the presence of CSRF tokens, we searched for iframe and form elements in the response body of each crawled webpage.

3.2 Vulnerabilities and Weaknesses

For the assessment of vulnerabilities and weaknesses, we focus on the following ten measurements:

- **Vulnerable Remote JavaScript Inclusion:** A website that chooses to include JavaScript from untrustworthy third-party sources opens itself up to a range of security issues. Recent research by Nikiforakis et al. [21], identified four different types of vulnerabilities that are related to the practice of unsafe remote JavaScript inclusions. In our assessment, we searched for the most dangerous of these vulnerabilities, called "Stale Domain-name-based Inclusions", where remote JavaScript is requested from a domain that has expired and is available for registration, which means the attacker can buy the domain and use it to serve malicious JavaScript.
- **Mixed-content Inclusion:** When migrating to HTTPS, many websites fail to fully update their applications, resulting in mixed-content inclusions where the main webpage is sent over a secure HTTPS channel, while some additional content included on that page, such as images and scripts, are delivered over non-secured HTTP connections. As a result, an active network attacker can attack the TLS-enabled website by intercepting and modifying any of the mixed content that is loaded over HTTP [13].
- **SSL-stripping Vulnerable Form:** For performance reasons, some websites only implement HTTPS for certain webpages that contain sensitive information (such as a log-in page), which may result in forms vulnerable to SSL stripping [19]. In this scenario, the form is displayed on an HTTP page, however the form action points to an HTTPS link. As a result, a MitM attacker can replace all HTTPS form links on the HTTP page to HTTP links, which will allow the attacker to intercept the form data sent from the user's browser.
- **Insecure SSL Implementation:** SSL is important for website owners since it provides end-to-end security. At the same time, however, it turns out that it is not easy to deploy SSL correctly. According to Qualys' latest SSL survey of the most popular websites in December 2013, about half of the HTTPS

websites have security issues associated with their SSL implementations [6]. In our assessment, we use a fast SSL scanner called `sslyze` [7] to search for SSL implementation issues including the support of SSL v2.0, use of weak ciphers, and the vulnerability to the recently discovered BEAST [14] and CRIME [23] attacks.

- **Weak Browser XSS Protection:** Most modern browsers include security mechanisms to protect a user against reflected Cross-Site Scripting attacks [20], and these features are, in general, enabled by default. While web servers can instruct a user's browser to disable this protection by means of the `X-XSS-Protection` response header, we consider such behavior as a weakness of the website, because disabling it might allow an attacker to successfully exploit an, otherwise unexploitable, XSS vulnerability.

- **HTTP Parameter Pollution (HPP):** When a website fails to properly sanitize user input, they might be vulnerable to HPP attacks. These attacks consist of injecting encoded query string delimiters into other existing parameters. By doing so, an attacker is able to compromise the application logic to perform client-side and server-side attacks. In our assessment, we searched for HPP vulnerabilities in a manner similar to the methodology of Balduzzi et al. [9].

- **Outdated Server Software:** It is important to keep web servers up-to-date, since an outdated server usually contains vulnerabilities that may lead to attacks. In our assessment, we searched for outdated server software for popular web servers including Apache, Microsoft-IIS, and Nginx.

- **Outdated Content Manage Systems (CMSs):** Many popular websites nowadays are built using a CMS, since CMSs allow non-technical users to build dynamic websites, and are usually free of charge. Similar to web servers, it is also recommended to keep a CMS up-to-date, as outdated CMSs often contain vulnerabilities. In our assessment, we looked for outdated CMSs for websites using WordPress, Joomla, vBulletin, and MediaWiki.

- **Information Leakage:** Many websites generate error messages and display them to users, which may reveal implementation details or information that is useful to an attacker. In our assessment, we searched for various categories of information leakage including SQL error messages, website directory listings, IIS error messages, PHP/ASP/JSP source code and error messages.

- **Sensitive Files:** A website may accidentally expose sensitive files such as configuration files and source code to the public, when moving files from the development server to the production server. The degree of vulnerability depends on the sensitive file that is exposed, ranging from information disclosure, to disclosure of source code containing credentials. In our assessment, we searched for the following files that were most likely to contain sensitive information: `phpinfo.php` or `test.php`, containing system information from the `phpinfo()` function, website configuration files, such as `Web.config`, and two version control system folders, namely `.svn/` and `.git/`.

Most of the aforementioned vulnerabilities and weaknesses can be discovered through passive analysis with PhantomJS visiting webpages, except for the finding of HPP vulnerabilities and sensitive files, where we actively scanned a limited number of webpages from each website, taking the necessary precautions not to stress or harm websites.

3.3   Scoring System Details

The scoring system used to estimate the state of security of websites is based on the Common Weakness Scoring System (CWSS) [3]. The CWSS provides a quantitative measurement of security weaknesses in software applications, and is mainly used to prioritize the remediation of reported weaknesses. In essence, the score appointed to a weakness by the CWSS aims to reflect the impact and likelihood of exploitation by adversaries. For instance, not "escaping" user-controlled data in an HTML document could lead to Cross-Site Scripting attacks, and may allow an attacker to extract sensitive user information. This weakness obviously has a high impact and is remotely exploitable; thus it will receive a higher score than, say, an insecure SSL implementation weakness.

The reason for using the CWSS over other scoring systems as a base for our scoring system is twofold. First, the CWSS is a well-established and commonly used mechanism to give a quantitative score to weaknesses. It has been extensively reviewed, which gives, to a certain extent, a guarantee that the score appointed to a weakness reflects the magnitude of the induced threat. Second, the CWSS gives scores to weaknesses, rather than to actual vulnerabilities as is done in the Common Vulnerability Scoring System (CVSS) [2]. This is important because most features we analyzed are security indicators rather than actual vulnerabilities.

The CWSS uses 18 different factors across three metric groups to calculate the total score for a weakness. The first group, named the "Base Finding" group, reflects the risk of the weakness, the finding confidence and the presence of built-in defense mechanisms. The second group, called the "Attack Surface" group, reflects the exploitability of a weakness. A vulnerability which is easy to exploit, such as a stale JavaScript inclusion, will consequently receive a higher score for this group. The last group, named the "Environmental" group, indicates, among others, the impact on the business in case the weakness is exploited, as well as the likelihood of discovery and exploitation. Each group is appointed a subscore which constitutes of a weighted score of its factors. The total score appointed to a weakness is calculated by multiplying the score for the "Base Finding" group (value between 0 and 100) by the two other groups (values between 0 and 1).

In order to give a metric to security features on a similar scale as weaknesses, the CWSS was also used to appoint scores to these defense mechanisms. As the CWSS only works for weaknesses, we calculated the score for security measures by determining the metric for the vulnerability or weaknesses they attempt to prevent. Additionally, we took the effectiveness of the countermeasure into account, as security features that completely block certain attacks should receive a better score. For instance, the HttpOnly flag on cookies may prevent sensitive cookies to be stolen in Cross-Site Scripting attacks, but it will not mitigate all consequences of these attacks, something that a properly written Content Security Policy may do.

Table 1. Calculated scores for defense mechanisms and vulnerabilities

Defense Mechanism	Score
Content Security Policy	58.93
X-Frame-Options	45.21
HTTP Strict-Transport-Security	33.52
CSRF tokens	32.73
Secure cookies	31.84
HttpOnly cookies	28.21
Iframe sandboxing	25.32
X-Content-Type-Options	8.02

Vulnerabilities and Weaknesses	Score
Vulnerable remote JavaScript inclusion	67.50
Sensitive files	41.81
SSL-stripping Vulnerable Form	30.16
X-XSS-Protection	28.33
Outdated CMS	18.30
Insecure SSL implementation	18.10
HTTP Parameter Pollution	18.06
Mixed-content inclusions	13.42
Information leakage	9.44
Outdated Server Software	8.71

Table 2. Results from the analyzed websites that enable security features

Security mechanism	# of websites	% of websites	Estimated year of adoption
HttpOnly cookie	7,658	33.51	2007
CSRF token	3,815	16.70	NA
Secure cookies	1,217	5.33	2007
X-Frame-Options	1,029	4.50	2008
X-Content-Type-Options	467	2.04	2008
Strict-Transport-Security	116	0.50	2010
Content Security Policy	13	0.06	2011
Iframe sandboxing	10	0.04	2010

Table 1 shows the score appointed to each defense mechanism and weakness. Due to reasons of brevity, we limit the discussion of the rationale for the calculated scores to one example. As can be seen in the table, the vulnerable inclusion of remote JavaScript received the highest score (67.50). The high impact, i.e., the execution of arbitrary JavaScript code on multiple web pages, and the ease of exploitability, i.e., the registration of a stale domain name, are the main factors that contribute to this high score. Additionally, no control mechanisms (e.g. Content Security Policy) were found on the vulnerable websites that attempt to mitigate this vulnerability. Consequently, a score of 90 was calculated for the "Base Finding" group subscore. As victims will be exploited upon visiting the vulnerable web site, a score of 1 was appointed to the "Attack Surface" group. The score for the "Environmental" group is 0.75. The main factor that contributed to this score is the business impact, which is mostly case-specific. While the execution of arbitrary JavaScript code may have a very high impact on security-sensitive websites (e.g. a banking website), the potential impact on a purely informational website that stores no sensitive data is considerably less. The total score, 67.50, is then calculated by multiplying the three subscores (90 * 1 * 0.75).

4   Findings

4.1   General Findings

Out of the 22,851 analyzed websites, we found that 10,539 (46.12%) enabled at least one security feature. As can be seen in Table 2, the most popular defense mechanism is the HttpOnly attribute on cookies, which was present in 33.51% of the evaluated websites. This defense mechanism is followed in popularity by the presence of a CSRF token in forms, which was found in 16.70% of the websites. Interestingly, these two most popular security features are mitigations for the most critical web application flaws according to the OWASP Top 10 project [4]. This table also shows that, in general, the popularity of a defense mechanism is related to the time it was adopted by popular browsers, i.e., the older a security feature, the more widely it is used.

In our evaluation, we found that 12,885 (56.39%) websites contained at least one vulnerability or weakness. Table 3 shows the distribution of the number of websites found to be vulnerable. While only 5,113 websites provided at least one page over HTTPS, we found that the majority (80.32%) had content originating from an insecure channel on their website, or had SSL implementation issues. Likewise, although we only evaluated 17,910 websites for the presence of HTTP Parameter Pollution (HPP) vulnerabilities, we found 15.24% of these websites to be vulnerable. As HPP is very closely related to XSS in the sense that they are both caused by improper encoding of certain characters, we manually analyzed a subset of the webpages vulnerable to HPP for XSS vulnerabilities. This showed us that approximately 75% of the websites vulnerable to HPP are also vulnerable Cross-Site Scripting attacks.

4.2   Incorrect Security-Header Usage

By making use of headers, website administrators are capable of instructing a user's browser to enable a certain security feature. Browsers, however, require the value of the security-header to be correct. Values that are incorrect, for example headers containing a typing error or headers with incorrect syntax, will be ignored by the browser. The presence of such headers in websites is a strong indication that the website administrator is under the impression that he successfully secured his website. Nonetheless, if the security-header contains

Table 3. Results from the analyzed websites that contain vulnerabilities

Vulnerability	# of websites	% of websites
Outdated server Software	6,412	28.06
Mixed-content inclusion	3,442	15.06
SSL-stripping Vulnerable Form	2,884	12.62
HTTP Parameter Pollution	2,731	11.95
Outdated CMS	2,041	8.93
Insecure SSL implementation	1,945	8.51
Information leakage	1,231	5.39
Sensitive files	1,068	4.67
Vulnerable remote JS inclusion	91	0.40
X-XSS-Protection	91	0.40

a syntactical or typographical error, adversaries might be able to successfully exploit a vulnerability on a website.

In our analysis, we found several instances where the website operator tried to protect his website against ClickJacking attacks by using the X-Frame-Options header, but failed to do so by using an incorrect directive, for instance specifying SAME-ORIGIN, instead of the correct SAMEORIGIN directive.

Additionally, we found that 15 out of 116 (12.93%) analyzed websites that make use of the Strict-Transport-Security header to prevent SSL-stripping attacks, used the header in an improper fashion. The majority of these websites sent the Strict-Transport-Security header over an HTTP connection, without referring the user to an SSL-connection. Since browsers will ignore HSTS headers that are sent over an unencrypted channel, users of these websites can still fall victim to SSL-stripping attacks. The remainder of websites that implemented HSTS incorrectly, either forgot the max-age directive, or set this directive to the value 0, which signals the user's browser to delete the HSTS policy associated with the website.

4.3   Security by Alexa Rank

As the set of evaluated websites is distributed over the Alexa's list of the top 1 million websites, we evaluated how the rank of a website relates to the score we appoint it. We found that on average, the rank of a website is positively correlated with the positive score we appoint it, i.e., a high-ranked website is more likely to have a relatively high positive score. Contrastingly, we found that the negative score of a website is unrelated to its popularity according to Alexa. This indicates that popular websites try to improve their security by the adoption of defense mechanisms, rather than by tackling vulnerabilities. Figure 1 depicts the relation between the security score and the Alexa rank. Each entry coincides with the average positive or negative metric of the evaluated websites that fall within a range of 10,000 Alexa ranks.

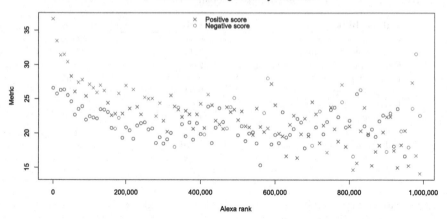

Fig. 1. Average metric by analyzed websites grouped by 10,000 Alexa entries

Additionally, we found that, in general, there is no correlation between the positive metric and negative score of a website, which strengthens the indication that websites try to improve their security by adding security mechanisms in an ad-hoc fashion. Moreover, we found that a large number of websites apply a certain defense mechanism to a limited fraction of the URLs we visited, e.g. the majority of websites that make use of the `X-Content-Type-Options` header to prevent XSS attacks in Internet Explorer due to MIME sniffing, only add the header to a small fraction of their pages.

4.4   Security by Country

We found that the scores for websites located in different countries were similar. Figure 2 shows the cumulative distribution function of both the positive as well as the negative score for websites of a set of four randomly selected countries. From this set, Germany has more websites with a higher positive score than the other countries. However, the same country scores worse than the rest on the negative score. This again shows that there is no relation between the number of enabled security features and the number of weaknesses or vulnerabilities we were able to find on a website.

The variance of scores between different countries are most likely due to the unequal distribution of the countries' websites over the Alexa rank. The distribution of Alexa rank for the subset of four countries is shown in Figure 3. Compared to the distribution of the positive score, it is clear that the countries with the most high-ranked websites have a better positive score. This indicates that, in general, the security of a website is unrelated to its geographical location or the policies its hosting country may have.

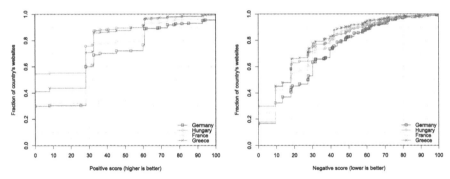

Fig. 2. Distribution of positive and negative score for several countries' websites

4.5   Novel Attack Techniques

In the course of our analysis, we encountered a new attack technique in the Cross-Origin Resource Sharing mechanism as well as two variations on the insecure inclusion of remote JavaScript code on a webpage. Both are related to remote trust relations in the sense that the website operator trusts a certain domain or URL to be benign, which may become malicious in the future.

By sending out the `Access-Control-Allow-Origin` header, a website operator can instruct a browser to allow a third-party website to make XHR-requests towards his website and read out the result. When the `Access-Control-Allow-Credentials` header is included as well, these requests can be authenticated. It is in the best interest of a website administrator to only allow trusted websites to extract the response of an XHR-request targeting his website. Interestingly, we found a case where a website sent out the `Access-Control-Allow-Origin` containing a `.local` domain. This allows an attacker to trick a user on the local network in visiting his webpage located at the `.local` domain. The attacker is then able to make the victim's browser send XHR-requests to the vulnerable website while being able to read out CSRF-tokens from forms.

In the aforementioned work by Nikiforakis et al. [21], the authors analyzed the inclusion of JavaScript files from expired domains. In the course of our analysis, we encountered two variations on this type of attack. More specifically, we found that several websites remotely include JavaScript files from domains that were marked as "for sale" by their owner on `sedo.com`, a large domain marketplace. Similar to the attack described by the authors, an attacker is able to buy such a domain, and serve malicious JavaScript to unsuspecting users. The second variation on this type of attack occurs when websites include JavaScript files directly from project hosting websites, such as GitHub or Google Code. The files hosted on these services are linked to a project or a user. However, upon deletion, that project or account, becomes again available for registration. This way, an adversary is able to host malicious JavaScript, which may be included by a large set of websites. To show the importance of this type of attack, we registered a stale project on Google Code, and made available the last available version

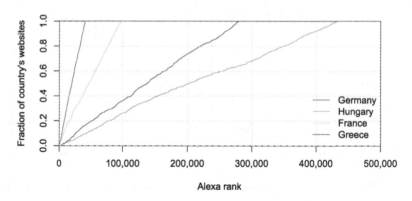

Fig. 3. Distribution of Alexa rank for several countries

of project's JavaScript files, with a minor addition which allowed us to analyze the number of including websites and affected users. During a month's time, we registered a total of 3,879,701 requests, originating from 1,104,497 unique IP addresses. In total, there were 3,400 websites, including a prominent Chinese news website, which directly included JavaScript files from this Google Code project. In every single one of these requests, an attacker could have have served malicious JavaScript that steals a user's cookies, exfiltrates private user information and even attempts to launch a drive-by download.

4.6 Miscellaneous

In our analysis, we found that the presence of certain security features, such as the `HttpOnly` attribute in the `Set-Cookie` header, is more common in websites that are powered by frameworks which facilitate the system-wide usage of these security features [25]. More precisely, through the `X-Powered-By` header we found that although the majority (49.53%) of the analyzed websites are powered by PHP, only 16.36% of these websites enable the `HttpOnly` attribute. The second most popular framework is ASP.NET, used by 22.80% of the crawled websites. Interestingly, we found that 54.74% of these ASP.NET websites enable `HttpOnly` (three times as much as PHP sites).

5 Limitation and Challenges

5.1 Accuracy of Passive Analysis

Due to legal and ethical considerations, our analysis of vulnerabilities in websites was limited to a passive analysis, with a few exceptions. Consequently, the results described in the previous section only show an estimation on the state of security of European websites. In order to assess the accuracy of these estimates, we compared the scores of websites likely to be insecure, to websites expected to be secure. The set of most-likely vulnerable websites consisted of websites with a Cross-Site Scripting vulnerability which was publicly known and had not been patched in over one year.[1] The set of websites probable to be secure, was made up from a set of 20 respectable banking websites. This comparison showed that the average positive score for the known-vulnerable set (35.21) was lower than that of the set of banking websites (41.62). Also the average negative score, which was 27.22 on the insecure set and 12.80 on the probably secure websites, indicates that, despite the fact that only a fraction of a website's state of security could be assessed, we were still able to differentiate between vulnerable and secure websites. At the same time, we are aware of the coarse-granularity of our analysis and we highlight the antithesis between the invasiveness of an external security assessment, and the coverage obtained by it. It would be worthwhile to investigate whether website administrators would be willing to consent to a more invasive security assessment, in return for obtaining the results free of charge.

5.2   Scoring System

In order to evaluate the general state of security of a website, we developed a scoring system based on CWSS, as was described in Section 3.3. However, this scoring system is subject to two types of limitations. Firstly, the total positive score assigned to a website originates from an individually assigned score of eight security features, while the total negative score is derived from a score attributed to ten potential weaknesses and vulnerabilities. As a result, the positive score for a website is on a different scale from the negative score. This prevents us from being able to compare the positive score, to the negative score. Moreover, as the total score appointed to a website originates from a limited set of factors, the total score may not always reflect the actual state of security of a website. However, as we evaluate diverse aspects which are highly related to a website's security, we believe that our scoring system provides a good estimate on the general state of security of a website.

The metric appointed to each weakness and security measure is derived from a list of 18 factors, some of which are subject to the opinion of the authors or are often case-specific. For instance, the impact of exploiting a certain vulnerability may differ based on the type of website. In order to account for these differences, each metric was calculated for a general website. Consequently, the appointed metrics are not website-specific and the score of one feature is relative to the other scores. This allows us to appoint a comparable score which gives an estimation of the state of security for each tested website.

6   Related Work

To the best of our knowledge, there exists no large-scale analysis which evaluates security features as well as weaknesses in a broad range of websites. Nonetheless,

---

[1] http://www.xssed.com

several evaluations on the presence of specific vulnerabilities in web applications have been carried out. For instance, WhiteHat Security evaluates, on a yearly basis, the data on several types of vulnerabilities they collect from their customers [31]. Contrastingly to our research, their security analysis has the permission of their clients and is thus more aggressive, which enables them to find additional types of vulnerabilities, such as SQL Injections and XSS errors.

Another large-scale evaluation of websites in a specific demographic area is presented in research by Alarifi et al. [8], that evaluates the security of popular Arabic websites. Their analysis explores the presence of phishing and malware pages in 7,000 domains. To detect malicious scripts hosted on webpages, they make use of APIs offered by known website scanners. Kals et al. developed the SecuBat tool, which was used for an automated detection of XSS and SQL Injection vulnerabilities in a selection of 100 security-sensitive websites [16]. Similarly, Zeller et al. performed an analysis on the presence of CSRF vulnerabilities in popular websites [32], finding vulnerabilities in four major websites. Nikiforakis et al. presented a large-scale analysis of remote JavaScript inclusions [21]. Additionally, in their paper, they also proposed a metric called Quality of Maintenance (QoM) to characterize a website's security consciousness. Their QoM adopts several features such as `HttpOnly` cookies, `X-Frame-Options`, that are also included in our assessment. As earlier discussed, the presence of these defensive mechanisms give an indication for a website's security.

Vasek and Moore found that some website features, such as server software and CMSs, can serve as positive risk factors for webserver compromise [29]. Their study shows that some server types and CMS types are more risky than others (e.g., servers running Apache and Ngnix are more likely to be compromised than those running Microsoft IIS).

Lekies et al. performed a large-scale detection of DOM-based XSS vulnerabilities in the top 5,000 Alexa websites [17]. In their evaluation, they found a total of 6,167 unique vulnerabilities distributed over 480 domains, demonstrating that 9.6% of the evaluated websites are vulnerable to this type of attack. Son et al. analyzed the implementation of the HTML5 `postMessage` mechanism in the Alexa top 10,000 [26]. They found that 84 popular websites were exploitable to several attacks, including XSS and content injection, due to the lack of proper checks in the cross-origin communication mechanism.

A feature that we did not include in our study was the security of a site's hosting provider. Sites situated on shared hosting environments are expected to be at a greater risk of compromise, since a vulnerability of another co-located tenant can be used to attack the entire server. Canali et al. recently investigated the ability of shared hosting providers to detect compromised sites hosted on their servers [12], finding that the vast majority of providers cannot detect even the most straightforward attacks.

7   Conclusion

Websites have become the main target for numerous attacks originating from adversaries who attempt to monetize a user's sensitive data and resources.

In order to protect themselves from this threat, website operators are provided with several security mechanisms to defend against a wide range of vulnerabilities. In this paper, we evaluated the usage of security features, as well as the presence of vulnerabilities and weaknesses, in 22,851 EU websites. We found that a large part of the evaluated websites showed weaknesses, and some even contained severe vulnerabilities. Moreover, we discovered that the state of security of a website is unrelated to its demographic characteristics. In spite the fact that popular websites are more likely to prevent attacks by implementing security features, we found that the presence of weaknesses and vulnerabilities is unrelated to a site's popularity. We hope that our study can inspire similar systems at a country- or sector-level, and help the owners of sites to discover and prioritize the adoption of security mechanisms, and the correction of existing vulnerabilities.

Acknowledgements. We want to thank the anonymous reviewers for the valuable comments. This research was performed with the financial support of the Prevention against Crime Programme of the European Union (B-CCENTRE), the Research Fund KU Leuven, and the EU FP7 projects NESSoS, WebSand, and STREWS.

References

1. Bing Search API, http://datamarket.azure.com/dataset/bing/search
2. Common Vulnerability Scoring System (CVSS), http://www.first.org/cvss
3. Common Weakness Scoring System (CWSS), https://cwe.mitre.org/cwss/
4. OWASP Top Ten Project,
   https://www.owasp.org/index.php/Category:OWASP_Top_Ten_Project
5. Phantomjs: Headless webkit with javascript api, https://www.phantomjs.org/
6. SSL Pulse, https://www.trustworthyinternet.org/ssl-pulse/
7. sslyze, https://github.com/iSECPartners/sslyze
8. Alarifi, A., Alsaleh, M., Al-Salman, A.: Security analysis of top visited arabic web sites. In: 2013 15th International Conference on Advanced Communication Technology (ICACT), pp. 173–178. IEEE (2013)
9. Balduzzi, M., Gimenez, C.T., Balzarotti, D., Kirda, E.: Automated Discovery of Parameter Pollution Vulnerabilities in Web Applications. In: 18th Annual Network and Distributed System Security Symposium, San Diego, USA (2011)
10. Barth, A.: HTTP state management mechanism. IETF RFC (2011)
11. Barth, A., Jackson, C., Mitchell, J.C.: Robust defenses for cross-site request forgery. In: Proceedings of the 15th ACM conference on Computer and communications security, CCS 2008, pp. 75–88. ACM, New York (2008)
12. Canali, D., Balzarotti, D., Francillon, A.: The role of web hosting providers in detecting compromised websites. In: Proceedings of the 22nd International Conference on World Wide Web, WWW 2013, pp. 177–188 (2013)
13. Chen, P., Nikiforakis, N., Huygens, C., Desmet, L.: A Dangerous Mix: Large-scale analysis of mixed-content websites. In: Proceedings of the 16th Information Security Conference, ISC 2013, Dallas, USA (2013)
14. Thai Duong and Juliano Rizzo. Here Come The ⊕ Ninjas (2011)

15. Hodges, J., Jackson, C., Barth, A.: HTTP strict transport security (HSTS). IETF RFC (2012)
16. Kals, S., Kirda, E., Kruegel, C., Jovanovic, N.: Secubat: a web vulnerability scanner. In: Proceedings of the 15th International Conference on World Wide Web, pp. 247–256. ACM (2006)
17. Lekies, S., Stock, B., Johns, M.: 25 million flows later: large-scale detection of dom-based xss. In: Proceedings of the 2013 ACM SIGSAC Conference on Computer & Communications Security, pp. 1193–1204. ACM (2013)
18. Lundeen, R., Ou, J., Rhodes, T.: New ways i'm going to hack your web app. (2011)
19. Marlinspike, M.: New tricks for defeating ssl in practice. Blackhat (2009)
20. Microsoft: IE8 Security Part IV: The XSS Filter (2008)
21. Nikiforakis, N., Invernizzi, L., Kapravelos, A., Acker, S.V., Joosen, W., Kruegel, C., Piessens, F., Vigna, G.: You are what you include: large-scale evaluation of remote javascript inclusions. In: Proceedings of the 2012 ACM Conference on Computer and Communications security, CCS 2012, pp. 736–747. ACM, New York (2012)
22. Nikiforakis, N., Younan, Y., Joosen, W.: HProxy: Client-side detection of SSL stripping attacks. In: Proceedings of the 7th Conference on Detection of Intrusions and Malware & Vulnerability Assessment, DIMVA 2010 (2010)
23. Rizzo, J., Duong, T.: Crime: Compression ratio info-leak made easy. In: Ekoparty Security Conference (2012)
24. Ross, D., Gondrom, T.: HTTP Header X-Frame-Options. IETF RFC (2013)
25. Sellers, D.: ASP.NET 2.0 and the new HTTP-only property. MSDN Blogs (March 2006)
26. Son, S., Shmatikov, V.: The postman always rings twice: Attacking and defending postmessage in html5 websites
27. Stamm, S., Sterne, B., Markham, G.: Reining in the web with content security policy. In: Proceedings of the 19th International Conference on World Wide Web, WWW 2010, pp. 921–930. ACM, New York (2010)
28. Sterne, B., Barth, A.: Content Security Policy 1.0. W3C Candidate Recommendation (2012)
29. Vasek, M., Moore, T.: Identifying Risk Factors for Webserver Compromise. In: Proceedings of the Eighteenth International Conference on Financial Cryptography and Data Security, FC 2014 (2014)
30. West, M.: Play safely in sandboxed iframes (2013)
31. WhiteHat. Website Security Statistics Report, https://www.whitehatsec.com/resource/stats.html
32. Zeller, W., Felten, E.W.: Cross-site request forgeries: Exploitation and prevention. The New York Times, 1–13 (2008)

Towards a Vulnerability Tree Security Evaluation of OpenStack's Logical Architecture

Doudou Fall, Takeshi Okuda, Youki Kadobayashi, and Suguru Yamaguchi

Internet Engineering Laboratory, Nara Institute of Science and Technology, Japan
{doudou-f,okuda,youki-k,suguru}@is.naist.jp

Abstract. Cloud computing's rapid development has favored the emergence of many other technologies like OpenStack, which is the most popular open-source cloud management software. OpenStack has received a lot of praise lately thanks to its ease of use and its vibrant community, but it has also started garnering attention in the national vulnerability database. Furthermore, OpenStack has a logical architecture in which, the degree of interconnectedness within and between the components is a source of many security concerns. To prevent the damages that can be caused by the combination of these security issues, we proposed a vulnerability tree security analysis of OpenStack's logical architecture that allowed us to generate ready-to-use vulnerability trees of the major services or components of the architecture. We also suggested an amendment of OpenStack's vulnerability naming, because the current naming does not cope well with our proposal.

Keywords: OpenStack, Vulnerability Tree, security.

1 Introduction

Cloud computing has burgeoned to become the dominant paradigm in Information Technology (IT). The rapid development of cloud computing has permitted the emergence of other important paradigms in IT like cloud management stacks. A cloud management stack is a set of components that work together to facilitate the management of a cloud infrastructure system. A cloud management stack is, at least, composed of the following components: an external application programming interface (API) that assures the communication between the cloud services and external users; a compute service that takes in charge the management of the virtual machines (VMs) on the host machines in terms of features like creation, deletion or suspension of VMs; an image service for managing the deployment or registration of VM images; a volume service that maps persistent storage used by the VMs; and a network service that helps with the management of the networks used by the VMs. In addition to the intrinsic aforementioned components, cloud management stacks rely on some external services that are critical for functioning. Among those external services, the hypervisor is regarded as the most important. Popular cloud computing management stacks

T. Holz and S. Ioannidis (Eds.): TRUST 2014, LNCS 8564, pp. 127–142, 2014.

include OpenStack [1], OpenNebula [3], CloudStack [4], or again Eucalyptus [2]. In this paper, our focus is on OpenStack because it is the most deployed cloud management software, plus it has a vibrant community that provides all the necessary documentation. People in the academia and the industry are profusely using OpenStack to deploy their private clouds. However, with its rapid adoption, OpenStack is also rapidly beginning to garner attention in the National Vulnerability Database (NVD) [6] as its number of vulnerabilities continues to increase as schematised in Figure 1. Elsewhere, OpenStack has an architecture with a high dependency between the different components, which means that an attack in a particular component could spread out to the other interconnected components. To overcome this issue, we propose to perform a fault (or vulnerability) tree security analysis of OpenStack's logical architecture. In our study, we were able to generate the different security vulnerability trees of the components that compose the architecture, and we were also able to make some recommendations on a better nomenclature of OpenStack's vulnerabilities. Because with the current nomenclature format, we are not able to fully evaluate the security of the architecture. In other words, this research paper lays the foundations of the security evaluation of OpenStack by providing security vulnerability trees that are ready to be used given the right vulnerability nomenclature.

The remainder of the paper is structured as follows. In Section 2, we detail the very few related works that we have found in this field. Section 3 contains our motivation and the proposal. Section 4 is entirely dedicated to the security analysis of the architecture. In Section 5, we propose a discussion of our findings and give a hint of our future work. Section 6 concludes the paper.

2   Related Work

We have to confess that most of the work related to this study comes from reliability system analysis. Indeed, we make use of the fault tree to perform our security analysis, which is similar to applying fault tree in a highly critical system like nuclear power plant system. To our knownledge, besides Fall et al. [10], we are not aware of a similar work that has been conducted in cloud computing, particularly in OpenStack's architecture. Nevertheless, there is some work in OpenStack's security that we can cite as reference.

Zhai el al. [12] produced the closest work to this research. They proposed a structural reliability auditing (SRA) technique that permits to quantify the vulnerabilities of interdependent infrastructures in a cloud platform. The operating of the system is divided in three steps: infrastructure dependency data collection, construction of a fault tree based on the gathered data, and analysis of the fault tree to estimate the probability of failure of the top event. They demonstrated the practicality of their system by implementing it, which also showed the lack of privacy measures for the data that is being used. Xiao et al. [13] fixed the issue by adding a privacy aspect to the SRA system. They re-engineered the 3-step process of [12]'work by adding privacy to each step and using Secure Multi-Party Computation (SMPC). They were able to evaluate an implemented version of their proposal on the Sharemind SecretC platform.

Khan et al. [14] proposed an OpenId authentication mechanism for OpenStack. in their system, OpenId provides authentication for the user solely while the cloud provider manages the access control policies. Sasko et al. [15] performed an Open-Stack security assessment. They set up a system running OpenStack with virtual machines that separetely have Ubuntu, CentOS, Fedora and Windows operating systems. After running a vulnerability scan, they concluded that the later operating system was more subject to vulnerabilities than the others.

On the same spirit, Donevski et al. [16] proposed a security assessment for virtual machines in open source clouds. They also used openstack and performed their assessment in two different network situations for the virtual machines: same IP address for floating and fixed IPs, and two different IPs for both. They were able to label out different test cases that gave different results that they classified qualitatively and quantitatively by using the CVSS.

Aryan et al. [17] evaluated the degree of compromission of a cloud environment knowing that, at least, one of the components is compromised.

In the other hand, despite the fact that it is out of the scope of this research, we wanted to mention that Fault Mode and Effects Analysis (FMEA) [19] and Root Cause Analysis (RCA) [20] compete with Fault Tree Analysis (FTA) [7] on modeling failures in a given system. We prefer FTA because we contend that it is more suitable for our research.

3   Motivation and Approach

OpenStack is the most popular open-source cloud computing management platform. Its latest release, HAVANA whose architecture is considered in this work, has nine different services which are as follows:

- Dashboard: also called Horizon, provides a web portal for the management of the underlying OpenStack services.
- Compute: or Nova, facilitates the management of OpenStack's instances;
- Networking: codenamed neutron, this service, not only permits network connection between OpenStack's services, but also allows users to configure networks by putting an API into their disposition;
- Object Storage: helps with the storage and retrieval of arbitrary unstructured data objects. It is also known as Swift.
- Block Storage: or Cinder, provisions persistent block storage to running instances;
- Identity Service: is responsible of the identity management (authentication, authorization, endpoints) for the other OpenStack's services. This service is codenamed Keystone.
- Image Service: codenamed Glance, takes in charge the storage and the retrieval of virtual machine disk images;
- Telemetry: codenamed Ceilometer, helps monitoring and metering the business aspects of OpenStack like billing or benchmarking.
- Orchestration: or Heat, facilitates the orchestration of multiple composite cloud applications.

OpenStack has a vibrant community that keeps on proposing new services to further ease the management of a cloud system. Additionally, many universities and small businesses are deploying OpenStack, which reflects the good dynamism of its adoption. However, recently we have noticed an accumulation of OpenStack vulnerabilities in the National Vulnerability Database (NDV) [6]. Indeed, OpenStack has a total of 75 vulnerabilities that have scores ranging from 7.5 to 1.9 in the Common Vulnerability Scoring System (CVSS) [5]. Figure 1 gives a visual describtion of the former statement. Furthermore, the logical architecture of OpenStack, described in Figure 2, reveals a deep level of interconnectedness between its different components (services) and subcomponents. We contend that these two situations, mixed together, could jeopardize the security of the cloud systems of the different adopters of OpenStack. Due to this level of interconnectedness, a successful attack in one component can turn out to be a successful attack on the entire architecture (Figure 2). We propose a fault or vulnerability security analysis of OpenStack's logical architecture. Fault tree [7,8] is overwhelmingly used to quantify the faultiness of mission critical systems like nuclear power plant or aircraft space systems. It is so because it has demonstrated its effectiveness as a tool capable of generating a quantifiable model that can help engineers to take precautionary measures to anticipate on future catastrophes. In our paper [10], we demonstrated how useful fault tree analysis could be once applied in a cloud infrastructure. The amendment we made is to replace fault by vulnerability in order to be more inline with security. In a nutshell, in this research, we are intrigued to discover the results of a fault/vulnerability tree analysis of OpenStack's logical architecture. In the following subsections, we describe the differents needs to accomplish our goal.

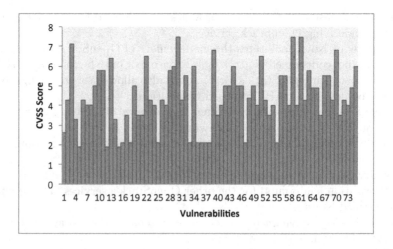

Fig. 1. OpenStack Presence in the NVD

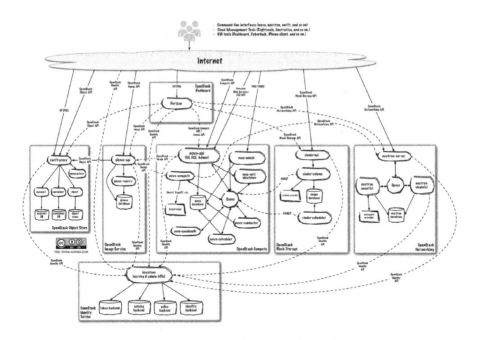

Fig. 2. OpenStack Logical Architechture [1]

3.1   NVD and CVSS

The National Vulnerability Database is a publicly available database for computer related vulnerabilities. It is a property of the United States (US) government, which manages it throughout the U.S. National institute of Science and Technology (NIST) computer security division. The NVD is also used by the U.S. government as content repository for the Security Content Automation Protocol (SCAP). The primary sources of the NVD are as follows: Vulnerability Search Engine (Common Vulnerability Exposure (CVE) and CCE misconfigurations), National Checklist Program (automatable security configuration guidance in XCCDF and OVAL), SCAP and SCAP compatible tools, Product dictionary (CPE), Common vulnerability Scoring System for impact metrics, and Common Weakness Enumeration (CWE).

The Common Vulnerability Scoring System (CVSS) is a vendor-neutral open source vulnerability scoring system. It was established to help organizations to efficiently plan their responses regarding security vulnerabilities. The CVSS is comprised of three metric groups classified as base, temporal, and environmental. The base metric group contains the quintessential characteristics of a vulnerability. The temporal metric group is used for non-constant characteristics of a vulnerability, and the environmental metric group defines the characteristics of a vulnerability that are tightly related to the user's environment. The temporal and environmental base metric groups intervene after a vulnerability is exploited, therefore they do not feature prominently in our research. The remaining metric group regroups essential metrics that are used to compute the score of a vulnerability: Access Vector (AV), Access Complexity (AC), Authentication (Au), Confidentiality Impact (C), Integrity Impact (I), and Availability Impact (A).

3.2 Fault Tree Analysis

A fault tree is a basic tool used as part of a quantitative analysis of a system. It gives rise to a pictorial representation of an undesirable event in a system in Boolean logic. The analysis of the fault tree is the process of developing a deterministic description of the occurrence of an undesirable event, the top event, in terms of the occurrence or non-occurrence of other events called intermediate events. Furthermore, the intermediate events are deeply explored until the basic events, which represent the lowest events of the tree, are reached. Each node in a fault tree represents either an event or a logic gate. The logic gates determine the logical relationship among the events. The events can be fundamentally different but should belong to the same family, i.e., when the top event is a successful attack on an infrastructure, the basics events are successful attacks on some of the components that constitute the infrastructure. Additionally, since fault tree is an expression in Boolean logic, its usage implies that the events are binary, that is, true or false. Fault tree construction requires different symbols and notations, which, some of them are illustrated in Figure 3. Practically, the use of various gates can be helpful to construct a well-detailed fault tree but, in principle, it is possible to construct any fault tree from the combination of AND and OR gates. Figure 4 is an example of fault tree. Hereafter, we provide some definitions that are necessary for a better comprehension of fault tree analysis.

Definition 1. *A cut set is a collection of basic events such that if these events occur together then the top event will certainly occur.*

Definition 2. *: A minimal cut set is a collection of basic events forming a cut set such that if any of the basic events is removed, then the remaining set is no longer a cut set.*

Definition 3. *: A path set is a collection of basic events such that if none of these events occur then the top event will certainly not occur.*

Definition 4. *: A minimal path set is a path set such that if any of the events is removed then the remaining will no longer be a path set.*

The minimal cut and path sets are primordial for quantifying the probability of the top event. Suppose that we have a fault tree representation with a top event T and several cut sets $C_1, \ldots, C_n$. From the aforementioned definitions, we know that:

$$T = C_1 \cup C_2 \cup \ldots \cup C_n. \tag{1}$$

By applying the inclusion-exclusion law of probability [9] to Equation 1, we obtain Equation 3:

$$P[T] = P(C_1 \cup C_2 \cup \ldots \cup C_n). \tag{2}$$

$$P[T] = \sum_{i=1}^{n} P[C_i] - \sum_{i<j<k} P[C_i \cap C_j \cap C_k] - \ldots + (-1)^{n+1} P[C_1 \cap C_2 \cap \ldots \cap C_n]. \tag{3}$$

In the subsequent security analysis, we will use this formulation for the different components of OpenStack's architecture. We will also write vulnerability instead of fault tree in order to be more in line with security but, the intrinsic concepts of fault tree remain intacts. Finally, we will consider the CVSS score of the vulnerabilities as $P[C_i]$.

4 Security Analysis

This section is the quintessential part of this paper. Within it, we will elucidate the security interconnections that exist in OpenStack's logical architecture.

Figure 2 depicts OpenStack's logical architecture. This architecture is comprised of seven main components (note that we use component instead of service to fit more into the spirit of vulnerability tree analysis). We use that architecture to run our security evaluation mechanism, which consists of using vulnerability trees into the different components of OpenStack. The architecture helps us understand the degree of interconnectedness that exists between the different components. That interconnectedness can be dangerous to the entire architecture as it gives the possibility for an attacker, who succeeds to exploit a vulnerability in one component, to then, as a domino effect, proceed and exploit the other components because of the tight relations. The background of the main components has already been clarified in Section 3. We mostly used the Boolean operator OR to construct our vulnerability trees. That choice is made to give ourselves more flexibility. The use of other Boolean operators like AND, as instance, would suggest a very strong dependency between the subcomponents, which implies that the failure of the entire component happens if and only if all the subcomponents are vulnerable. Nevertheless, we consider the Boolean operator used in our analysis to be inclusive. We made the assumption that all

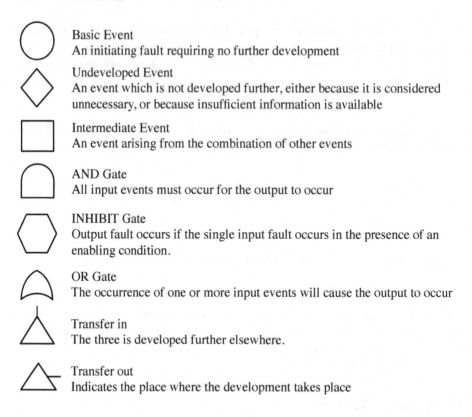

Basic Event
An initiating fault requiring no further development

Undeveloped Event
An event which is not developed further, either because it is considered unnecessary, or because insufficient information is available

Intermediate Event
An event arising from the combination of other events

AND Gate
All input events must occur for the output to occur

INHIBIT Gate
Output fault occurs if the single input fault occurs in the presence of an enabling condition.

OR Gate
The occurrence of one or more input events will cause the output to occur

Transfer in
The three is developed further elsewhere.

Transfer out
Indicates the place where the development takes place

Fig. 3. Non Exhaustive List of Standard Fault Tree Symbols

the components (respectively subcomponents) that have a direct connection to the Internet (the end users) are susceptible of being attacked. That assumption ensued in the construction of 7 vulnerability trees that we examine hereafter. Due to space limitations and the fact that the process of evaluation is similar, we only provide details of the top events for two cases. A clear comprehension of Section 3 allows a better understanding of this section.

4.1   Security Evaluation of Swift

Swift or OpenStack Object Store, is intrinsically composed of seven subcomponents that are named: memcached, account, container, objetct, account DB, container DB, and Object DB. The three last mentioned subcomponents are respectively bound to the three other subcomponents that precede them. The resulting vulnerability tree is described in Figure 4. As Swift is attached to Keystone, the vulnerability tree can be developed further in respect to that attachment.

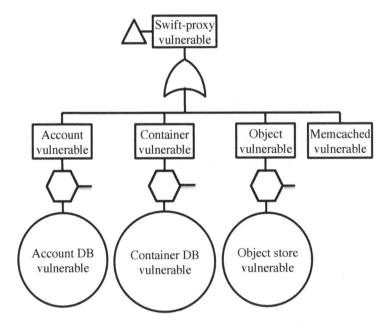

Fig. 4. Swift Vulnerability Tree

4.2 Security Evaluation of Glance

Glance is very simple in its composition, consequently the vulnerability tree, which is schematised in Figure 5, is easy to generate. Glance has connections with Swift, Horizon, Nova, and Keystone. As a result, the tree can be further expanded in any of those directions.

4.3 Security Evaluation of Nova

OpenStack Compute or Nova turns out to be the most complicated component of OpenStack in terms of the high level of interconnection between its contents plus the fact that it can be accessed from the Internet in two ways. We have constructed one vulnerability tree that describes the former situation. The subcomponent nova-api, which we consider as the main subcomponent, is linked to the subcomponents nova-database, Queue, and nova-cert/objectstore. Queue, in its turn, is linked to the subcomponents nova-consoleauth, nova-scheduler, nova-conductor, nova-compute, nova-console. The fault tree that resumes this narrative is depicted in Figure 6. We indicate that the tree can be extrapolated due the connections that Nova has with other components.

4.4 Security Evaluation of Cinder

The vulnerability tree of OpenStack Block Storage, also known as Cinder, is simple to construct and is represented in FIgure 7. Cinder is composed of the

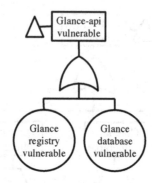

Fig. 5. Glance Vulnerability Tree

subcomponents cinder-api, cinder volume, volume provider, cinder database and cinder scheduler. The tree can be developed further as Cinder has connections with Nova and Keystone.

4.5 Security Evaluation of Neutron

OpenStack Network Service, codenamed Neutron, also has a simple composition that facilitates the construction of the vulnerability tree showed in Figure 8. Neutron has connections with Horizon, Nova, and Keystone. Consequently, the tree can be extended further towards those components.

4.6 Security Evaluation of Keystone

Keystone, which is the security guard of OpenStack, is composed of the subcomponents keystone, tocken backend, catalog backend, policy backend, and identity backend. The vulnerability tree is described in Figure 9. Keystone is connected to all the other components thus, the three is subject to be developed further to accomplish a deeper analysis. We denote the top event (Keystone vulnerable) K, the basics events: Token backen vulnerable, Catalog backen vulnerable, Policy backend vulnerable, and Identity backend vulnerable, are respectively denoted K_1, K_2, K_3, and K_4. By following the details in Subsection 3.2, we are able to derive the security evaluation, which is given by Equation 4.

$$
\begin{aligned}
P[K] = {} & P[K_1] + P[K_2] + P[K_3] + P[K_4] - P[K_1]P[K_2] \\
& - P[K_1]P[K_3] - P[K_1]P[K_4] - P[K_2]P[K_3] \\
& - P[K_2]P[K_4] - P[K_3]P[K_4] + P[K_1]P[K_2]P[K_3] \\
& + P[K_1]P[K_2]P[K_3] + P[K_1]P[K_2]P[K_4] + \\
& P[K_2]P[K_3]P[K_4] - P[K_1]P[K_2]P[K_3]P[K_4].
\end{aligned} \tag{4}
$$

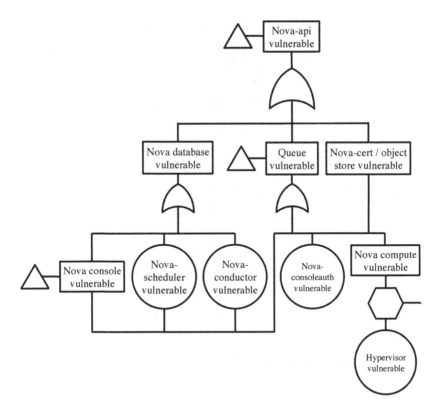

Fig. 6. Nova Vulnerability Tree

Let us remind that the numerical value of $P[K_1]$, as instance, is the score of the vulnerability in question in the CVSS. Unfortunately, we can not have a use case because of the vulnerability issue (5) we encountered in this study.

4.7   Security Evaluation of Horizon

Horizon or OpenStack's dashboard is very intriguing because it does not have any particular subcomponent but is linked to all the other major components, which makes it one of the most critical component of the architecture. Its vulnerability tree is depicted in Figure 10. All the events are deemed intermediate because they could be extended further. Let's denote the top event (Horizon vulnerable) by H. The intermediate events Swift vulnerable, Glance vulnerable, Nova vulnerable, Cinder vulnerable, Neutron vulnerable, and Keystone vulnerable are respectively denoted S, G, No, C, Ne, and K. The ensuing security evaluation is given in Equation 5. As in the previous subsection, Equation 5 can not be used with the current naming of OpenStack's vulnerabilities.

Let us remind that P[S], P[G], P[No], P[C], P[Ne], and P[K] respectively represents the security evaluation of Swift, Glance, Nova, Cinder, Neutron, and

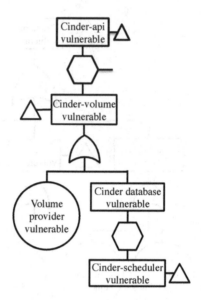

Fig. 7. Cinder Vulnerability Tree

Keystone. The security evaluation of Horizon, P[H], can be seen as the security evaluation of the entire OpenStack logical architecture.

$$
\begin{aligned}
P[H] ={}& P[S] + P[G] + P[No] + P[C] + P[Ne] + P[K] - P[S]P[G] - \\
& P[S]P[No] - P[S]P[C] - P[S]P[Ne] - P[S]P[K] - P[G]P[No] - \\
& P[G]P[C] - P[G]P[Ne] - P[G]P[K] - P[No]P[C] - P[No]P[Ne] - \\
& P[No]P[K] - P[C]P[Ne] - P[C]P[K] - P[Ne]P[K] + P[S]P[G]P[No] + \\
& P[S]P[G]P[C] + P[S]P[G]P[Ne] + P[S]P[G]P[K] + P[S]P[No]P[C] + \\
& P[S]P[No]P[Ne] + P[S]P[No]P[K] + P[S]P[C]P[Ne] + \\
& P[S]P[C]P[K] + P[S]P[Ne]P[K] + P[G]P[No]P[C] + P[G]P[No]P[Ne] + \\
& P[G]P[No]P[K] + P[G]P[C]P[Ne] + P[G]P[C]P[K] + P[G]P[Ne]P[K] + \\
& P[No]P[C]P[Ne] + P[No]P[C]P[K] + P[No]P[Ne]P[K] + P[C]P[Ne]P[K] - \\
& P[S]P[G]P[No]P[C] - P[S]P[G]P[No]P[Ne] - P[S]P[G]P[No]P[K] - \\
& P[S]P[No]P[C]P[Ne] - P[S]P[No]P[C]P[K] - P[S]P[C]P[Ne]P[K] - \\
& P[G]P[No]P[C]P[Ne] - P[G]P[No]P[C]P[K] - \\
& P[No]P[C]P[Ne]P[K] + P[S]P[G]P[No]P[C]P[Ne] + \\
& P[S]P[G]P[No]P[C]P[K] + P[G]P[No]P[C]P[Ne]P[K] - \\
& P[S]P[G]P[No]P[C]P[Ne]P[K].
\end{aligned}
\tag{5}
$$

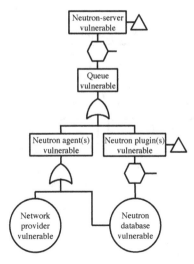

Fig. 8. Neutron Vulnerability Tree

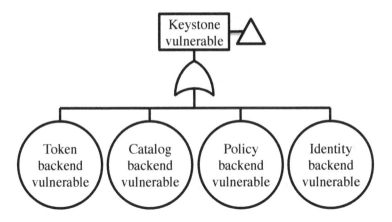

Fig. 9. Keystone Vulnerability Tree

4.8   In a Nutshell

Overall, the security analysis of OpenStack's logical architecture is a daunting task. One must know the intricacies of each component and the different liaisons between the components. We decided to use the Boolean operator OR to give ourselves more room to flexibly operate the security analysis but a deeper analysis of the architecture can yield a more on-the-point security analysis by using more precise Boolean operators. . Some components contain subcomponents that have redundant connections with other subcomponents. That situation was hard to design in the fault tree, and we forcibly have to ignore that redundancy while generating the likelihood of the top event.

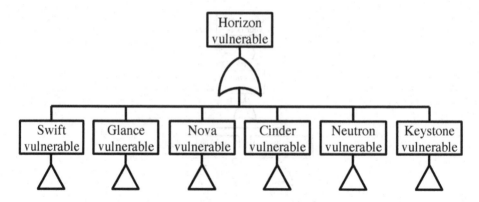

Fig. 10. Horizon Vulnerability Tree

```
<cpe-lang:fact-ref name="cpe:/a:openstack:swift:1.4.6"/>
<cpe-lang:fact-ref name="cpe:/a:openstack:swift:1.4.7"/>
<cpe-lang:fact-ref name="cpe:/a:openstack:swift:1.4.8"/>
```

Fig. 11. Current Vulnerability Naming of OpenStack

```
<cpe-lang:fact-ref name="cpe:2.3:a:openstack:swift:1.10.0:*:*:*:*:*:*:*"/>
<cpe-lang:fact-ref name="cpe:2.3:a:openstack:swift:1.10.0:memcached:*:*:*:*:*:*"/>
<cpe-lang:fact-ref name="cpe:2.3:a:openstack:swift:1.10.0:account:*:*:*:*:*:*"/>
<cpe-lang:fact-ref name="cpe:2.3:a:openstack:swift:1.10.0:account:accountDB:*:*:*:*"/>
<cpe-lang:fact-ref name="cpe:2.3:a:openstack:swift:1.10.0:container:*:*:*:*:*:*"/>
<cpe-lang:fact-ref name="cpe:2.3:a:openstack:swift:1.10.0:container:containerDB:*:*:*:*"/>
<cpe-lang:fact-ref name="cpe:2.3:a:openstack:swift:1.10.0:object:*:*:*:*:*:*"/>
<cpe-lang:fact-ref name="cpe:2.3:a:openstack:swift:1.10.0:object:objectDB:*:*:*:*"/>
```

Fig. 12. Proposed Nomenclature for OpenStack Vulnerabilities

5   Discussion and Future Work

In the previous section, we have deployed our security analysis mechanism and
generated the different vulnerability trees that could allow someone to quantify
the security of OpenStack depending on how many components she wants to use.
One of the first issues we have noticed is the complication of the interconnectedness of the components. Indeed, if they are taken individually, we can affirm
that the vulnerability trees developed in the previous section are corrects. But
when we take them collectively, we have some components that come back re-
dundantly, hence compromising our vulnerability tree. The result of the security
evaluation in this case will not be optimal because we do not really know how
that redundancy is impacting the evaluation.

The other point of contention is the nomenclature of the vulnerabilities. In
our security evaluation, the equations depend heavily on the subcomponents.
Whereas the naming of the vulnerabilities in the NVD does not give any indication on which subcomponent was affected by the vulnerability. The descriptions

of OpenStack's vulnerabilities often only indicate the components that are vulnerable (Figure 11). The naming of the vulnerabilities is effectuated by using the Naming specification of the Common Platform Enumeration (CPE) [11]. CPE is a standard that is used for the identification and the description of classes of applications, operating systems, and hardware devices. The latest version of CPE (CPE 2.3) uses the well-formed CPE name (WFN), which is an abstract logical construction, to represent the name of the classes of products. There are two methods for binding WFNs into machine-readable encodings: Uniform Resource Identifier (URI) binding and formatted string binding. URI binding is used for backward compatibility with CPE 2.2 [18]; that is why it has monopolistic presence in the NVD. Based on these facts, the equations for each component would be 'mono-parametric'. Additionally, the equation of the entire architecture will be simpler yet hiding many information i.e., it will not be accurate. Therefore, a new way of naming OpenStack's vulnerabilities is needed. That way should take into account all the different subcomponents that compose OpenStack. As future work, we will propose to use a nomenclature system that is adequate to our security evaluation. The formatted string binding appears to be a good choice. Figure 12 gives a hint on what a better nomenclature for OpenStack's vulnerabilities, by using the formatted string binding, should look like. But, the intrinsic definitition of the CPE forbids the usage of its binding methods to name a class of product in a very detailed way. What means that a new binding method is definitely needed for our proposal.

Our last discussion point revolves around the case of vulnerability masking. Indeed, one might argue that in case of networked-system the vulnerabilities might not factor in i.e. the security evaluation is useless in that situation. That theory is true that is why in the introduction of section 4, we made the assumption that only the Internet-facing components are considered in our security evaluation. An Internet-facing component, in our research, is a component that has a direct connection to the Internet there is no intermediary infrastructure like a firewall.

Finally, the architecture we considered in this work does not contain all the services of OpenStack. Indeed, Heat and Ceilometer are not part of the architecture consequently, we did not consider them in our security evaluation.

6   Conclusions

We proposed a vulnerability tree security evaluation of OpenStack's logical architecture. By applying our methology, we were able to generate ready-to-use vulnerability trees of the main components of the architecture. Unfortunately, we were not able to conduct the security analysis from inception to completion due to a nomenclature issue of OpenStack's vulnerabilities – nomenclature that does not consider the subcomponents of the major services of OpenStack. That issue has serendipituously opened for us doors to new research horizons on the naming of OpenStack's vulnerabilities.

References

1. OpenStack (2014), http://www.openstack.org
2. Eucalyptus (2014), http://www.eucalyptus.com
3. OpenNebula (2014), http://opennebula.org
4. Apache Foundation, CloudStack, http://cloudstack.apache.org
5. Mell, P., Scarfone, K., Romanosky, S.: A Complete Guide to the Common Vulnerability Scoring System (CVSS) Version 2.0 (2007), http://www.first.org/cvss/cvss-guide
6. U.S National Institute of Science and Technology (NIST), National Vulnerability Database (NVD), http://nvd.nist.gov
7. Vesely, W.E., Goldberg, F.F., Roberts, N.H., Haasl, D.F.: In: Fault tree handbook. No. NUREG-0492. Nuclear regulatory commission washington dc (1981)
8. Vesely, W.: Fault Tree Analysis (FTA): Concepts and Applications. NASA document, http://www.hq.nasa.gov/office/codeq/risk/ftacourse.pdf (accessed April 2014)
9. Bedford, T., Cooke, R.: Probabilistic Risk Analysis: Foundations and Methods. Cambridge University Press (2011)
10. Fall, D., Chaisamran, N., Okuda, T., Kadobayashi, Y., Yamaguchi, S.: Security Quantification of Complex Attack. In: Infrastructure as a Service Cloud Computing. In: 3rd International Conference on Cloud Computing and Services Science (June 2013)
11. Cheikes, B.A., Waltermire, D., Scarfone, K.: Common Platform Enumeration: Naming Specification Version 2.3, NISTIR 7695 (2011)
12. Zhai, E., Wolinsky, D.I., Xiao, H., Liu, H., Su, X., Ford, B.: Auditing the structural reliability of the clouds. Technical Report YALEU/DCS/TR-1479, Department of Computer Science, Yale University (2013), http://www.cs.yale.edu/homes/zhai-ennan/sra.pdf
13. Xiao, H., Ford, B., Feigenbaum, J.: Structural cloud audits that protect private information. In: Proceedings of the 2013 ACM Workshop on Cloud Computing Security Workshop, pp. 101–112. ACM (2013)
14. Khan, R.H., Ylitalo, J., Ahmed, A.S.: OpenID Authentication as a Service in openStack. In: 2011 7th International Conference on Information Assurance and Security (IAS), pp. 372–377. IEEE (2011)
15. Ristov, S., Gusev, M., Donevsky, A.: OpenStack Cloud Security Vulnerabilities From Inside and Outside. In: The Fourth International Conference on Cloud Computing, GRIDs, and Virtualization, CLOUD COMPUTING 2013, pp. 101–107 (2013)
16. Donevski, A., Ristov, S., Gusev, M.: Security assessment of virtual machines in open source clouds. In: 2013 36th International Convention on Information & Communication Technology Electronics & Microelectronics (MIPRO), pp. 1094–1099. IEEE (2013)
17. TaheriMonfared, A., Jaatum, M.G.: As Strong As The Weakest Link: Handling Compromised Components in OpenStack. In: Proceedings of the Third IEEE International Conference on Cloud Computing Technology and Science, CloudCom (2011)
18. Buttner, A., Ziring, N.: Common Platform Enumeration (CPE) - Specification Version 2.2 (March 2009)
19. Failure mode and effects analysis, http://en.wikipedia.org/wiki/Failure_mode_and_effects_analysis
20. Root cause analysis, http://en.wikipedia.org/wiki/Root_cause_analysis

PrivLoc: Preventing Location Tracking in Geofencing Services

Jens Mathias Bohli, Dan Dobre, Ghassan O. Karame, and Wenting Li

NEC Laboratories Europe, Germany
firstname.lastname@neclab.eu

Abstract. Location-based services are increasingly used in our daily activities. In current services, users however have to give up their location privacy in order to acquire the service.

The literature features a large number of contributions which aim at enhancing user privacy in location-based services. Most of these contributions obfuscate the locations of users using spatial and/or temporal cloaking in order to provide k-anonymity. Although such schemes can indeed strengthen the location privacy of users, they often decrease the service quality and do not necessarily prevent the possible tracking of user movements (i.e., direction, trajectory, velocity). With the rise of Geofencing applications, tracking of movements becomes more evident since, in these settings, the service provider is not only requesting a single location of the user, but requires the movement vectors of users to determine whether the user has entered/exited a Geofence of interest.

In this paper, we propose a novel solution, PrivLoc, which enables the privacy-preserving outsourcing of Geofencing and location-based services to the cloud without leaking any meaningful information about the location, trajectory, and velocity of the users. Notably, PrivLoc enables an efficient and privacy-preserving intersection of movement vectors with any polygon of interest, leveraging functionality from existing Geofencing services or spatial databases. We analyze the security and privacy provisions of PrivLoc and we evaluate the performance of our scheme by means of implementation. Our results show that the performance overhead introduced by PrivLoc can be largely tolerated in realistic deployment settings.

Keywords: Privacy, Geofencing, location tracking, location-based services.

1 Introduction

Location-based services (e.g., Foursquare [1] and Yelp [5]) are gaining increasing importance recently. Several applications enable users (e.g., using mobile devices) to discover and communicate their locations to a server in the cloud; in turn, the server uses this information to return data relevant at the users' locations. For instance, a number of existing services can only be acquired by users who are located within a specific geographical area; these include banking services, Youtube, and content delivery services, among many others. Location information also proves to be useful for a number of security-critical services such as police investigations, e-voting, etc.

T. Holz and S. Ioannidis (Eds.): TRUST 2014, LNCS 8564, pp. 143–160, 2014.

However, while many devices (e.g., smartphones, tablets) are capable of discovering and reporting their locations, a considerable number of users shy away from reporting their locations in the fear of being tracked or profiled by service providers [7]. This problem is even more evident when the service provider wishes to outsource his spatial services to the cloud (e.g., [4]). Service providers have considerable incentives to rely on hosted services in the cloud, since this enables them to maximize the availability of the service while minimizing the costs for acquisition of hardware and operation. Indeed, the cloud offers a low barrier for small and medium enterprises to offer location-based services and enables its clients to avoid huge upfront investments to accommodate for peak usage. However, hosting the spatial service in the cloud raises serious privacy concerns with respect to the leakage of client location information to the cloud provider.

The literature comprises a plethora of contributions which strengthen the privacy of users in location-based services. Most of these contributions focus on anonymizing user locations by means of a trusted location anonymizer server [6, 15, 20, 22, 34]. After registering with the service, users can send their exact locations to the server, which "blurs" these location reports and sends the cloaked location to a remote database server. The server also filters the database's response and subsequently sends the exact answers back to the users when needed. Existing location anonymization techniques can be categorized according to three different approaches: (i) inserting false dummies [21], where the server sends n location updates for each location reported by the user ($(n-1)$ reports of which are dummy), (ii) location blurring [6, 10, 15, 20, 33] where the location of the user is blurred into a spatial area (using spatial or temporal cloaking), and (iii) landmark obfuscation [19] where the server sends the location of a near-by landmark instead of the location of the user.

While these techniques can provide users with k-anonymity guarantees, existing techniques (i) often require changes to the database server in order to efficiently process the anonymized queries, or (ii) reduce the accuracy of the location-based service (e.g., when relying on spatial cloaking), or (iii) do not prevent location tracking [22]. Location tracking could be performed e.g., by inferring the direction of the movement/path followed by the user, the velocity of the user, etc., which might de-anonymize users. Such information leakage is particularity damaging in location-based services where service providers are interested in the events of users entering/exiting a given area (e.g., Geofencing applications [2, 3, 23, 28, 29]). These applications are gaining increasing importance for e.g., targeted advertisements, and typically take as inputs vectors of movements performed by users and enable service providers to extract various statistics about their customers, such as visit durations, start, end, etc.

In this paper, we address this problem, and we propose a novel solution, PrivLoc, which efficiently enables the privacy-preserving use of Geofencing services in the cloud without incurring any modifications to spatial indexing techniques, and without leaking any meaningful information about the location, trajectory, and/or velocity of the users to the cloud provider. More specifically, we consider a typical Geofencing setting, whereby a spatial database hosted on the cloud receives regular movement vectors from users, and checks if these movements cross a Geofenced area which has been subscribed to within the database. If so, the provider issues a notification informing the appropriate subscriber that a user has exited/entered the subscribed area of interest. Note that this can be achieved in existing spatial databases by querying for intersection between the user movement vector and the Geofenced area. PrivLoc leverages the presence of a private trusted service which performs efficient specially-crafted transformations of location reports to interface with the cloud-hosted Geofencing service without exposing the privacy of users. As such, PrivLoc can be used by companies and individuals to prevent information leakage towards spatial databases hosted in clouds, such as Google, Amazon, etc. In this respect, PrivLoc enables a privacy-preserving intersection of movement vectors with any polygon of interest, while leveraging functionality from existing cloud-based spatial databases. We analyze the security and privacy provisions of PrivLoc and we evaluate its performance in a realistic setting. Our results show that our scheme scales well with the number of users and subscriptions in the system and does not incur considerable computational overhead on the trusted server.

The remainder of the paper is organized as follows. In Section 2, we outline our system and adversarial model. In Section 3, we introduce and analyze our solution, PrivLoc, which efficiently enables users to acquire privacy-preserving Geofencing services hosted in the cloud. We evaluate its performance by means of an implementation in Section 4. In Section 5, we overview related work in the area, and we conclude the paper in Section 6.

2   Model

In this section, we describe our system and adversarial model, and we outline the security requirements that our solution should satisfy.

2.1   Spatial Databases

Spatial databases are instances of databases optimized to store and query data which represents objects defined in a geometric space. Examples of spatial databases include MongoDB, MySQL, PostgreSQL, among others. To efficiently handle and store spatial data, spatial databases rely on a Spatial Database Management System (SDBMS) which extends upon the capabilities of a traditional database management system. SDBMS typically supports three types of queries: *(i)* set operators (e.g., disjoint, touch, contains), *(ii)* spatial analysis (e.g., distance, intersection), and *(iii)* other basic functions such as envelope, boundary, etc. This is efficiently achieved through the reliance on spatial indices (e.g., R-tree, X-tree, GiST). For instance, R-trees [18] represent objects with their minimum bounding rectangle in the next higher level of the tree. The main intuition here is that a query which does not intersect the bounding rectangle also cannot intersect any of the contained objects.

While there are a number of spatial indexing techniques, all techniques require the database server to check a series of coordinate equalities and inequalities in order to determine its spatial index. This clearly poses a problem when dealing with encrypted data objects. For instance, standard encryption of the coordinate system with a semantically secure cryptosystem such as AES, would not preserve any relationship (i.e., to check for equality/inequality) between two points in the coordinate system. While this would be ideal from a cryptographic point of view, it would not be useful for spatial databases, since no "efficient" indexing would be possible on objects.

2.2 System Model

We consider the following system: we assume the existence of mobile nodes $\mathcal{M}$ (e.g., mobile devices, sensors) which "publish" periodic location reports to a Geofencing service that is hosted in the cloud and consists of multiple database servers. In the sequel, we denote by $\mathcal{D}_i$ the i-th database server; for clarity of presentation, we also denote by $\mathcal{D}$ the "logical" database comprising the various database servers. For simplicity and without loss of generality, we assume a 2D bounded area where the nodes can freely move. Each node $M_i \in \mathcal{M}$ periodically sends location beacons to the database servers. These beacons consist of tuples of the form $\langle \text{ID}_i, \text{Loc}_i \rangle$, where ID_i is an identifier of M_i, Loc_i is a vector of the last movement performed by M_i (e.g., Loc could comprise the last and the current coordinates of M_i). We assume that the movement of node M_i is characterized by a velocity distribution $\mathcal{V}_i$, and a path distribution $\mathcal{P}_i$. For simplicity and without loss of generality, we assume that the movement of M_i between two reported coordinates corresponds to a straight line. Current Geofencing applications require indeed that nodes report their last and the current coordinates; by doing so, the Geofencing server can be a stateless server which does not memorize the last coordinate of each node. As we show in this paper, this also serves to increase the privacy of the entire system.

We assume that $\mathcal{D}$ offers location-based services to customers, denoted in the sequel by $\mathcal{S}$. Here, we assume that customers can "subscribe" to events that occur within a specific sub-area of the map for instance, customers want to be notified when users enter/exit their subscribed Geofences.

In the sequel, we denote by S_i the ith subscriber in $\mathcal{S}$; upon receiving a location report from node M_i, $\mathcal{D}$ checks if M_i's reported coordinates are located within a subscribed area. More specifically, $\mathcal{D}$ relies on existing spatial database functionality which can efficiently compute the intersection between a line and polygons. If the movement vector of a node results in non-empty intersection, $\mathcal{D}$ issues a notification message to S_k (e.g., using a URL of S_k stored at $\mathcal{D}$).

2.3 Adversarial Model and Security Requirements

Throughout our analysis, we assume that the nodes are trusted to report their locations correctly. That is, we assume that these devices cannot be compromised by the adversary. Moreover, we assume that the cloud providers (operating the database servers) are honest-but-curious. More specifically, we assume that each database server will correctly follow the protocol (i.e., authenticate the nodes, output correct notifications) but is interested in acquiring information about the locations of the nodes in the system, and about the queries that are issued by the customers. Ideally, different database servers do not collude; this assumption especially holds when the database servers are hosted by different clouds (e.g., Amazon, Google). Moreover, we assume that the adversary cannot physically track the mobile users to acquire information about their movements. Finally, we assume that the adversary is computationally bounded (i.e., she cannot acquire secrets, break secure encryption functions, etc.).

As mentioned earlier, the main premise behind our work is to design a privacy-preserving solution for a Geofencing service hosted in the cloud, *without* incurring any modifications on the database servers, and while ensuring that $\mathcal{D}$ does not learn any meaningful information about the location of the users and subscriptions in the system. Since the adversary can compromise a database server, we can express these security properties using the following requirements:

Requirement 1—Confidentiality of Stored Records: Each database server should not learn any meaningful information about the stored subscriptions. This can be ensured if the transcript of interaction between $\mathcal{D}$, $\mathcal{M}$, and $\mathcal{S}$ is (computationally) independent of the actual subscription coordinates.

Requirement 2—Confidentiality of Queries: Similar to Requirement (1), each database server should not learn any meaningful information about the location of the nodes. This includes the direction of the movement, the trajectory taken by each node, the distance travelled by each node, etc.

Recall that both Requirements (1) and (2) should be achieved without compromising the functionality of the database server, i.e., while enabling efficient geo-spatial indexing, search over encrypted data, etc. (cf. Section 2.1).

Note that both Requirements (1) and (2) can only ensure confidentiality of the input/output, but do not prevent the possible correlation between the inputs and outputs of the database when subject to location queries by the nodes. This is the case since $\mathcal{D}$ can learn whether a given publish event matches an encrypted subscribe event. In this work, we do not aim at preventing such information leakage. As far as we are aware, the literature features a number of solutions for this problem. These include delaying some queries to ensure k-anonymity [17, 31, 32], relying on bogus queries/subscription to probabilistically provide input/output unlinkability [21], among many others.

3 PrivLoc: Privacy-Preserving Outsourced Geofencing Services

In this section, we introduce PrivLoc, our solution which enables the privacy-preserving outsourcing of Geofencing services to the cloud and we thoroughly analyze its security and privacy provisions.

3.1 Overview of PrivLoc

PrivLoc requires that $\mathcal{D}$ only implements the standard Geofencing functionality specified in Section 2.1 without any modification, given inputs from the mobile users. Thus, we see $\mathcal{D}$ as a Geofencing service hosted in the cloud. Nevertheless, PrivLoc ensures that no meaningful information about the location of the devices and subscriptions in the system is leaked to any entity, including $\mathcal{D}$.

In order to achieve these goals, PrivLoc relies on a trusted server $\mathcal{T}$, which mediates the exchange of information between the devices/subscribers on one side, and $\mathcal{D}$ on the other side. More specifically, $\mathcal{T}$ translates both the mobile device locations, and the subscriptions into "scrambled" inputs that are then stored and processed by $\mathcal{D}$. Although the inputs are subsequently hidden from $\mathcal{D}$, PrivLoc ensures that they can be processed using existing geo-spatial indexing algorithms and always result in a correct database lookup. More specifically, the various operations undergone in PrivLoc are:

Table 1. Global system parameters of PrivLoc

κ	the security parameter, e.g. 128 bit
L	the width and height of a tile
m	the number of tiles in a column, i.e. the height of the map
n	the number of tiles in a row, i.e. the width of the map

- Upon receiving each subscription request, $\mathcal{T}$ translates the subscription requested by the subscribers into the appropriate coordinates and stores them at $\mathcal{D}$.
- Upon receiving each sensor location beacon, $\mathcal{T}$ translates the location into the appropriate coordinates and only forwards the transformed beacon to $\mathcal{D}$.

We see $\mathcal{T}$ as an additional service which is run locally to prevent information leakage towards spatial database servers hosted in clouds, such as Google, Amazon, etc. Clearly, for our solution to be effective, the overhead on $\mathcal{T}$ should be minimal. Indeed, in PrivLoc, $\mathcal{T}$ simply has to apply a series of transformations on the received subscriptions and location reports. We stress at this point that the role of $\mathcal{T}$ can be emulated by the mobile nodes and the subscribers themselves, in case these entities pre-share keys. Otherwise, the presence of a trusted service which orchestrates the key management among users and subscribers of the database is required (see [6, 10, 15, 20, 33] for similar assumptions).

PrivLoc introduces two granularity levels when encrypting locations. On the coarse-granular level, PrivLoc relies on a pseudo-random permutation to emulate a strong encryption function, while on the fine-granular level PrivLoc relies on a weaker notion—order-preserving encryption—to preserve the relative location of closely-related points within a sub-area—referred to as *tiles* —so that the spatial operations performed by $\mathcal{D}$ can be applied within each tile without modification. As we describe in Section 3.2, PrivLoc relies on multiple database servers to ensure that any two consecutive location reports can be fitted to at least one tile. The combination of our techniques ensure that location reports pertaining to each tile can be processed using existing functionality of $\mathcal{D}$, without revealing the location or direction of movements. In the following paragraphs, we discuss in details the various translation operations and the load incurred by $\mathcal{T}$ in PrivLoc.

3.2   PrivLoc: Protocol Specification

PrivLoc unfolds as follows. $\mathcal{T}$ first proceeds to dividing the original map by a regular grid into fixed-size square tiles. For privacy reasons, the area covered by a tile should fall above a given threshold. In the sequel, we assume the global system parameters shown in Table 1. Furthermore, PrivLoc makes use of the following functions:

- a pseudorandom function PRF : $\mathcal{K} \times \{0,1\}^* \times \ell \to \{0,1\}^\ell$, which can be realized by a HMAC construction.
- a pseudorandom permutation PRP : $\mathcal{K} \times \{0,1\}^N \to \{0,1\}^N$, where $N = \lceil \log_2(nm) \rceil$. Exemplary PRP constructions can be found in [8].

In the setup phase, $\mathcal{T}$ generates key k as a uniformly random bit string of a length depending on the intended security level κ.

As mentioned earlier, PrivLoc requires that $\mathcal{T}$ encrypts the coordinates reported by devices before transmitting them to $\mathcal{D}$. Besides hiding location information, one important goal here is to hide the fine-grained user movements (i.e., direction and distance of movement). Recall that, in our setting, the subscribers are interested in knowing whether a device has crossed a Geofence. For the database servers to determine that, it is therefore necessary for them to be able to compare the relative coordinates between the origin and the destination of every sensor movement segment along with the boundaries of Geofences (or subscriptions).

PrivLoc achieves the aforementioned goals by dividing the map into tiles and distorting the original coordinate system into three different variant maps (for the reasoning why, see following paragraphs). By doing so, PrivLoc encrypts the location of each tile within the maps, but ensures that every received location report can be fitted to at least one full tile in one of the maps. Subscriptions that cross more than one tile are also subsequently split to several smaller Geofences that are completely contained in a single tile. Within that tile, PrivLoc further distorts the direction and distance of the user movement while enabling the spatial database to find all intersections between the movement vector and translated Geofences in the distorted tile using existing indexing techniques.

More specifically, PrivLoc applies the encrypt procedure (Algorithm 1); encrypt takes as input real world coordinates (x, y) and transforms them into obfuscated coordinates $(newx, newy)$. encrypt is executed on *(i)* movement vectors to translate the movement end-points, and on *(ii)* subscriptions to translate the south-west, and the north-east coordinates that define the minimum bounding box of each Geofence.

The algorithm encrypt consists of four main routines:

– permuteTiles is used to divide the map into equal-sized tiles and permute these tiles. By doing so, permuteTiles hides the location of the devices within the map.
– rotateTile and flipTile are used to rotate and flip each tile in the distorted map. Both routines serve to hide the direction of devices' movements within the original map.
– OPE is used to hide the distance between any two locations within each tile.

Here, permuteTiles, rotateTile, and flipTile hide the location and direction of the movement of each device from $\mathcal{D}$, while OPE distorts the distances within each tile. All four routines, however, enable $\mathcal{D}$ to rely on existing indexing techniques (c.f. Section 2.1) to compare different locations *within each tile*.

Hiding Movements within a Tile

Recall that PrivLoc operates on movement vectors reported by the users. Upon receiving the vector from devices, $\mathcal{T}$ encrypts the vector, by applying the encrypt procedure in Algorithm 1, to both the start and end-point of the movement vector. These points are represented by 2D coordinates (x, y). The encryption function invokes the procedure coordinatesOnTile, which returns the tile number Num of the tile where the point (x, y) lies on, and the relative coordinates (dx, dy) on the respective tile. As the map is split in $n \times m$ tiles, we have $Num \in \mathbf{Z}_{n \times m}$. This coordinate translation is achieved by means of Algorithm 2.

Algorithm 1. Coordinate Encryption in PrivLoc

Require: Coordinates x, y, map offset z, master key k
Ensure: Encrypted location $newx, newy$
1: **procedure** ENCRYPT(x, y, z, k)
2:     $(Num, dx, dy) \leftarrow$ COORDINATESONTILE(x, y, z)
3:     $Num \leftarrow PRP(k; n \times m; Num)$
4:     $(dx, dy) \leftarrow$ ROTATETILE(dx, dy, Num, k)
5:     $(dx, dy) \leftarrow$ FLIPTILE(dx, dy, Num, k)
6:     $(dx, dy) \leftarrow$ OPE(dx, dy, Num, k)
7:     $newx \leftarrow (Num \bmod n) \times L + dx$
8:     $newy \leftarrow (Num \textbf{ div } n) \times L + dy$
9:     **return** $newx, newy$
10: **end procedure**

Algorithm 2. Coordinate Translation

Require: Coordinates x, y and offset z of the respective map
Ensure: Num of the tile where x, y lies and relative coordinates dx, dy on the tile
1: **procedure** COORDINATESONTILE(x, y)
2:     $x0 \leftarrow (x - z \bmod L \times m) \textbf{ div } L$
3:     $y0 \leftarrow (y - z \bmod L \times n) \textbf{ div } L$
4:     $Num \leftarrow (x0 + y0 \cdot n)$
5:     $(dx, dy) \leftarrow x \bmod L, y \bmod L$
6:     **return**($x0, y0, dx, dy$)
7: **end procedure**

As the first step of hiding the location of these points within the map, $\mathcal{T}$ permutes the tiles using the key k by applying the pseudorandom function: $PRP(k; n \times m; Num)$. Note that k is only held by the trusted server $\mathcal{T}$. This function computes a pseudorandom permutation of the numbers in $\mathbf{Z}_{n \times m}$ and outputs the new position Num for the tile T.

To further hide the linkability between two consecutive location reports (i.e., to prevent leakage of movement information), $\mathcal{T}$ first rotates each tile using rotateTile (rotation chosen at random among $0, \pi/2, \pi, 3\pi/4$), and then (individually) flips them using flipTile, in order to obfuscate the direction of the movement. Both operations result in a transformation entropy of three bits per tile. When combined with permuteTile, this results in a total of $3 \lfloor \log_2(nm) \rfloor$ bits of entropy per tile.

rotateTile is described in Appendix A. rotateTile takes the output of permuteTile; the position of the tile T is not changed in this algorithm. The rotation angle of T is determined using the key-based pseudo-random function PRF.

$\mathcal{T}$ then applies tile flipping (Algorithm 3). Given the outputs of rotateTile, flipTile outputs the newly flipped coordinates $(newx, newy)$. Note that flipTile is analogous to rotateTile, except that the coordinates are transformed by a mirror matrix.

In order to hide the distances of movements executed by devices, PrivLoc further relies on the use of order-preserving encryption (OPE) within each tile. Order-preserving

---

Algorithm 3. Tile Flipping

Require: Coordinates dx, dy and Num
Ensure: Coordinates dx, dy after flipping the tile
1: **procedure** FLIPTILE(x, y, k)
2:      $flip \leftarrow$ PRF(k; "flip", Num; 1)
3:      **if then**$flip = \text{'}1\text{'}$
4:          $dx' \leftarrow (L - 1) - dx$
5:      **end if**
6:      **return**(dx', dy)
7: **end procedure**

---

encryption has the property that the relative order among coordinates is preserved after encryption. That is, let OPE(p) denote the order-preserving encryption of plaintext p. Then, the following holds:

$$\begin{cases} \text{OPE}(p_1) \leq \text{OPE}(p_2) \ if p_1 \leq p_2, \\ \text{OPE}(p_1) > \text{OPE}(p_2) \ if p_1 > p_2. \end{cases}$$

Hiding Cross-Tile Movements

Clearly, encrypt can only hide the trajectory, and distance exhibited by location reports from $\mathcal{D}$ when they fall within the same tile. However, if two consecutive location reports cross the boundary of a single tile and are matched to different tiles, then *(i)* $\mathcal{D}$ cannot compare the relative location advertised by these reports and *(ii)* $\mathcal{D}$ might be able to guess that these tiles correspond to physically connected tiles in the original map.

Thus, a query for a movement which crosses the tile boundary must be avoided in PrivLoc. To achieve that, PrivLoc relies on more than one tiling of the same map (see Figure 1); although a movement might cross the boundary of one map tiling, PrivLoc ensures that there is at least one tiling, in which the movement falls completely within a single tile. Here, by different map tilings, we refer to slightly shifted variants of the original map, which have been processed (i.e., using the encrypt routine) by means of different keys (cf. Figure 1). As shown in Figure 1, the maximum magnitude of a movement vector that PrivLoc accepts is bounded by $l = t/3 + \epsilon$, where t is the length of one tile. Thus, all vectors with magnitude $d(x, y) < r = t/3$ can be located within one complete tile stored at least on one of the three servers. Within that tile, this enables the comparison between all closely located points x and y, where $d(x, y) < t/3$, while ensuring that the movement from location x to y does not cross the tile[1]. An example of a map with three tilings is depicted in Figure 1. As shown in Figure 1, we point out that relying on two tilings of the same map is not enough. This is the case since there exist movement vectors which can still cross two different tiles in any two map tilings. However, it is easy to show that given three shifted tilings of the same map, there is no point where all boundaries intersect, thus ensuring that every movement can be fitted to one tile pertaining to at least one tiling. This is exactly why PrivLoc requires the presence of three database servers $\mathcal{D}_1$, $\mathcal{D}_2$, and $\mathcal{D}_3$, which store subscriptions pertaining to the three map tilings.

---

[1] Thus, this ensures that an adversary who can observe consecutive movements cannot acquire information about the relative position of the actual tiles in each transformed map.

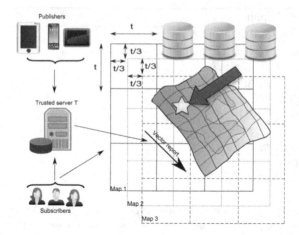

Fig. 1. Example of three tilings of the original map. Notice here that the movement vector crosses the boundaries of tiles in "Map 1" (shown in solid lines) and "Map 2" (shown in dotted lines) but can be fitted complexity within a tile in "Map 3" (shown in dashed lines).

All received subscriptions are stored encrypted with three different keys k_1, k_2 and k_3 on all three servers respectively. Whenever $\mathcal{T}$ receives a location report, it will choose to query the database server $\mathcal{D}_i, i \in \{1, 2, 3\}$ for whom this report falls in a full tile (see Appendix B for the algorithm). Here, $\mathcal{T}$ can efficiently find out which server to query for each movement (by essentially performing two integer divisions, cf. Section 4).

As a by-product, we point out that the reliance on multiple database servers in our scheme inherently achieves load balancing of the load on the servers and increases the load capacity of the entire system. This is the case since $\mathcal{T}$ only queries one server for each received location report.

Encrypting Subscriptions

We now proceed to describing how $\mathcal{T}$ encrypts subscriptions and stores them at the database servers $\mathcal{D}$. Clearly, for $\mathcal{D}$ to be able to use existing functionality to compute the intersections of the movements with subscriptions, the subscriptions must be encrypted using the same routine that is used to process the location reports.

More specifically, $\mathcal{T}$ uses the encrypt routine to encrypt the north-east and the south-west coordinates which define the minimum bounding box for each subscription. This is done using the three keys k_1, k_2, and k_3, respectively. The resulting encrypted coordinates are stored in database servers $\mathcal{D}_1$, $\mathcal{D}_2$, and $\mathcal{D}_3$ (see Figure 2). Here, $\mathcal{T}$ must ensure that:

- In case a subscription crosses the boundaries of tiles for the map tiling at a database server, the subscription needs to be split into parts, that each completely fit within one tile of the corresponding map tiling. This process has to be repeated for each of the three servers independently. While this incurs additional storage overhead per server to store the tiles, we show in Section 4 that the storage blowup incurred by PrivLoc can be, to a large extent, tolerated in realistic settings.

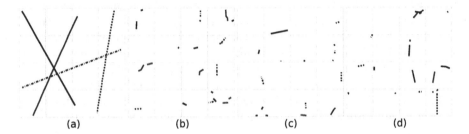

Fig. 2. Exemplary run of PrivLoc with four different movements. Each path displayed in (a) consists of 20 movement reports, each of a length of 30% of the tile width. We depict the snapshots seen by database servers $\mathcal{D}_1$, $\mathcal{D}_2$, and $\mathcal{D}_3$ in (b), (c) and (d), respectively. Note that the marking of the vectors in (b)-(d) is only for visualisation, since different location reports cannot be linked by the database.

- $\mathcal{T}$ batches the upload of $\bar{k}$ subscriptions to the three database servers. Here, $\bar{k}$ denotes a desired privacy threshold. As we show later, this ensures that database servers cannot temporally correlate various subscriptions.

3.3   Security Analysis

Before analyzing the security of PrivLoc, we capture Requirements (1) and (2) (cf. Section 2.3) using the following security game, $\mathrm{Priv}^{\mathcal{A}}$, which involves a p.p.t adversary $\mathcal{A}$ and a challenger $\mathcal{C}$. In our game, $\mathcal{C}$ simulates location reports and subscription requests and emulates the role of the trusted server $\mathcal{T}$ which interacts with $\mathcal{D}$. More specifically, the $\mathrm{Priv}^{\mathcal{A}}$ game unfolds as follows.

Setup. The challenger $\mathcal{C}$ sets up 3 database servers $\mathcal{D}_1$, $\mathcal{D}_2$ and $\mathcal{D}_3$ and generates the respective master keys k_1, k_2 and k_3 using the setup routine.

Run. The challenger $\mathcal{C}$ simulates location reports and subscriptions. More specifically, $\mathcal{C}$ simulates the presence of N nodes with distribution $(\mathcal{V}, \mathcal{P})$, and S subscriptions. On input a location report (x, y), $\mathcal{C}$ executes chooseServer and encrypt(x, y, k).

Compromise. $\mathcal{A}$ chooses *one* server $\mathcal{D}_i^{\mathcal{A}}$, $i \in \{1, 2, 3\}$ at time t. Starting from time t, $\mathcal{A}$ acquires a trace consisting of all inputs and outputs to/from $\mathcal{D}_i^{\mathcal{A}}$.

Challenge. $\mathcal{A}$ then chooses a location report r that arrived at $\tilde{t} > t$ and sends r as a challenge to $\mathcal{C}$.

Response. Upon reception of r, $\mathcal{C}$ locates the node M_k which issued r, and randomly flips a bit b. If $b = 0$, then $\mathcal{C}$ sends to $\mathcal{A}$ a trajectory of movement vectors followed by node M_k. Otherwise, if $b = 1$, $\mathcal{C}$ creates a randomly generated trajectory comprising of movement vectors derived from the distributions $\mathcal{V}_k$ and $\mathcal{P}_k$.

We define the advantage of $\mathcal{A}$ in the above game $\mathrm{Priv}^{\mathcal{A}}$ by:

$$\mathrm{Adv}_{\mathrm{Priv}^{\mathcal{A}}} = \mathrm{Prob}[b' \leftarrow \mathcal{A} : b = b']$$

Definition 1. *Location Tracking*
We say that a system prevents ϵ-tracking if $\mathrm{Adv}_{\mathrm{Priv}^{\mathcal{A}}} = \frac{1}{2} + \epsilon.$

Clearly, a system perfectly prevents location tracking when ϵ is negligible. Definition 1 captures Requirements (1) and (2) in Section 2.3. Here, $\mathcal{A}$ can compromise one database server. After observing the transcript of interactions with the compromised server, our goal is to prevent $\mathcal{A}$ from acquiring information about the trajectory followed by any node M_k of her choice. This is captured by the fact that the probability that $\mathcal{A}$ can distinguish the trajectory adopted by M_k from any random path is negligible. Notice that $\text{Priv}^{\mathcal{A}}$ captures the ability of the adversary to infer information about the trajectory taken by users using side-information like the velocity of movement, the distance traveled, etc.

Security Analysis: We informally analyze the security of our scheme with respect to the aforementioned $\text{Priv}^{\mathcal{A}}$ game.

Notably, our goal is to show that an adversary $\mathcal{A}$ which compromises one database server $\overline{\mathcal{D}_i}$ and has access to the inputs/outputs of $\overline{\mathcal{D}_i}$ cannot acquire meaningful information about the trajectory of users. Recall that the communication between users, subscribers, and $\mathcal{T}$ is performed over confidential and authenticated channels, which does not give $\mathcal{A}$ any advantage in acquiring information about the (plaintext) location reports and the subscriptions in the system.

In analyzing the advantage of $\mathcal{A}$ in $\text{Priv}^{\mathcal{A}}$, two cases emerge:

1) *Analyzing single location reports:* Having received an encrypted location vector from $\mathcal{T}$, we note that $\mathcal{A}$ cannot infer the location of the corresponding user whom generated it in the original map. This is the case since the keyed PRP used in the permuteTiles function ensures that the adversary cannot guess the actual location of the tile which hosts the report in the original map. Moreover, OPE ensures that $\mathcal{A}$ cannot acquire the actual distance travelled by the user while the keyed tile rotation and flipping ensure that $\mathcal{A}$ cannot guess the direction of the user movement given the received location vector.

2) *Correlating two or more location reports:* Recall that $\overline{\mathcal{D}_i}$ will only receive location reports which correspond to a complete tile given the tiling hosted by $\overline{\mathcal{D}_i}$. As mentioned earlier, the combined use of the permuted tile location of the report, the OPE-obfuscated distance travelled by the user, and tilted/rotated movement direction does not offer any distinguisher for $\mathcal{A}$ to correlate two or more location reports.

Similarly, it is easy to show that $\mathcal{A}$ cannot acquire any meaningful information about the subscriptions in the system. Note that when tiling and permuting tiles at each server, each subscription might be split into a number of smaller subscriptions within each tile. However, assuming that the system hosts a number of subscriptions, this does not give any advantage to $\mathcal{A}$ in inferring information about the subscriptions. Note, here, that $\mathcal{A}$ can acquire considerable information as $\mathcal{T}$ populates $\overline{\mathcal{D}_i}$. For instance, it is straightforward for $\mathcal{A}$ to guess with high probability that consecutive subscriptions in $\overline{\mathcal{D}_i}$ correspond to the same actual subscription which was subsequently split by $\mathcal{T}$ to prevent subscriptions from crossing tile borders. This is exactly why PrivLoc requires that $\mathcal{T}$ batches the processing of $\overline{k}$ (genuine) subscriptions at a time. On one hand, this enhances the anonymity of the subscriptions, and on the other hand, this prevents $\mathcal{A}$ from correlating stored encrypted subscriptions (e.g., map them to the same subscription) and acquiring information about the tile permutation.

As mentioned in Section 2.3, PrivLoc can only ensure confidentiality of the input/output, and does not prevent the correlation among the inputs and outputs of $\overline{\mathcal{D}_i}$. That is, $\mathcal{A}$ can learn whether a given location report has triggered a response from $\overline{\mathcal{D}_i}$ and therefore corresponds to a user entering/exiting a Geofence. The literature features a number of solutions for this problem (see [17, 21, 31, 32]).

4 Implementation and Evaluation

In this section, we implement PrivLoc and we evaluate the performance of our implementation in comparison to the setting where the Geofencing service is not outsourced to the cloud, but is locally offered using an existing spatial database.

4.1 Implementation Setup

We implement the PrivLoc service using Java. In our implementation, we set $\kappa = 128$, we adapt the OPE from [9], and we use HMAC-SHA1 as the PRF in the rotateTile and flipTile routines. The tile permutation is achieved by an array permutation given a secure random number generator. In our setup, we deploy PrivLoc on an 8-core Intel Xeon E3-1230 with 16 GB RAM; the various clients issuing location reports and/or subscriptions were co-located with $\mathcal{T}$ on the same machine.

We chose a square $100km \times 100km$ map in which the maximum size of a subscription is $100m \times 100m$ (this was also the tile size in our implementation). Conforming with Section 3.2, we set the maximum movement distance of a user between two consecutive location reports to $\frac{t}{3} \approx 30m$. We rely on the random waypoint model to simulate node mobility. More specifically, for each user in the system, we assume a random initial location in the map; for each subsequent movement, the movement vector angle is chosen randomly from [0,360] degrees, while the distance of each movement is chosen randomly from [0,30] meters. Throughout our evaluation, we assume a realistic setting where the ratio of location reports to incoming subscription requests is 19:1.[2]

Based on this setup, we measure the throughput achieved by PrivLoc with respect to the average latency incurred on $\mathcal{T}$ due to a location report or a subscription. To increase the load on $\mathcal{T}$, we vary the number of concurrent clients from 1 to a maximum of 256. In our experiments, we are interested in assessing the performance of PrivLoc when the links between $\mathcal{T}$ and the database servers are not the bottleneck. For that purpose, we short-circuit the database servers and we abstract away the time to upload the location reports by $\mathcal{T}$ to the database servers. Under these settings, we compare the throughput and latency achieved by PrivLoc to the traditional case where the spatial database is entirely hosted locally; here, we compare the performance of PrivLoc to (i) a stand-alone MySQL spatial database (with R-tree indexing) and (ii) a PostgreSQL database (with GiST indexing). Both databases were deployed within our 8-core Intel Xeon E3-1230 with 16 GB RAM; we report their performance with different subscription table sizes (i.e., initial number of records). We also evaluated PrivLoc when compared to MongoDB. Since the performance exhibited MongoDB was far inferior to that of MySQL and PostgreSQL, we omit these measurements from our evaluation.

---

[2] We conducted experiments where the ration between where location reports and subscriptions is 1:1. Our results were similar to the setting featuring a ratio of 19:1.

4.2 Evaluation Results

We start by evaluating the performance of PrivLoc w.r.t. to the MySQL and PostgreSQL databases while varying the initial number of stored subscriptions. This experiment captures the performance of PrivLoc compared to locally hosted spatial databases as the number of subscription populating these databases increases with time. For that purpose, we measure the peak throughout (PT) exhibited by PrivLoc and compare it with that of

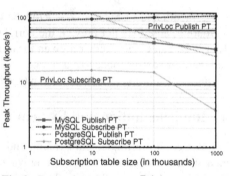

Fig. 3. Comparison between PrivLoc and local MySQL and PostgreSQL databases

MySQL, and PostgreSQL respectively, in settings where the initial number of stored subscriptions varies from 1,000 to 1,000,000. Our results are depicted in Figure 3. Our findings show that the PT of PrivLoc is superior to MySQL when processing location reports, irrespective of the number of stored subscriptions. Here, PrivLoc outperforms PostgreSQL as the number of subscriptions stored by the PostgreSQL database increases beyond 50,000 records. This is also the case when processing subscription requests. Nevertheless, our results indicate that, even when the initial number of subscriptions stored in the MySQL, and PostgreSQL databases is as low as 1,000, the relative PT achieved by PrivLoc can be easily tolerated.

In a second experiment, we evaluate the relative performance of PrivLoc in the realistic case where the Geofencing service has been running for some time, and has accumulated the subscriptions from a large number of subscribers. To simulate this case, we insert 1,000,000 subscription records in the databases. Figure 4 depicts the latency incurred in PrivLoc for the processing of location reports and subscriptions in the system with respect to the achieved throughput (measured in the number of 1000 operations per second). For comparison purposes, we also include the performance achieved by a local MySQL and a PostgreSQL spatial database in the same setup. Our results (cf. Figure 4(a)) show that PrivLoc is at least twice faster than locally processing location reports on both spatial databases. Moreover, the peak throughput achieved in PrivLoc is more than 2 times higher than that achieved by the MySQL and PostgreSQL databases. However, our results in Figure 4(b) show that the latency and peak throughput achieved by PrivLoc are modest when inserting subscriptions, compared to the local MySQL database. This is due to the blow-up in the number of subscriptions. Notably, since $\mathcal{T}$ splits the map into small tiles, a subscribed area might be further split by $\mathcal{T}$ if it crosses multiple tiles. Note that each subscribed area results in an average of 6.75 subscribed areas which will be encrypted by PrivLoc and pushed to the $n = 3$ database servers. This blow-up is dependent on the number of database servers, and the size of the subscribed area with respect to the size of the tiles. More specifically, the average area of a subscription in our setup is $1/4$ of the area of a tile; this means that the average number of partitions of a subscribed area on each database server is $N_p = 1 \cdot \frac{1}{4} + 2 \cdot \frac{2}{4} + 4 \cdot \frac{1}{4} = 2.25$. The total blowup in terms of subscriptions is subsequently $3N_p = 6.75$.

In spite of the storage blowup, our findings nevertheless show that PrivLoc considerably outperforms a local PostgreSQL database.

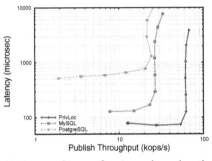 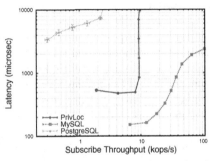

(a) Average latency for processing a location report by $\mathcal{T}$ with respect to the throughput.

(b) Average latency for processing a subscription by $\mathcal{T}$ with respect to the throughput.

Fig. 4. Throughput and latency in PrivLoc. Here, we assume a subscription table size of 1,000,0000 records. Each data point in our measurements is averaged over 10 independent measurements; we present the corresponding 95% confidence intervals.

5   Related Work

In what follows, we briefly overview existing contributions in the area. In [7], Barkkuus and Dey show that users were concerned about the ability of services to track them.

Most privacy-enhancing solutions for location-based services rely on a trusted "location anonymizer" service which hides the location of users. These services either provide k-anonymity [13, 17, 26, 31, 32] or spatial/temporal cloaking with an area of interest [6, 10, 15, 20, 33]. A number of solutions rely on inserting fake queries in order to prevent a database server from learning the actual location reports (e.g., [21]). While these solutions provide k-anonymity, they incur significant additional costs on the database server. Other solutions rely on location perturbation/obfuscation; these solutions map the location reports to a set of pre-defined landmarks [19] or blur the user location into a spatial area using linear transformations [6, 15, 20, 22, 34] Such solutions indeed hide the location of users but might affect the accuracy of the location-based service. Moreover, these solutions can only hide the location of a user, but do not aim at hiding the user movement.

To prevent location tracking, Gruteser and Liu [16] propose disclosure control algorithms which hide users' positions in sensitive areas and withhold path information that indicates which areas they have visited. Other schemes rely on Private Information Retrieval (PIR) algorithms in order to enable privacy-preserving queries in spatial databases [14, 24]. PIR schemes allow a querier to retrieve information from a database server without revealing what is actually being retrieved from the server. However, these solutions are computationally intensive and require modifications to the database server in order to process the blurred location queries.

In [25], Pfitzmann *et al.* define unlinkability and privacy in pseudonymous systems. Dwork [12] define differential privacy and quantify information leakage from the query access of individuals. In [30], Shokri *et al.* quantify location privacy using the error of the adversarial estimate from the ground truth. In [11, 27], various entropy-based metrics are introduced to assess the communication privacy in anonymous networks.

6   Conclusion

In this paper, we proposed a novel solution, PrivLoc, which enables privacy-preserving outsourcing of location-based services to the cloud without leaking any meaningful information to the cloud provider. PrivLoc goes one step beyond existing solutions in the area and targets Geofencing services where users send a vector of their movements for the service provider to detect whether a user has crossed a given Geofence. We analyze the security and provisions of PrivLoc and show that PrivLoc does not leak information about the location, movement, trajectory, and/or velocity of the users to the Geofencing database. Our evaluation of PrivLoc shows that the overhead incurred by our solution can be largely tolerated in realistic deployment settings.

Acknowledgements. This work was supported by the EU FP7 SMARTIE project (contract no. 609062).

References

1. Foursquare, http://foursquare.com/
2. Keep Track of Your Kids With Geofences, http://netsecurity.about.com/od/ newsandeditoria2/a/ Keeping-Tabs-On-Your-Kids-With-Geofences.htm
3. Location Based Notifications, http://www.plotprojects.com/
4. Valtus Spatial Data Cloud Services, http://www.valtus.com/products/ vault-spatial-data-cloud-services/
5. Yelp, http://www.yelp.com/
6. Bamba, B., Liu, L., Pesti, P., Wang, T.: Supporting Anonymous Location Queries in Mobile Environments with Privacygrid. In: Proceedings of the 17th International Conference on World Wide Web, WWW 2008, pp. 237–246. ACM, New York (2008)
7. Barkhuus, L., Dey, A.: Location-based services for mobile telephony: a study of users' privacy concerns. In: INTEREACT, pp. 709–712 (2003)
8. Black, J.A., Rogaway, P.: Ciphers with Arbitrary Finite Domains. In: Preneel, B. (ed.) CT-RSA 2002. LNCS, vol. 2271, pp. 114–130. Springer, Heidelberg (2002)
9. Boldyreva, A., Chenette, N., Lee, Y., O'Neill, A.: Order-preserving symmetric encryption. In: Joux, A. (ed.) EUROCRYPT 2009. LNCS, vol. 5479, pp. 224–241. Springer, Heidelberg (2009)
10. Chow, C.-Y., Mokbel, M.F.: Enabling Private Continuous Queries for Revealed User Locations. In: Papadias, D., Zhang, D., Kollios, G. (eds.) SSTD 2007. LNCS, vol. 4605, pp. 258–275. Springer, Heidelberg (2007)
11. Díaz, C., Seys, S., Claessens, J., Preneel, B.: Towards measuring anonymity. In: Dingledine, R., Syverson, P.F. (eds.) PET 2002. LNCS, vol. 2482, pp. 54–68. Springer, Heidelberg (2003)
12. Dwork, C.: Differential privacy: A survey of results. In: Agrawal, M., Du, D.-Z., Duan, Z., Li, A. (eds.) TAMC 2008. LNCS, vol. 4978, pp. 1–19. Springer, Heidelberg (2008)
13. Gedik, B., Liu, L.: Protecting Location Privacy with Personalized k-Anonymity: Architecture and Algorithms. IEEE Transactions on Mobile Computing 7(1), 1–18 (2008)

14. Ghinita, G., Kalnis, P., Khoshgozaran, A., Shahabi, C., Tan, K.-L.: Private Queries in Location Based Services: Anonymizers Are Not Necessary. In: Proceedings of the 2008 ACM SIGMOD International Conference on Management of Data, SIGMOD 2008, pp. 121–132. ACM (2008)

15. Gruteser, M., Grunwald, D.: Anonymous Usage of Location-Based Services Through Spatial and Temporal Cloaking. In: Proceedings of the 1st International Conference on Mobile Systems, Applications and Services, MobiSys 2003, pp. 31–42. ACM, New York (2003)

16. Gruteser, M., Liu, X.: Protecting Privacy in Continuous Location-Tracking Applications. IEEE Security and Privacy 2(2), 28–34 (2004)

17. Guha, S., Jain, M., Padmanabhan, V.N.: Koi: A Location-privacy Platform for Smartphone Apps. In: Proceedings of the 9th USENIX Conference on Networked Systems Design and Implementation, NSDI 2012, p. 14. USENIX Association, Berkeley (2012)

18. Guttman, A.: R-trees: A Dynamic Index Structure for Spatial Searching. In: Proceedings of the 1984 ACM SIGMOD International Conference on Management of Data, SIGMOD 1984, pp. 47–57. ACM, New York (1984)

19. Hong, J.I., Landay, J.A.: An Architecture for Privacy-sensitive Ubiquitous Computing. In: Proceedings of the 2nd International Conference on Mobile Systems, Applications, and Services, MobiSys 2004, pp. 177–189. ACM, New York (2004)

20. Kalnis, P., Ghinita, G., Mouratidis, K., Papadias, D.: Preventing Location-Based Identity Inference in Anonymous Spatial Queries. IEEE Trans. on Knowl. and Data Eng. 19(12), 1719–1733 (2007)

21. Kido, H., Yanagisawa, Y., Satoh, T.: An Anonymous Communication Technique using Dummies for Location-based Services. In: ICPS, pp. 88–97 (2005)

22. Mokbel, M.F., Chow, C.-Y., Aref, W.G.: The New Casper: Query Processing for Location Services Without Compromising Privacy. In: Proceedings of the 32nd International Conference on Very Large Data Bases, pp. 763–774. VLDB Endowment (2006)

23. Myllymaki, J., Kaufman, J.: High-performance spatial indexing for location-based services. In: Proceedings of the 12th International Conference on World Wide Web, WWW 2003, pp. 112–117. ACM, New York (2003)

24. Olumofin, F., Tysowski, P.K., Goldberg, I., Hengartner, U.: Achieving Efficient Query Privacy for Location Based Services. In: Atallah, M.J., Hopper, N.J. (eds.) PETS 2010. LNCS, vol. 6205, pp. 93–110. Springer, Heidelberg (2010)

25. Pfitzmann, A., Hansen, M.: Anonymity, Unlinkability, Undetectability, Unobservability, Pseudonymity, and Identity Management? A Consolidated Proposal for Terminology. Fachterminologie Datenschutz und Datensicherheit, 111–144 (2008)

26. Samarati, P.: Protecting Respondents' Identities in Microdata Release. IEEE Trans. on Knowl. and Data Eng. 13(6), 1010–1027 (2001)

27. Serjantov, A., Danezis, G.: Towards an information theoretic metric for anonymity. In: Dingledine, R., Syverson, P.F. (eds.) PET 2002. LNCS, vol. 2482, pp. 41–53. Springer, Heidelberg (2003)

28. Shekhar, S., Chawla, S., Ravada, S., Fetterer, A., Liu, X., Lu, C.-T.: Spatial databases-accomplishments and research needs. IEEE Trans. on Knowl. and Data Eng. 11(1), 45–55 (1999)

29. Sheth, A., Seshan, S., Wetherall, D.: Geo-fencing: Confining Wi-Fi Coverage to Physical Boundaries. In: Tokuda, H., Beigl, M., Friday, A., Brush, A.J.B., Tobe, Y. (eds.) Pervasive 2009. LNCS, vol. 5538, pp. 274–290. Springer, Heidelberg (2009)

30. Shokri, R., Theodorakopoulos, G., Le Boudec, J., Hubaux, J.P.: Quantifying location privacy. In: Proceedings of the IEEE Symposium on Security and Privacy (2011)

31. Sweeney, L.: Achieving K-anonymity Privacy Protection Using Generalization and Suppression. Int. J. Uncertain. Fuzziness Knowl.-Based Syst. 10(5), 571–588 (2002)

32. Sweeney, L.: K-anonymity: A Model for Protecting Privacy. Int. J. Uncertain. Fuzziness Knowl.-Based Syst. 10(5), 557–570 (2002)
33. Wang, Y., Xu, D., He, X., Zhang, C., Li, F., Xu, B.: L2P2: Location-aware location privacy protection for location-based services. In: INFOCOM, pp. 1996–2004 (2012)
34. Yiu, M.L., Ghinita, G., Jensen, C.S., Kalnis, P.: Enabling Search Services on Outsourced Private Spatial Data. The VLDB Journal 19(3), 363–384 (2010)

A   Tile Rotation in PrivLoc

Require: Coordinates dx, dy and Num
Ensure: Coordinates dx, dy after rotating the tile
```
 1: procedure ROTATETILE(x, y, k)
 2:     rotation ← PRF(k; "rotate", Num; 2)
 3:     if rotation = '00' then
 4:         dx' ← dx
 5:         dy' ← dy
 6:     else if rotation = '01' then
 7:         dx' ← dy
 8:         dy' ← (L − 1) − dx
 9:     else if rotation = '10' then
10:         dx' ← (L − 1) − dx
11:         dy' ← (L − 1) − dy
12:     else if rotation = '11' then
13:         dx' ← (L − 1) − dy
14:         dy' ← dx
15:     end if
16:     return (dx', dy')
17: end procedure
```

B   Querying the Appropriate Database Server in PrivLoc

Require: Coordinates $x0, y0$ and $x1, y1$ describing a movement
Ensure: Server where $x0, y0$ and $x1, y1$ are on the same tile or $\perp$
```
 1: procedure chooseServer(x, y)
 2:     for all D_i, z_i with i = 1, 2, 3 do          ▷ Server D with tile offset z
 3:         nx ← (x0 − z_i mod L × m) div L
 4:         ny ← (y0 − z_i mod L × n) div L
 5:         Num0 ← (nx + ny · n)
 6:         nx ← (x1 − z_i mod L × m) div L
 7:         ny ← (y1 − z_i mod L × n) div L
 8:         Num1 ← (nx + ny · n)
 9:         if Num0 = Num1 then
10:             return i
11:         end if
12:     end for
13:     return ⊥
14: end procedure
```

Hiding Transaction Amounts
and Balances in Bitcoin

Elli Androulaki[1] and Ghassan O. Karame[2]

[1] IBM Research Zurich, CH-8803 Rüschlikon, Switzerland
lli@zurich.ibm.com
[2] NEC Laboratories Europe, 69115 Heidelberg, Germany
ghassan.karame@neclab.eu

Abstract. Bitcoin is gaining increasing adoption and popularity nowadays. In spite of its reliance on pseudonyms, Bitcoin raises a number of privacy concerns due to the fact that all of the transactions that take place in the system are publicly announced.

The literature contains a number of proposals that aim at evaluating and enhancing user privacy in Bitcoin. To the best of our knowledge, ZeroCoin (ZC) is the first proposal which prevents the public tracing of coin expenditure in Bitcoin by leveraging zero-knowledge proofs of knowledge and one-way accumulators. While ZeroCoin hardens the traceability of coins, it does not hide the amount per transaction, nor does it prevent the leakage of the balances of Bitcoin addresses. In this paper, we propose, EZC, an extension of ZeroCoin which *(i)* enables the construction of multi-valued ZCs whose values are only known to the sender and recipient of the transaction and *(ii)* supports the expenditure of ZCs among users in the Bitcoin system, without the need to convert them back to Bitcoins. By doing so, EZC hides transaction values and address balances in Bitcoin, for those users who opt-out from exchanging their coins to BTCs. We performed a preliminary assessment of the performance of EZC; our findings suggest that EZC improves the communication overhead incurred in ZeroCoin.

Keywords: Bitcoin, ZeroCoin, user-privacy, hiding transaction amounts, hiding Bitcoin balances.

1 Introduction

First introduced in 2008, Bitcoin is the most widely adopted digital currency in history. Indicatively, Bitcoin is currently integrated across a number of businesses [1] and has several exchange markets (e.g., MtGox [2], Bitstamp [3]).

Bitcoin is a Proof-of-Work (PoW) based currency which allows users to generate digital coins by performing computations. Users execute payments by digitally signing their transactions and are prevented from double-spending their coins through a distributed time-stamping service [38]. This service operates on top of the Bitcoin Peer-to-Peer (P2P) network which ensures that all transactions and their order of execution are available to all Bitcoin users. In this way,

T. Holz and S. Ioannidis (Eds.): TRUST 2014, LNCS 8564, pp. 161–178, 2014.
© Springer International Publishing Switzerland 2014

Bitcoin transactions form chains of digital signatures, which enables the public tracing of the expenditure of individual coins (BTCs).

The literature contains a number of proposals that analyze the privacy offered in Bitcoin [4, 34, 37]. ZeroCoin [32] is the first proposal to enhance the privacy in Bitcoin and has received increasing attention recently; ZeroCoin leverages zero-knowledge proofs of knowledge (ZKPoK) protocols and cryptographic accumulators in order to hide the expenditure of coins. More specifically, ZeroCoin transforms each single BTC in the system into a ZeroCoin (ZC); this ZC can be proven (using zero-knowledge techniques) to originate from a valid, and unspent BTC, but it is computationally infeasible for any adversary to trace the ZC to the corresponding BTC.

Here, each ZC corresponds to one BTC (or a predefined number of BTCs); transactions whose values are larger than the ZC's would therefore result in several back-to-back ZeroCoin transactions. This results in significant overhead in propagating the corresponding transactions in the network and including them in valid blocks. Moreover, it is easy to see that while ZeroCoin indeed prevents the traceability of coins, it does not conceal the transaction amounts; multiple ZC payments for the same transaction are likely to be linked in time and the total amount per payment can be recovered (since each ZC corresponds to a single BTC). Furthermore, ZeroCoin does not hide the total number of BTCs redeemed by Bitcoin addresses, when the owners of these addresses transform their ZCs back to BTCs. A recent study [4] has shown that tracing coin expenditure is not the only source of information leakage in Bitcoin. More specifically, Androulaki *et al.* have shown that behavior-based clustering algorithms can be used to acquire considerable information about the user profiles in Bitcoin [4]. These algorithms mainly leverage user spending patterns, such as transaction amounts, transaction times, etc., in order to profile users. Clearly, ZeroCoin does not prevent such analysis, since the transaction times, transaction amounts, and address balances can still be derived from the block chain.

In this work, we address this problem and we propose an enhanced variant of ZeroCoin, dubbed EZC, which builds upon ZeroCoin to hide the transaction amount and address balances from the network. Similarly to ZeroCoin, EZC leverages accumulators and ZKPoK protocols to construct multi-valued ZCs. The resulting coins can be either spent as regular Bitcoins, or can be spent directly in the network without transforming them back to the corresponding BTC coins. Our construct ensures that the transaction amount is never revealed to any user in the system (except for the sender and recipient). Since the coins created in EZC do not have to be exchanged back to BTCs, our scheme also prevents the leakage of the balances of address who opt-out from exchanging their coins to BTCs. We analyze the security and privacy provisions of our proposal and we show that it incurs in considerably less communication overhead when compared to ZeroCoin, given the current usage patterns of Bitcoin.

The remainder of this paper is organized as follows. In Section 2, we briefly overview the main operations in Bitcoin and Zerocoin. In Section 3, we introduce our adversarial model, and the buildings blocks that we will use in the paper.

In Section 4, we introduce and analyze our extended version of ZeroCoin, EZC. In Section 5, we overview related work in the area and we conclude the paper in Section 6.

2   Background and Problem Description

In this section, we overview the main operations in Bitcoin and ZeroCoin, respectively. We also discuss the main shortcomings of ZeroCoin.

2.1   Bitcoin

Bitcoin is a P2P payment system [38] that was introduced in 2008. Electronic payments are performed by generating *transactions* that transfer Bitcoin coins (BTCs) among Bitcoin peers. These peers are referenced in each transaction by means of virtual pseudonyms—referred to as *Bitcoin addresses*. Generally, each peer has hundreds of different Bitcoin addresses that are all stored and managed by its (digital) wallet. Each address is mapped through a transformation function to a unique public/private key pair. These keys are used to transfer the ownership of BTCs among addresses.

Peers transfer coins to each other by issuing a transaction. A transaction is formed by digitally signing a hash of the previous transaction where this coin was last spent along with the public key of the future owner and incorporating this signature in the coin [38]. Any peer can verify the correctness of each Bitcoin transaction by checking the chain of signatures.

Transactions are included in Bitcoin *blocks* that are broadcasted in the entire network. To prevent double-spending of the same BTC, Bitcoin relies on a hash-based proof-of-work (PoW) scheme. More specifically, to generate a block, Bitcoin peers must find a nonce value that, when hashed with additional fields (i.e., the Merkle hash of all valid and received transactions, the hash of the previous block, and a timestamp), the result is below a given target value. If such a nonce is found, peers then include it (as well as the additional fields) in a new block thus allowing any entity to publicly verify the PoW. This process is referred to as *block mining*. Upon successfully generating a block, a peer is granted a number of BTCs. This provides an incentive for peers to continuously support Bitcoin. The resulting block is forwarded to all peers in the network, who can then check its correctness by verifying the hash computation. If the block is deemed to be "valid" (that is, the block contains correctly formed transactions that have not been previously spent, and has a correct PoW), then the peers append it to their previously accepted blocks.

Since each block links to the previously generated block, the Bitcoin block *chain* grows upon the generation of a new block in the network. Bitcoin relies on this mechanism to resist double-spending attacks. In fact, for malicious users to double-spend a BTC, they would not only have to redo all the work required to compute the block where that BTC was spent, but also they would need to recompute all the subsequent blocks in the chain. Further details on Bitcoin can be found in [5, 6, 38].

2.2   ZeroCoin

ZeroCoin was introduced by Miers *et al.* in [32] to prevent the public tracing of coin expenditure in the Bitcoin network.

ZeroCoin is a cryptographic extension to Bitcoin and leverages ZKPoP protocols and cryptographic accumulators. More specifically, ZeroCoin transforms each single BTC in the system into a ZeroCoin coin, referred to in the sequel by ZC, by adding it to a cryptographic coin mixer (essentially an accumulator that is publicly available). The resulting ZCs can be proven in zero-knowledge to have originated from a valid and unspent BTC, i.e., that they are part of the unspent subset of coins in the mixer. In this way an entity is prevented from linking a transaction with the BTC (and the corresponding address) that generated the zc used therein. In other words, ZeroCoin ensures that the origin of a zc is hidden among all BTCs that were converted to zcs. In addition, ZeroCoin preserves the security guarantees of Bitcoin (e.g., the doublespending resistance). That is, no party can spend more BTCs or ZCs than the ones he/she possesses. We refer the reader to Section 3.2 for a detailed presentation of the operations and security provisions of ZeroCoin.

2.3   Problem Description

As mentioned earlier, ZeroCoin prevents the linking of a given coin spending (or transaction) to the BTC associated with it; however, ZeroCoin does not entirely prevent the possible linking of different transactions.

Recently, Androulaki *et al.* have shown that behavior-based clustering algorithms leak considerable information about user profiles in Bitcoin [4] . These algorithms mainly leverage user spending patterns, such as transaction amounts, transaction times, etc. in order to profile users and link their addresses.

ZeroCoin does not prevent such analysis, since the transaction times and transaction amounts can still be acquired from the block chain. In fact, since each ZC corresponds to exactly one BTC, any payment for a value that exceeds one BTC will incur the issuing of multiple ZC transactions. At spending time, multiple ZC transactions will be broadcasted in the network back to back in time which *(i)* can be correlated in time by a user connected to the Bitcoin P2P network in order to acquire the actual transaction amounts and *(ii)* can be used to link all the recipient addresses. Indeed, this would give the adversary $\mathcal{A}$ a considerable advantage in linking two different addresses together.

In Section 4, we propose an extension to ZeroCoin which hardens behavior-based analysis by preventing the leakage of transaction amounts. As a by-product, our proposed extension also prevents the leakage of address balances.

3   Model and Building Blocks

In existing centralized payment systems [15, 17, 22], user privacy is often measured with respect to the honest-but-curious centralized entity (e.g., Bank of

Mint) that maintains the accounts of individuals. In these systems, privacy typically means guaranteeing the payer/payee anonymity with respect to the bank. However, existing privacy-preserving solutions in this area indirectly assume that although the bank can have complete view of daily or monthly withdrawals and deposits of individuals, it is not aware of *all* transactions that take place within the system.

In an open payment system, such as Bitcoin, this model is clearly not applicable. In particular, the centralized entity is substituted by the distributed time-stamping server which is governed by the "majority of the available computation power", and has the ability to confirm or reject transactions. This distributed mechanism requires that participants check the validity of *all* transactions that occur in the system. Therefore, the privacy adversary in this case should be adjusted to account for public view of all payments, although it may not be able to link payments to individuals. For instance, in Bitcoin, a user is only aware of the pseudonym (address) of the person he/she sends a payment to/receives a payment from, but does not know other addresses that pertain to that person.

In what follows, we introduce our adversary model and we introduce the various building blocks that we use in the paper.

3.1   Threat Model and Requirements

We observe the public log of Bitcoin, denoted by publLog, within a period of time Δt. During this period, a number of users participate in publLog. We assume that within Δt, a total of n_T transactions have taken place as follows:

$$T = \{\tau_1(S_1 \to R_1), \ldots, \tau_{n_T}(S_{n_T} \to R_{n_T})\},$$

where $\tau_i(S_i \to R_i)$ denotes a transaction with (unique) ID i and S_i and R_i denote the sets of senders' addresses and recipients' addresses, respectively.

We assume that the adversary $\mathcal{A}$ is motivated to acquire information about the addresses/transactions pertaining to all or to a subset of Bitcoin users. As such, $\mathcal{A}$ does not only have access to publLog, but is also *part of the Bitcoin system* and can participate in one or more transactions through Bitcoin. Furthermore, we assume that $\mathcal{A}$ can have access to the (public) addresses of some vendors along with (statistical) information such as the pricing of items or the number of their clients within a specified amount of time. We, however, assume that $\mathcal{A}$ is computationally bounded and as such cannot construct ill-formed Bitcoin blocks, double-spend confirmed transactions, or forge signatures, etc.

Given the aforementioned adversarial model, we identify the following security notions for Bitcoin: *balance, anonymity,* and *activity unlinkability.* Informally, the balance property requires that no p.p.t. adversary who has legitimately acquired a set of BTCs can spend more BTCs to other users than the ones that she possesses [32]. On the other hand, the unlinkability property refers to the fact that an adversary $\mathcal{A}$ should not be able to link two different transactions that pertain to a user of her choice. Finally, anonymity refers to the fact that the spending of a coin should not be linked to a particular coin. We refer the reader to Section 4.3 for the definitions of the aforementioned security properties.

3.2   Building Blocks

In the sequel, we will make use of the following building blocks.

Zero Knowledge Proofs of Knowledge and Signatures of Knowledge: Our protocols use zero-knowledge proofs, i.e., protocols that can be used by a prover to prove knowledge of a committed value v, without leaking any information on the value she proves knowledge of. We instantiate such zero-knowledge proofs using the technique of Schnorr [39], and its extensions [16,19,24,29], and convert them into non-interactive proofs by applying the Fiat-Shamir heuristic [28]. In the latter case, we refer to the resulting non-interactive proofs as signatures of knowledge as defined in [21].

In signatures of knowledge scheme, the knowledge of the (secret) committed value v is used as signing key. The unforgeability property of these schemes implies that no one but the party that has knowledge of v is able to provide a valid signature on any message, i.e., a signature for which the signature verification algorithm accepts.

In the following, we will use the notation of Camenisch and Stadler [11,19,21] when referring to these proofs. Namely, NIZKPoK$\{(\alpha, \beta) : h = g^\alpha \wedge c = g^\beta\}$ denotes a non-interactive zero-knowledge proof of knowledge of the elements α and β that satisfy both $h = g^\alpha$ and $c = g^\beta$. All values not enclosed in ()s are known to the verifier. Similarly, the extension ZKSoK$[m]\{(\alpha, \beta) : h = g^\alpha \wedge c = g^\beta\}$ indicates a signature of knowledge on message m.

Accumulators: Cryptographic accumulators basically constitute one-way membership functions; these functions can be used to answer a query whether a given candidate belongs to a set without revealing any meaningful information about the other set members. We make use of the accumulator by Camenisch and Lysyanskaya [18] that supports the following operations:

- $\{N, u\} \leftarrow$ ACC.Setup(k). On input a security parameter k, sample primes p, q (with polynomial dependence on the security parameter), Setup computes the RSA modulus $N = pq$, and chooses value $u \in QR_N, \neq 1$. Finally, Setup outputs (N, u), which we will refer to as params.
- $\{Acc\} \leftarrow$ ACC.Accumulate(params, PN). On input params and a set of prime numbers $PN = \{p_1, ..., p_n | p_i \in [A, B]\}$, where A and B can be chosen with arbitrary polynomial dependence on k, as long as $2 < A$ and $B < A^2$ (see [20] for more details), ACC.Accumulate computes the accumulator $Acc = p_1 p_2 \cdots p_n \pmod{N}$.
- $\omega \leftarrow$ ACC.GenWitness(params, v, PN). On input params $= (N, u)$, a set of prime numbers PN as described above, and a value $v \in PN$, the witness ω is the accumulation of all the values in Acc besides v, i.e., $\omega =$ ACC.Accumulate(params, Acc|v).

- $\{0,1\} \leftarrow$ ACC.Verify(params, Acc, v, ω). On input params (N, u), an element v, and witness ω, ACC.Verify computes Acc$'$ $\leftarrow \omega^v$(modN), and outputs 1 if and only if Acc$'$ = Acc, v is prime, and v $\in$ [A, B].

Accumulators in [18] satisfy the strong collision-resistance property if the Strong RSA assumption is hard. Informally, this ensures that no p.p.t. adversary can produce a pair (v,ω) such that v $\notin$ PN and yet ACC.Verify is satisfied.

Camenisch and Lysyanskaya [18] describe an efficient zero-knowledge proof of knowledge which proves that a committed value is contained in an accumulator. Similar to [32], we convert this into a non-interactive proof using the Fiat-Shamir transform and refer to the resulting proof using the following notation:

$$\text{NIZKPoK}(\nu, \omega) : \text{Acc.Verify}((N, u), \text{Acc}, \nu, \omega) = 1.$$

ZeroCoin Operations: Our proposal, EZC, builds upon the ZeroCoin algorithms, which we describe below.

ZeroCoin consists of the following operations: Setup, where the system parameters are set, the Mint operation, where a Bitcoin (BTC) is converted to a ZeroCoin (ZC), the Spend operation, where a ZC is spent, i.e., deposited to Bitcoin address, and (automatically) converted to a (part of) BTC, and the Verify operation, through which the peers of Bitcoin can verify the validity of the ZC transaction and include it in a block. More specifically,

- params $\leftarrow$ ZC.Setup(1^k), where k is the security parameter. params include a group $\mathcal{G}$ of RSA modulus and of order o, and its generators $g, h : \langle g \rangle = \langle h \rangle = \mathcal{G}$.
- $\{$pub$_{zc}$, sec$_{zc}\} \leftarrow$ ZC.Mint(params, btc), tthrough which a BTC, btc, is converted to a ZeroCoin, zc of fixed value. The latter is associated to a secret token sec$_{zc}$ and a public token pub$_{zc}$. ZC.Mint is reflected to a Bitcoin transaction (e.g., Mint transaction), where the converted btc is the transaction input and pub$_{zc}$ that uniquely defines zc is the transaction output. Mint transactions are broadcasted in the entire network. Upon receiving the Mint transaction, the miners verify that the input btc is valid, i.e., that it is owned by the address who has signed the transaction and that it has not been spent before by that address. If btc is valid, then the Mint transaction (and thus pub$_{zc}$) is included in the next block using the same mining process as in Bitcoin. The public ZC-coin tokens that are included in blocks of the longest blockchain are automatically considered to be part of a public accumulator Acc.[1]. The public token related to zc, pub$_{zc}$ is actually a Pedersen commitment to a serial number s of the form zc = $g^s \cdot h^r$, where $s, r \leftarrow_R Z_o$. The secret information associated with zc is set to sec$_{zc}$ = (s, r) and is partially revealed in ZC.Spend operation.

---

[1] Note that the accumulator value is computed by the peers locally. Given the public parameters of the accumulator, and the confirmed ZCs, each peer can locally compute the accumulator value at any point in time.

- $\{\pi, s\} \leftarrow$ ZC.Spend(params, sec$_{zc}$, pub$_{zc}$, Acc), which is performed by the peer who wishes to spend a ZC coin, zc, with public information pub$_{zc}$. To do so, the peer reveals s and computes a ZKPoK π that s corresponds to a ZC-coin which has been confirmed into a block (i.e., is part of the accumulator). As such, ZeroCoin Spend transactions can be integrated in existing Bitcoin transactions as follows: (s, π) constitute the transaction input, while the Bitcoin address(es) that will receive the spent ZC coin, will constitute the transaction output(s). This special transaction is signed using the zero-knowledge π, and is released to the network to be confirmed into a block.
- $\{\pi, s\} \leftarrow$ ZC.Verify(params, s, π, Acc), which can be executed by every peer in the Bitcoin network to verify that the ZC-coin associated to serial number s and signature of knowledge derived from the ZKPoK π has not been spent before, i.e., that the signature of knowledge verification accepts and that the serial number s has not been used in another confirmed spending. Verified pairs of (π, s) are included by the Bitcoin miners in the next generated block, to establish the spending of the corresponding ZC-coin to all Bitcoin peers.

4   EZC: An Extension of ZeroCoin

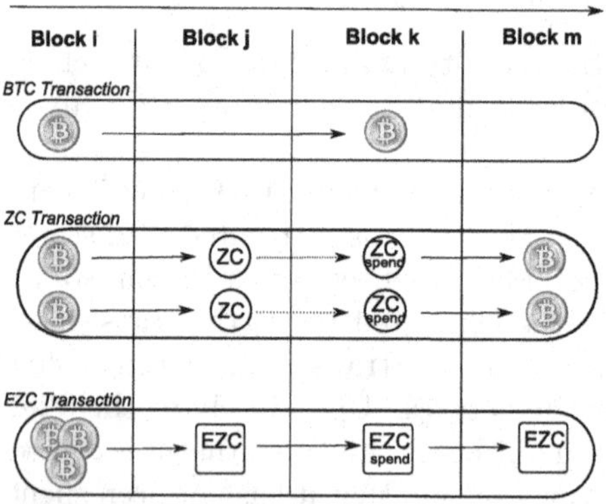

In what follows, we propose, EZC, an extended variant of ZeroCoin that *(i)* is not restricted to values equivalent to 1 BTC and can thus cope with any transaction amount v, and *(ii)* allows the direct spending of the v-valued ZCs into ZCs (i.e., without transforming them to BTCs first) while completely concealing the transaction amounts. Figure 1 compares the main operations of EZC to ZC.

Fig. 1. Comparison between EZC and ZC. Each ZC corresponds to a single BTC and can only be spent in the form of BTCs. EZC, on the other hand, enables the construction of a (multi-valued) eZC, and can be spent in eZCs without the need to transform them back to BTCs.

4.1   Overview

We now start by describing the main intuition behind EZC. In the following, we refer to an EZC coin by eZC.

EZC supports the following operations: *(i)* EZC.Mint, where arbitrary valued BTCs are converted to an EZC coin (eZC)[2], *(ii)* EZC.SpendEZCToBTC, where eZCs are spent in the form of BTCs, *(iii)* EZC.SpendEZCToEZC, where the payment recipient receives her

---

[2] This operation may also be thought of as a Bitcoin Spend operation where BTCs are spent in the form of eZC(s).

payment in the form of eZC(s), and *(iv)* EZC.SpendBTCToBTC where the payer provides BTC payments and the recipient receives its payment in the form of BTCs. Similarly to Bitcoin, the validity of each transaction is checked by the network peers, who subsequently work towards confirming valid transactions into blocks as in Bitcoin.

As in ZeroCoin, EZC generates parameters for a dynamic public accumulator Acc_{EZC} which absorbs all properly minted and confirmed eZCs. In particular, an eZC is added in this accumulator whenever a Mint transaction is validated, i.e., included in a block, while eZCs in Acc_{EZC} can be spent only once.

In EZC, the Mint transaction is constructed in a similar way to the corresponding transaction in ZeroCoin, and thus consists of an input (in BTCs) and an output which includes information related to the created eZCs. However, the coins generated through EZC.Mint can accommodate any payment value *val*. More specifically, the output of a Mint transaction in EZC, consists of a commitment c to *val* and to a serial number *ser*, and a zero-knowledge proof of c's correctness. As we show later, *val* is revealed by the peer who runs EZC.Mint to all the peers in the network but *ser* is kept private until the minted eZC is spent. The Mint transaction in EZC is signed using the private keys corresponding to the input Bitcoin address(es). The correctness of EZC.Mint transactions is checked by the rest of the peers in the network and valid transactions are included in the longest block chain, in which case the EZC.Mint transactions are deemed confirmed. After the confirmation of an EZC.Mint transaction, the commitment c is considered to be a valid member of Acc_{EZC}.

To spend an eZC in the form of BTCs of value *val*, the eZC-owner—who knows *ser* and the opening of c—constructs a proof π that *ser* corresponds to a commitment to a value *val* that is a member of Acc_{EZC}. She then constructs an EZC.SpendEZCtoBTC transaction by providing a signature of knowledge of π on a conventional Bitcoin transaction output where *val* is assigned to one or more Bitcoin addresses. Note that for peers of the network to be able to verify the correctness of such a transaction, the serial *ser* is revealed; nevertheless, no entity is able to link it to a particular EZC.Mint transaction, and, thus, to the btc-s that created it.

On the other hand, to spend an eZC in the form of a fresh eZC of the same or smaller value val', the payer reveals *ser*, and engages in a similar set of operations as in EZC.SpendEZCtoBTC to construct π. However, to accommodate the creation of the recipient's eZC, the two parties construct a commitment c' to a freshly generated serial ser' and to the payment amount val'. Here, π contains a proof that the payment amount does not exceed the value of the payer's coin. Finally, π is used to produce a signature of knowledge on the output commitment c' into an EZC.SpendEZCtoEZC transaction, which is released to the network with *ser*. As soon as the latter is confirmed, c' is considered by the peers to be a member of Acc_{EZC}. Here, as opposed to EZC.SpendEZCtoBTC, where *val* is revealed to the peers, *val* is kept private between the payer and the payment recipient, while ser' and the opening of c' is only known to the payment recipient.

4.2   Protocol Specification

In what follows, we detail the operations in EZC. In the following, we denote the public information (token) associated with an coin of EZC, eZC, by pub_{eZC}, and the corresponding private information (token) by sec_{eZC}.

Setup. The setup consists of operation EZC.Setup, which runs with input a security parameter λ and produces the system parameters params:

$$\{\text{params}\} \leftarrow \text{EZC.Setup}(1^\lambda)$$

More specifically, EZC.Setup runs ACC.Setup(λ) to obtain (N, u), and generates primes p, q, such that $p = 2^f \cdot q + 1, f \geq 1$. It then picks g, h, and w such that $\mathcal{G} = \langle g \rangle = \langle h \rangle = \langle w \rangle \subset Z_q^*$. Finally, it sets params $= \{N, u, p, q, g, h, w\}$.

Coin Conversion. Coin conversion is achieved using the EZC.Mint operation, which is executed by the owner u of a set of BTCs $\mathcal{I}_{BTC}$, that are converted into an eZC with public information pub_{eZC}, and private information sec_{eZC}:

$$\{\pi, \text{pub}_{eZC}, u(\text{sec}_{eZC})\} \leftarrow \text{EZC.Mint}(\mathcal{I}_{BTC}, \text{params}).$$

Here, u picks $ser, r \leftarrow_R \mathcal{G}$, where ser is the serial number of the generated eZC, and computes $\text{pub}_{eZC} = g^{ser} \cdot h^r \cdot w^{val}$, such that pub_{eZC} is prime, and a ZKPoK π asserting that pub_{eZC} is correctly formed:

$$\text{NIZKPoK}(\alpha, \beta) : \text{pub}_{eZC} = g^\alpha \cdot h^{val} \cdot w^\beta.$$

Note that, the EZC.Mint transaction is constructed similarly to a standard Bitcoin transaction, where the BTCs are used as input, and $\langle \text{pub}_{eZC}, \pi \rangle$ is used as output. Subsequently, peers verify that pub_{eZC} is correctly formed, by running the ZKPoK verification protocol for π, and by confirming that the input BTCs were not spent in the past, as is currently done in Bitcoin. If the transaction is deemed valid by the majority of the computation power of the network, pub_{eZC} is included in the block chain, and pub_{eZC} is considered as a valid member of the public accumulator Acc_{EZC}. User u's private output is $\text{sec}_{eZC} = \langle ser, r \rangle$, while $\{\text{sec}_{eZC}, val\}$ is stored in u's local memory.

Spending EZC(s) to BTCs: This is performed using the EZC.SpendEZCToBTC operation, which takes as input $(\text{sec}_{eZC_S}, \text{pub}_{eZC_S})$, and spends them in BTCs of value val to a set of Bitcoin addresses, $\mathcal{O}_{BTC}$.

$$\mathcal{O}_{BTC} \leftarrow \text{EZC.SpendToBTC}[\text{params}, ser_S, u_S(\text{sec}_{eZC_S}, \text{pub}_{eZC_S})].$$

Here, the sender u_S first computes the public accumulator value Acc_{EZC} locally, by running ACC.Accumulate($N, u, \{\text{pub}_{eZC}\}_{v \in \text{pubLog}}$) for the set of EZC commitments that have appeared in the output of a transaction in the longest block chain. The sender retrieves sec_{eZC_S} from her local memory, and runs ACC.GenWitness(params, $\{\text{pub}_{eZC}\}_{v \in \text{pubLog}}, \text{pub}_{eZC_S}$), to compute the witness

w_S for $\text{pub}_{\text{eZC}_S}$'s membership in Acc_{EZC}. Furthermore, u_S computes a ZKPoK π to show that ser_S corresponds to an eZC whose public information (here, $\text{pub}_{\text{eZC}_S}$) is part of Acc_{EZC}, and that it corresponds to a value val. Finally, it converts π to a signature of knowledge on $\mathcal{O}_{\text{BTC}}$:

$$\text{ZKSoK}[\mathcal{O}_{\text{BTC}}](\alpha, \beta, \gamma) : \alpha = g^{ser_S} h^{val} w^\beta \wedge \text{Acc.Verify}(N, u, \text{Acc}_{\text{EZC}}, \alpha, \gamma) = 1\}.$$

Finally, u_S announces the corresponding signature within a transaction to the EZC network, which, after confirming the transaction's correctness, it includes the latter into a block. [3]

Spending EZC(s) to EZC(s). This is achieved through the EZC.SpendEZCToEZC operation, which is an interactive process between a payment sender u_S and a payment recipient u_R. EZC.SpendEZCToEZC takes as input the information associated to an eZC of u_S, e.g., $\text{sec}_{\text{eZC}_S}$, and $\text{pub}_{\text{eZC}_S}$, and spends it in the form of a new eZC that belongs to u_R, eZC_R; if change should be incorporated in the payment, EZC.SpendEZCToEZC outputs additionally another eZC that would belong to u_S; we denote this eZC by eZC'_S:

$$\{\langle \text{pub}'_{\text{eZC}_S}, \text{pub}_{\text{eZC}_R}, u_S(\text{sec}'_{\text{eZC}_S}), u_R(\text{sec}_{\text{eZC}_R}) \rangle / \bot\} \leftarrow \text{EZC.SpendEZCToEZC}$$
$$(\text{params}, ser_S, \text{Acc}_{\text{EZC}}, u_S(val_R, val_S, r_S, ser'_S, r'_S), u_R(val_R, ser_R, r_R)).$$

Here, u_R's private input $\text{sec}_{\text{eZC}_R}$ consists of a serial number ser_R for her new coin, and a random number $r_S \in Z_{(p-1)/2}$ which will be used in her new coin's commitment. Assuming that $\langle ser_S, r_S, val_S \rangle$ is the entry for eZC_S in u_S's local memory, u_S announces the serial number ser_S of eZC_S, and privately contributes r_S and val_S to compute the eZC_S validity proof as in EZC.SpendEZCtoBTC. Finally, u_S's private input includes the values $\langle ser'_S, r'_S \rangle$ used for $\text{eZC}_{S'}$'s construction. We emphasize that $\text{sec}_{\text{eZC}_R}$ should be kept private even towards u_S so as the latter is not able to trace further spendings of eZC_R.

In more detail, the payment sender u_S and recipient u_R engage in the following sequence of actions:

1. u_S proves eZC_S's validity: u_S runs $\text{ACC.Accumulate}(N, u, \{\text{pub}_{\text{eZC}}\}_{\forall \text{pubLog}})$ for the set of eZC-commitments that appear in the EZC-blockchain, to compute the current public accumulator value Acc_{EZC}. Subsequently, u_S runs $\text{ACC.GenWitness}(\text{params}, \text{pub}_{\text{eZC}_S}, \text{sec}_{\text{eZC}_S}, \text{Acc}_{\text{EZC}})$, to extract a witness w_S that eZC_S has been confirmed into a block. Then, u_S computes π as described in the previous section, i.e.:

$$\text{NIZKPoK}(\alpha, \beta, \gamma, \delta) : \alpha = g^{ser_S} \cdot h^\beta \cdot w^\gamma \wedge \text{ACC.Verify}(N, u, \text{Acc}_{\text{EZC}}, \alpha, \delta) = 1.$$

2. u_S mints eZC'_S: u_S picks $ser'_S \leftarrow_R Z_{\text{p}-1}$, and $r'_S \leftarrow_R Z_{\text{p}-1}$, and computes the public information associated to eZC'_S, as $\text{pub}'_{\text{eZC}_S} = g^{ser'_S} h^{val'_S} w^{r'_S}$, such

---

[3] Note that, if fees are to be supported, the fee amount should be explicitly stated within the message in the signature (transaction).

that pub'_{eZC_S} is prime and $\textit{val}'_S = \textit{val}_S - \textit{val}_R$ is the change value. Note that pub'_{eZC_S} would be part of the transaction output. Finally, u_S updates π to include a proof that pub'_{eZC_S} is properly formed: $\text{NIZKPoK}(\alpha, \beta, \gamma, \delta, \epsilon, \zeta, \eta)$:

$$\alpha = g^{ser_S} \cdot h^\beta \cdot w^\gamma \wedge \text{ACC.Verify}(N, u, \text{Acc}_{EZC}, \alpha, \delta) = 1 \wedge$$

$$\text{pub}'_{eZC_S} = g^\epsilon \cdot h^\zeta \cdot w^\eta \wedge \zeta \in Z_{(p-1)/2}.$$

3. u_S enables u_R to privately mint for the payment coin eZC_R. Thus, u_S picks $r_{SR} \leftarrow_R Z_{p-1}$, computes the auxiliary token $\ell_{SR} = h^{\textit{val}_R} w^{r_{SR}}$, and updates ZKPoK π so as to include a proof of correctness of ℓ_{SR}:

$$\text{NIZKPoK}(\alpha, \beta, \gamma, \delta, \epsilon, \zeta, \eta, \theta) : \alpha = g^{ser_S} \cdot h^\beta \cdot w^\gamma \wedge \text{ACC.Verify}(N, u, \text{Acc}_{EZC},$$

$$\alpha, \delta) = 1 \wedge \text{pub}'_{eZC_S} = g^\epsilon \cdot h^\zeta \cdot w^\eta \wedge \zeta \in Z_{(p-1)/2} \wedge \ell_{SR} \cdot \text{pub}'_{eZC_S} = g^\epsilon \cdot h^\beta \cdot w^\theta.$$

Finally, u_S sends $\langle \pi, \ell_{SR}, r_{SR} \rangle$ to u_R. ℓ_{SR} is used by u_R, for the latter to prove that her privately minted eZC, is of value $\textit{val}_R$ without revealing $\textit{val}_R$ (to a third party), or the secret token of its minted eZC to u_S.

4. u_R mints eZC_R: u_R picks $ser_R \leftarrow_R Z_{p-1}$, and $r_R \leftarrow_R Z_{p-1}$ and computes $\text{pub}_{eZC_R} = g^{ser_R} \cdot h^{\textit{val}_R} \cdot w^{r_R}$ as described previously; she extends π to include proof of correctness of pub_{eZC_R} and collaborates with u_S to converts π into a ZKSoK to sign ser_S and pub_{eZC_R} and $\text{pub}_{eZC'_S}$ in the longest blockchain resulting into another transaction:

$$\text{ZKSoK}[ser_S, \text{pub}'_{eZC_S}, \text{pub}_{eZC_R}](\alpha, \beta, \gamma, \delta, \epsilon, \zeta, \eta, \theta, \iota, \kappa, \mu, \rho) : \alpha = g^{ser_S} \cdot h^\beta \cdot w^\gamma \wedge$$

$$\text{ACC.Verify}(N, u, \text{Acc}_{EZC}, \alpha, \delta) = 1 \wedge \text{pub}'_{eZC_S} = g^\epsilon \cdot h^\zeta \cdot w^\eta \wedge \ell_{SR} \cdot \text{pub}'_{eZC_S}$$

$$= g^\epsilon \cdot h^\theta \cdot w^\theta \wedge \ell_{SR} = h^\iota \cdot w^\kappa \wedge \text{pub}_{eZC_R} = g^\mu \cdot h^\iota \cdot w^\rho \wedge \zeta \in Z_{(p-1)/2} \wedge \iota \in Z_{(p-1)/2}.$$

The resulting transaction is announced to the network of EZC peers, who upon correct verification of its correctness, work towards its inclusion into a block. After such a transaction is included into a block, pub_{eZC_R} and $\text{pub}_{eZC'_S}$ are considered members of Acc_{EZC}.

4.3 Security Analysis

In this section, we instantiate the security properties described in Section 3.1 in the context of EZC, and we show how these properties are achieved in our scheme.

Anonymity: We adopt the definition of anonymity as presented in Zero-Coin, where the spending of an eZC should not be linked to a particular Mint operation— and the BTCs—which were involved in the eZCs' creation operation with non-negligible advantage.

More formally, the EZC anonymity game takes place between an adversary $\mathcal{A}$ and the challenger $\mathcal{C}$ as follows. Initially, the challenger runs EZC.Setup to generate the system parameters. We assume that $\mathcal{C}$ has correctly acquired two sets of BTCs, $\mathcal{I}_{\mathrm{BTC}}^{(0)}$, and $\mathcal{I}_{\mathrm{BTC}}^{(1)}$, which he converts through EZC.Mint into eZC_0 $(\mathrm{pub}_{\mathrm{eZC}_0}, \mathrm{sec}_{\mathrm{eZC}_0})$, and eZC_1 $(\mathrm{pub}_{\mathrm{eZC}_1}, \mathrm{sec}_{\mathrm{eZC}_1})$. Challenger $\mathcal{C}$ sends $(\mathrm{pub}_{\mathrm{eZC}_0},$ $\mathrm{pub}_{\mathrm{eZC}_1})$ to $\mathcal{A}$. Then, he picks $\theta \leftarrow_R \{0, 1\}$, and computes EZC.SpendEZCToEZC or EZC.SpendEZCToBTC for eZC_θ, outputting $\langle ser_\theta, \pi_\theta \rangle$, which is sent to $\mathcal{A}$. Finally, $\mathcal{A}$ outputs her guess θ' on θ, and wins the game if $\theta' = \theta$.

We say that EZC satisfies coin-anonymity property if and only if $\mathcal{A}$ has a negligible advantage over winning in the anonymity game described above.

Claim. If the underlying commitment scheme is perfectly-hiding, and the signature of knowledge π is at least computationally zero-knowledge, then EZC provides coin-anonymity.

Proof Sketch. If there is an adversary $\mathcal{A}$ who could win the coin-anonymity game with non-negligible advantage over choosing her answer at random, then such an adversary could be used by another adversary $\mathcal{S}$ to break the zero-knowledge property of the signature scheme on a commitment of a hidden value.

Transaction Unlinkability: According to this property, it should be computationally infeasible for a third party to decide whether two eZC-transactions EZC.SpendEZCToEZC (or EZC.SpendEZCToBTC) belong to the same user or not.

More formally, we construct the eZC-transaction unlinkability game in EZC, adapted from [4], as follows. $\mathcal{A}$ chooses an transaction of type EZC.SpendEZCtoEZC from pubLog denoted by τ_0. Let u_S, u_R denote the sender and recipient of τ_0. $\mathcal{C}$ picks $\theta \leftarrow_R \{0, 1\}$; if $\theta = 0$, $\mathcal{C}$ randomly chooses $\tau_1 \neq \tau_0$ from $\mathrm{T}_{u_S} \cup \mathrm{T}_{u_R}$, where T_u denotes the set of transactions in which u has participated in; otherwise $\mathcal{C}$ picks τ_1 randomly from $\{\mathsf{pubLog} - \{\mathrm{T}_S \cup \mathrm{T}_{u_R}\}\}$ to ensure that there are no transactions pertaining to u_S or u_R. $\mathcal{C}$ then sends τ_0, τ_1 to $\mathcal{A}$. The adversary responds with her guess on θ, θ', and wins if and only if $\theta = \theta'$.

Claim. If the underlying commitment scheme is perfectly-hiding, and the signature of knowledge π is at least computationally zero-knowledge, then EZC provides eZC-transaction unlinkability.

Proof Sketch. We point out that at an eZC creation, the eZC-owner contributes random numbers. Therefore, eZCs pertaining to the same user are statistically independent. It remains to show that it is computationally infeasible for a third party that does not know the secret token of an eZC to link the spending of the eZC (EZC.SpendEZCToEZC or EZC.SpendEZCToBTC) to another EZC.SpendEZCToEZC transaction. As mentioned earlier, this follows from the security of the underlying signature of knowledge. In particular, the zero-knowledge and proof-of-knowledge properties of the underlying signature of knowledge guarantee that as long as the signature is valid, *(i)* the signer of the transaction *knows* the secret token of the spent eZC and to which public token it corresponds to, and *(ii)* that he/she leaks no information related to the parts of the tokens that remain concealed (i.e., the randomness r, the value incorporated in the coin val, and $\mathrm{pub}_{\mathrm{eZC}}$). Given that in the EZC.SpendEZCtoEZC transaction, the signature of knowledge is constructed collaboratively by the sender and recipient of the payment, the former cannot trace the spending of the payment eZC (since the sender does not obtain the secret token of the recipient eZC). We emphasize that our analysis does not account for any possible linking that can be performed by analyzing the choice of Bitcoin addresses or of the payment amount in an EZC.SpendEZCToBTC (since this transaction reveals the addresses and the amounts). On the contrary, owing to the zero-knowledge property of the signature of knowledge used within the EZC.SpendEZCtoEZC operation, it is computationally infeasible for a third party to infer the payment amount in a given EZC.SpendEZCtoEZC transaction.

Balance: The balance property requires that no user or coalition of users can spend eZCs with higher value than their balance, i.e., the value of eZCs which they possess. More formally, we consider the following game for balance. The challenger runs EZC.Setup and sets the system parameters. The adversary participates in a set of n EZC.Mint operations, by providing Bitcoin inputs $\{\mathcal{I}_{BTC}^{(i)}\}_{i=1}^{i=n}$ that were executed correctly and receive $\{eZC_i\}_{i=1}^{i=n}$ ($\{pub_{eZC_i}, sec_{eZC_i}\}_{i=1}^{i=n}$) in response. Let ser_i, val_i denote the serial number and value of eZC_i. The adversary $\mathcal{A}$ engages in a series of eZC-spendings resulting in a set of m eZCs $\{eZC_i'\}_{i=1}^{i=m}$ corresponding to $\{pub_{eZC_i}', sec_{eZC_i}'\}_{i=1}^{i=n}$ with values $\{val_i'\}_{i=1}^{i=m}$. The adversary wins the game if and only if $\sum_{i=1}^{n} val_i < \sum_{i=1}^{i=m} val_i'$. Clearly, we require that no probabilistic polynomial time algorithm $\mathcal{A}$ wins the balance game with non-negligible probability.

Claim. If the underlying zero-knowledge signature of knowledge scheme is sound, and the construction of the dynamic accumulator used is secure, EZC satisfies balance of payments.

Proof Sketch. Balance in EZC is satisfied by the security properties of the dynamic accumulator and the used ZKPoK schemes. More specifically, dynamic accumulators guarantee that no user can produce a valid witness of a coin which has not been previously added to the accumulator. This prevents the user from spending a coin which has never been confirmed. Thus, to double-spend a coin, the adversary should present the same serial number twice which would immediately reveal her intentions.

On the other hand, the security of ZKPoK protocols guarantee that if the protocol succeeds then the user indeed has knowledge of the secret values, and that the user does not overspend the value of a given eZC. More specifically, the ZKPoK used within our EZC guarantees, that in each transaction the amount of the input equals the output amount (either in BTCs or in EZCs). This is guaranteed by requiring that the amount included in the payment eZC and the eZCused for change is of a value below $\frac{(p-1)}{2}$. Such a requirement avoids attacks where the sender and recipient collude and generate arbitrary payment amounts whose sum wraps around the prime modulus p. Note that, for reasonable choices of p, $\frac{(p-1)}{2}$ corresponds to large payment values, which never typically occur in Bitcoin.

4.4   Performance Comparison to ZeroCoin

By enabling the construction of multi-valued ZCs, EZC clearly results in a smaller number of broadcasted transactions in the network when compared to ZeroCoin. That is, for a user to spend a transaction worth v BTCs in ZeroCoin, the user client actually broadcasts v separate Spend transactions. EZC only incurs, on the other hand, a single EZC.SpendZCtoZC transaction in order to spend the eZC whose value is worth v BTCs.

To better assess the performance gains brought by EZC when compared to ZeroCoin, we computed the average transaction amounts incurred in Bitcoin. For that purpose, we modified the block chain parser in [7] and we parsed the first 239,200 Bitcoin blocks (June 2013). Our results show that transactions in Bitcoin currently spend 9.47 BTCs on average. This means that EZC results in 9.47 times less transactions broadcast in the network, on average, when compared to ZeroCoin.

On the other hand, EZC incurs similar computational costs when compared to ZeroCoin in both the Mint and the Setup operations. Spending coins in EZC is more computationally expensive than ZeroCoin, since EZC requires an additional zero-knowledge proof that the input coins amount to the output coins. We argue, however, that this overhead is much lower than that incurred by performing ZC spendings given the current usage patterns in Bitcoin. Indeed, since current Bitcoin transactions transfer on average 9.47 BTCs, an average spending in ZC will result in the need to construct and verify almost 10 zero-knowledge proofs of knowledge.

5   Related Work

Bitcoin has received considerable attention in the literature. In [10], Elias investigates the legal aspects of privacy in Bitcoin. In [12], Babaioff et al. address the lack of incentives for Bitcoin users to include recently announced transactions in a block, while in [9], Syed et al. propose a user-friendly technique for managing Bitcoin wallets. In [8], Karame et al. thoroughly investigate double-spending attacks in Bitcoin and show that double-spending fast payments in Bitcoin can be performed in spite of the measures recommended by Bitcoin developers. In [13], Welten et al. compile countermeasures to detect double spending attacks. In [25], Wattenhofer et al. connect to a subset of the Bitcoin network and measure the propagation delay of blocks.

Clark et al. [23] propose the use of the Bitcoin PoW to construct verifiable commitment schemes. Reid and Harrigan [36] analyze the flow Bitcoin transactions in a small part of Bitcoin log, and show that external information, i.e., publicly announced addresses, can be used to link identities and organizations to some transactions.

In [4], Androulaki et al. evaluate user privacy in Bitcoin and show that Bitcoin leaks considerable information about the profiles of user. In an attempt to deal with the privacy leaks in ZeroCoin, Garman et al. briefly describe a ZKPoK based technique which enables the construction of transactions between anonymous coins [30]. Nevertheless, the scheme of [30] is only described at high level, and their anonymous coins' transactions only refer to transactions that self-spend coins (i.e., that originate from a user to herself); in this case, the output coins are allowed to be traced by the sender. In [37], Ron and Shamir this paper analyze the behavior of users (i.e., how they acquire and how they spend their BTCs) and investigate how users move BTCs between their various accounts in order to better protect their privacy. In [34], Ober et al. studied the time-evolution properties of Bitcoin by analyzing its transaction graph. Finally, in [33], Moore and Christin study the economic risks that investors face due to Bitcoin exchanges.

ECash [15,17,22] and anonymous credit cards were the first attempts to define privacy-preserving transactions. Privacy in ECash consists of user anonymity and transaction unlinkability; by relying on a set of cryptographic primitives ECash ensures that payments pertaining to the same user cannot be linked to each other or to the payer, provided that the latter does not misbehave. In [35], Pfitzmann et al. define unlinkability and privacy in pseudonymous systems. Dwork [27] defined differential privacy and quantified the information leakage from the query access of individuals. In [41], Shokri et al. quantify location privacy by assessing the error of the adversarial estimate from the ground truth. In [26,40] the authors further introduce entropy-based metrics to assess the communication privacy in anonymous networks.

In [14], Belenkiy et al., introduce an ECash-based P2P payment scheme that provides accountability at the cost of privacy. In [31], Karame et al. propose a novel micropayment model based on verifiable microcomputations.

6   Conclusion

In this paper, we presented EZC which builds atop Bitcoin in order to hide the transaction amounts and address balances in the system. More specifically, EZC enables the construction of a multi-valued ZeroCoin, which can be either spent as a regular Bitcoin, or can be spent directly in another ZC to ZC transaction. ESZ strengthens user privacy in the system, and minimizes information leakage that might arise from behavior based analysis.

We performed a preliminary assessment of the performance of EZC; our findings suggest that EZC considerably improves the communication overhead incurred in ZeroCoin. In the near future, we plan to implement EZC and integrate it within the Bitcoin system in order to better evaluate its performance.

Acknowledgements. The author would like to thank Srdjan Capkun for the valuable discussions. The author would also like to thank Kristiyan Haralambiev for the various discussions on ZKPoP, and Arthur Gervais for his help in parsing the Bitcoin block chain.

References

1. Trade - Bitcoin, `https://en.bitcoin.it/wiki/Trade`
2. Mt. Gox – WIkepedia, `http://en.wikipedia.org/wiki/Mt._Gox`
3. Bitcoin Charts, `http://bitcoincharts.com/`
4. Evaluating User Privacy in Bitcoin, Financial Cryptography and Data Security Conference (FC) (2013), `http://eprint.iacr.org/2012/596.pdf`
5. Protocol Rules – Bitcoin, `https://en.bitcoin.it/wiki/Protocol_rules`
6. Protocol Specifications – Bitcoin, `https://en.bitcoin.it/wiki/Protocol_specification`
7. znort987 Bitcoin Blockchain parser, `https://github.com/znort987/blockparser`
8. Two Bitcoins at the Price of One? Double-Spending Attacks on Fast Payments in Bitcoin, `http://eprint.iacr.org/2012/248.pdf`
9. Bitcoin Gateway, A Peer-to-peer Bitcoin Vault and Payment Network (2011), `http://arimaa.com/bitcoin/`
10. Bitcoin: Tempering the Digital Ring of Gyges or Implausible Pecuniary Privacy (2011), `http://ssrn.com/abstract=1937769`
11. Au, M.H., Susilo, W., Mu, Y.: Proof-of-Knowledge of Representation of Committed Value and Its Applications. In: Steinfeld, R., Hawkes, P. (eds.) ACISP 2010. LNCS, vol. 6168, pp. 352–369. Springer, Heidelberg (2010)
12. Babaioff, M., Dobzinski, S., Oren, S., Zohar, A.: On Bitcoin and Red Balloons. In: CoRR (2011)
13. Bamert, T., Decker, C., Elsen, L., Wattenhofer, R., Welten, S.: Have a Snack, Pay with Bitcoins. In: 13th IEEE International Conference on Peer-to-Peer Computing (2013)
14. Belenkiy, M., Chase, M., Erway, C., Jannotti, J., Küpçü, A., Lysyanskaya, A., Rachlin, E.: Making P2P Accountable without Losing Privacy. In: Proceedings of WPES (2007)
15. Brands, S.: Electronic Cash on the Internet. In: Proceedings of the Symposium on the Network and Distributed System Security (1995)
16. Brands, S.: Rapid Demonstration of Linear Relations Connected by Boolean Operators. In: Fumy, W. (ed.) EUROCRYPT 1997. LNCS, vol. 1233, pp. 318–333. Springer, Heidelberg (1997)
17. Camenisch, J.L., Hohenberger, S., Lysyanskaya, A.: Compact E-Cash. In: Cramer, R. (ed.) EUROCRYPT 2005. LNCS, vol. 3494, pp. 302–321. Springer, Heidelberg (2005)
18. Camenisch, J., Lysyanskaya, A.: Dynamic accumulators and application to efficient revocation of anonymous credentials, pp. 61–76 (2002)
19. Camenisch, J.: Group Signature Schemes and Payment Systems Based on the Discrete Logarithm Problem. PhD thesis, ETH Zurich. ETH Series in Information Security and Cryptography (1998)
20. Camenisch, J., Lyasyanskaya, A.: Dynamic accumulators and application to efficient revocation of anonymous credentials (2002)
21. Chase, M., Lysyanskaya, A.: On signatures of knowledge. In: Dwork, C. (ed.) CRYPTO 2006. LNCS, vol. 4117, pp. 78–96. Springer, Heidelberg (2006)
22. Chaum, D., Roijakkers, S.: Unconditionally secure digital signatures. In: Menezes, A., Vanstone, S.A. (eds.) CRYPTO 1990. LNCS, vol. 537, pp. 206–214. Springer, Heidelberg (1991)
23. Clark, J., Essex, A.: (Short Paper) CommitCoin: Carbon Dating Commitments with Bitcoin. In: Proceedings of Financial Cryptography and Data Security (2012)

24. Cramer, R., Damgård, I.B., Schoenmakers, B.: Proof of partial knowledge and simplified design of witness hiding protocols. In: Desmedt, Y.G. (ed.) CRYPTO 1994. LNCS, vol. 839, pp. 174–187. Springer, Heidelberg (1994)
25. Decker, C., Wattenhofer, R.: Information Propagation in the Bitcoin Network. In: 13th IEEE International Conference on Peer-to-Peer Computing (2013)
26. Díaz, C., Seys, S., Claessens, J., Preneel, B.: Towards measuring anonymity. In: Dingledine, R., Syverson, P.F. (eds.) PET 2002. LNCS, vol. 2482, pp. 54–68. Springer, Heidelberg (2003)
27. Dwork, C.: Differential privacy: A survey of results. In: Agrawal, M., Du, D.-Z., Duan, Z., Li, A. (eds.) TAMC 2008. LNCS, vol. 4978, pp. 1–19. Springer, Heidelberg (2008)
28. Fiat, A., Shamir, A.: How to prove yourself: Practical solutions to identification and signature problems. In: Odlyzko, A.M. (ed.) CRYPTO 1986. LNCS, vol. 263, pp. 186–194. Springer, Heidelberg (1987)
29. Fiat, A., Shamir, A.: How to Prove Yourself: Practical Solutions to Identification and Signature Problems. In: Odlyzko, A.M. (ed.) CRYPTO 1986. LNCS, vol. 263, pp. 186–194. Springer, Heidelberg (1987)
30. Garman, C., Green, M., Meiers, I., Rubin, A.: Rational zero: Economic security for zerocoin with everlasting anonymity. In: Financial Cryptography and Data Security Conference (2014)
31. Karame, G., Francillon, A., Čapkun, S.: Pay as you Browse: Microcomputations as Micropayments in Web-based Services. In: Proceedings of WWW (2011)
32. Miers, I., Garman, C., Green, M., Rubin, A.D.: Zerocoin: Anonymous Distributed E-Cash from Bitcoin (2013)
33. Moore, T., Christin, N.: Beware the middleman: Empirical analysis of bitcoin-exchange risk. In: Sadeghi, A.-R. (ed.) FC 2013. LNCS, vol. 7859, pp. 25–33. Springer, Heidelberg (2013)
34. Ober, M., Katzenbeisser, S., Hamacher, K.: Structure and anonymity of the bitcoin transaction graph. Future Internet 5(2), 237–250 (2013)
35. Pfitzmann, A., Hansen, M.: Anonymity, Unlinkability, Undetectability, Unobservability, Pseudonymity, and Identity Management-A Consolidated Proposal for Terminology. Fachterminologie Datenschutz und Datensicherheit, 111–144 (2008)
36. Reid, F., Harrigan, M.: An Analysis of Anonymity in the Bitcoin System. In: CoRR (2011)
37. Ron, D., Shamir, A.: Quantitative analysis of the full bitcoin transaction graph. In: Sadeghi, A.-R. (ed.) FC 2013. LNCS, vol. 7859, pp. 6–24. Springer, Heidelberg (2013), http://eprint.iacr.org/2012/584.pdf
38. Nakamoto, S.: Bitcoin: A Peer-to-Peer Electronic Cash System (2009)
39. Schnorr, C.-P.: Efficient signature generation for smart cards. Journal of Cryptology, 239–252 (1991)
40. Serjantov, A., Danezis, G.: Towards an information theoretic metric for anonymity. In: Dingledine, R., Syverson, P.F. (eds.) PET 2002. LNCS, vol. 2482, pp. 41–53. Springer, Heidelberg (2003)
41. Shokri, R., Theodorakopoulos, G., Le Boudec, J., Hubaux, J.P.: Quantifying location privacy. In: Proceedings of the IEEE Symposium on Security and Privacy (2011)

Integration of Data-Minimising Authentication into Authorisation Systems*

Dhouha Ayed[1], Patrik Bichsel[2], Jan Camenisch[2], and Jerry den Hartog[3]

[1] Thales, France
dhouha.ayed@thalesgroup.com
[2] IBM Research – Zurich, Switzerland
{pbi,jca}@zurich.ibm.com
[3] TU Eindhoven, The Netherlands
j.d.hartog@tue.nl

Abstract. Authentication and authorisation are essential ingredients for effective protection of data in distributed information systems. Currently, they are being treated as separate components with specified input and output relations. Traditional authorisation components require all of the users' information that is possibly relevant to an authorisation decision and consequently the authentication components need to fully identify the users and collect all available information about them. This destroys all the potential privacy and security benefits of data-minimising authentication technologies such as private credential systems. In this paper, we discuss different ways to address this problem. More precisely, we sketch two possibilities of integrating data-minimising authentication into a traditional authorisation system such that the overall system becomes data-minimising.

Keywords: authentication, authorisation, access control, privacy, XACML.

1 Introduction

In the past years we have seen a tremendous growth in the usage of digital information processing systems in all areas of our lives, resulting in enormous amounts of data being communicated, processed, or stored. In most cases it is in the interest of the data owner (e.g., a private person) as well as the data holder (e.g., a company or a government) that data is protected at all times. An important ingredient thereby are appropriate authorisation and access control (AC).

There are different AC models that allow for the implementation of rules to enforce that only authorised entities are able to access stored data or, more generally, any kind of resource. Some allow for a fine-grained specification of a subject's required attributes for being granted access to each resource. While such detailed specification are an ideal basis for data-minimisation authorisation, current implementations unfortunately require all *potentially relevant* attributes to be revealed to the authorisation system. This poses serious security and privacy problems to users and their employers as information systems are increasingly used for daily private and corporate tasks, on the one hand,

---

* This work has been supported by the EU FP7 project AU2EU (#611659).

T. Holz and S. Ioannidis (Eds.): TRUST 2014, LNCS 8564, pp. 179–187, 2014.

and require expensive efforts to properly protecting sensitive personal information, on the other hand. Consequently, there is a need for performing authorisation and access control using only the *strictly relevant* data about a subject.

Private or anonymous credentials [7,8,10] allow for data-sparse authentication of users. Using certified attributes contained in credentials, users are able to just prove properties about themselves (e.g., being over 18) while hiding all other information (such as birthdate, name, and address). Private credentials achieve (1) the goal of providing only the information relevant to a given (authentication) process, and (2) a high level of assurance in the communicated data through the use of certification. However, leveraging the benefits of data-minimising authentication in an authorisation system is challenging because of a mismatch in the respective expectations: the authorisation system requires all possibly relevant information about a subject to be present whereas the authentication system requires a declaration of the properties a subject must fulfil before it produces (cryptographic) evidence that proves such properties.

In this paper we provide a brief overview of data-minimising authentication (§2) as well as authorisation systems (§3). In §4 we show two possible approaches to solve the issues related to the integration of data-minimisation into an authorisation system. After sketching our approaches we compare their merits with a focus on the intrusiveness w.r.t. XACML-based access control systems.

Related Work. Access control systems differ in the *policy* language and model that they use. Systems such as Role Based Access Control (RBAC) [14] aim to improve over discretionary or mandatory access control in terms of manageability of policies by allowing indirect specification of rights based on properties (the roles) of entities. Systems such as the eXtensible Access Control Markup Language (XACML) [12] take this a step further allowing specification of users, resources and rights in terms of attributes. Most systems consider authentication and authorisation as distinct processes in which the authorisation part leverages information gained through the authentication process. Ardagna et al. [1] are an exception. They propose changes to the XACML framework that aim at including data-minimising authentication functionality into the XACML standard. In contrast, we do not rely on changing the XACML language.

2 Data-Minimising Authentication

Traditional authentication mechanisms have various drawbacks w.r.t. users' privacy, data quality, and the necessary protection of the collected data. Attribute-based authentication systems [9] allow for a selective disclosure of attributes certified in credentials, which make it possible to overcome these drawbacks. When it comes to the selection of the underlying technology, *anonymous credentials systems* as introduced in [7,8,10] offer the most comprehensive set of privacy preserving features [4]. They allow users to merely prove *properties* about the attributes certified in their credentials. As sensitive data disclosed in an authentication transaction can be reduced to a minimum, we call the use of private credentials *data-minimising authentication*.

We depict the message flow of an authentication transaction as well as the components of a data-minimising authentication system in Fig. 1. Given a user who is in possession of credentials issued to her by identity providers, the process of her trying to use a service (e.g., access to a medical database record) hosted on a server is depicted. For using its service, the provider requires the user to authenticate w.r.t. a service-specific *authentication policy*. This policy is formulated in terms of properties of the user's attributes, e.g., a policy could specify that only medical staff according to a credential issued by certain hospitals may use the service.

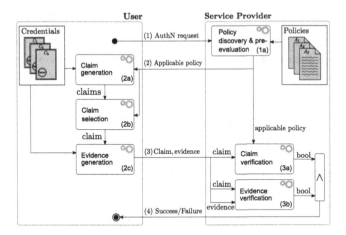

Fig. 1. User and a service provider components of a data-minimising authentication system [4]

Upon receiving an authentication request (1) for a service the server pre-evaluates the applicable authentication policy (1a) by resolving references to static content, such as the current date, to generate the policy that is sent to the user (2). After receiving the policy, the user's system determines which *claims*, i.e., statements about a subset of attributes of one or more of the available credentials, can be made that fulfil the given policy (2a). For example, a policy requiring the user to be medical staff of a hospital may be fulfilled by means of a user's employer credential. The favoured claim is selected (2b) interactively by the user [5] or automatically by a heuristics capable of finding the most privacy-preserving one. Based on the claim (credential technology-specific) *evidence* (2c) is generated. Claim and evidence are sent to the service provider (3), who verifies that the claim implies the policy (3a) and checks whether the claim's evidence is valid (3b). Note that some credential technologies require the issuer to be online and involved when evidence is created. After successful verification, the user is authenticated (4) as someone fulfilling the authentication requirements dictated in the policy. The strength of anonymous credential systems lies in the fact that they can strictly supply the information that is requested. For example, the only information the service provider learns about the user is the fact the she or he is indeed a currently employed as a medical staff at one of the collaborating hospitals. Thus, the user has minimised the information revealed about herself w.r.t. the given authentication policy. Ideally, the policy also reflects the minimal information necessary for conducting the scenario at hand.

3 Authorisation Systems

The authorisation problem typically arises when dealing with critical sensitive and confidential information. Current mechanisms [13] aim to protect *resources* by ensuring only *entities* with the correct *rights* get access. Attribute-based access control is a flexible model where permissions can be acquired dynamically according to actual user's attributes. Its capacity to accommodate real-time environmental states (such as user location and time) as access control parameters is one of its advantages. In this paper we focus on eXtensible Access Control Markup Language (XACML), an OASIS standard [12] which defines a flexible attribute-based framework for access control. In this section we provide a brief summary of the XACML policy language and framework.

XACML policies are expressed in an XML syntax. A *policy set* may contain further policy sets as well as *policies*, which in turn contain rules. Each of those elements has targets which specify what requests it (may) apply to. For example, a policy can apply to any read action on a medical record. If a request matches the target of a policy, policy set, or rule, the respective element is said to *apply* and it is evaluated. For a policy (set) this means its components are evaluated. For a rule its condition; e.g., 'it is daytime and the requester is a doctor' is checked and if satisfied, its effect (permit or deny) is used. As there may be multiple policy sets/policies/rules that apply, a combining algorithm (e.g.,'deny overwrite', 'first applicable') is used at each level to resolve any conflicts that may occur. XACML is attribute-based, i.e., each of the four components (subject, action, resource, environment) in a target as well as the condition are expressed using attributes. These attributes may be combined in different ways, e.g., 'the sensitivity level of the resource is less than the clearance level of the requester' or 'the time of request + requested duration of use is less than 17:00'. XACML distinguishes subject attributes, resources attributes, etc. and places some limitation on how, what type of attributes, can be used where.

Optional additional components of a policy (or policy set) are obligations. An obligation specifies an action that should be executed when the policy applies. For example, the policy may permit access to a resource but have the obligation that the owner of the resource is notified.

Policy enforcement in XACML is performed by a policy enforcement point (PEP), which intercepts requests for a resource and enforces the relevant policies according to the interpretation above. To enable this, the XACML framework uses the components detailed in the following.

The policy decision point (PDP) is responsible for the actual evaluation of policies relevant for the request which it obtains from the policy administration point (PAP). The context handler is responsible for formatting the request in XACML (rather than the application specific format the PEP intercepts) and retrieving the values of relevant attributes (e.g., by asking the policy information point (PIP)), either on its own initiative or when requested by the policy decision point (PDP). The PEP enforces the access decision and gives the corresponding obligations to the obligation handler to perform.

4   Integrated Architecture

As mentioned in the introduction, the integration of data-minimising authentication into any authorisation framework poses a major challenge due to the difference in the assumed information flow. While currently implemented authorisation systems expect all *possibly* relevant information on the user requesting access to be present, the data-minimisation principle requires that a user releases only the information minimally required for the operation at hand. The integration of data-minimisation into an authorisation system, consequently, requires changes of the current architecture or the communication flow.

We propose two approaches for realising *data-minimising authorisation* with an XACML-based system. The first one uses existing extension points to achieve the integration, whereas the second one diverges from the traditional XACML information flow and requires changes in the architecture of the system. After sketching both solutions in §4.1 and §4.2, respectively, we compare their advantages and drawbacks in §4.3.

There are some limitations to the degree to which data-minimisation can be applied. For instance, XACML allows for negative statements which deny requests containing certain attributes and in such cases it is essential that such attributes are always provided for security reasons. Also, different types of access (e.g., read, write) may have different types of requirements. For example, consider an activity program service for seniors. It may be accessed if a person is over 65 and a member, while it may be changed by a doctor only. Privacy is key for access, accountability is key for change.

4.1   Approach I: Use of Obligations

XACML allows for using obligations (cf. §3) in the authorisation process. One can instruct the PEP to only authorise access to a resource if an obligation is fulfilled. In the following we sketch a method for using this mechanism to integrate data-minimising authentication (cf. Fig. 2).

Where data-minimised access is allowed, the XACML policy would include an obligation with attributes that specify the corresponding authentication policy (or a reference to it) and its relevant arguments (e.g., the current date may be needed for an age check). For example, a usage policy with data-minimised access would look as follows (in explanatory shorthand notation):

```
<Policy><Rule Effect="Permit"/>
   <Obligation Id="xacml:abc:privatecred" FullfillOn="Permit">
   <AuthPolicyRef>MemberAndSenior</AuthPolicyRef>
   <Date>GetCurrentDateAttribute()</Date>
   <Contact>GetRequestorContactAttribute()</Contact>
</ObligationExpression></Policy>
```

The policy for changing programs by the doctor would not need to change (though we could also use an authentication policy that identifies the doctor or allows for the revocation of anonymity). The authentication policy needs to be in a format that can be processed by the data-minimising authentication system (e.g., the ABC4Trust presentation policy language [3], the language currently supporting the most comprehensive set of privacy-preserving features).

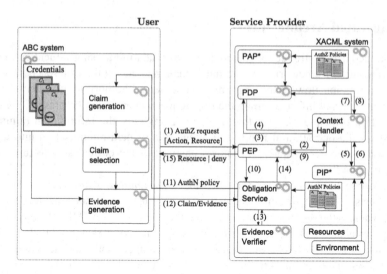

Fig. 2. Obligations approach: sequence of a resource request

In terms of communication flow (cf. Fig. 2) this means. First, in an authorisation operation an entity (i.e., a user or a system) issues a request providing information about the *resource* it wants to access as well as the *action* it intends to perform (1). Subject attributes such as an identity, role or pseudonym that relate the current request to a previous one are entirely optional. Second, the authorisation system runs as usual except that the PDP may return an obligation indicating there is not enough information about the subject (8). The obligation contains a (pointer to an) authentication policy that needs to be fulfilled. Of course, multiple obligations may be returned in which case all must be satisfied. Third, the PEP receives the obligations from the context handler (9) and relays them to the obligation component (10). Fourth, the obligation service extracts the authentication policies referred in the obligations and requests the authorisation subject to issue a claim as well as the accompanying evidence (called presentation token in [3]) by sending the extracted authorisation policy (11). For processing the evidence received from the subject (12), the obligations service contacts an evidence verifier component (13) that, given the authentication policy and the corresponding claim/evidence pair, decides on whether the latter complies with the subject attributes required by the authorisation system. Finally, the obligations service forwards the result of the verification to the PEP (14), which will either return the requested resource or deny access, depending on the obtained result (15).

Caching of a user's attribute values that result from an authentication query helps improving performance for repetitive access of resources. While this can be done in the obligations service itself, storing them in the PIP is beneficial but requires more integration with the XACML system. Note, anonymous credentials in general, and the Identity Mixer library [2]) in particular, support a broad range of possibilities when it comes to revealing data about their holder. Using the most privacy-preserving setting, e.g., only proving ownership of a certain credential in an way that several transactions of the same user cannot be linked, does not allow the authorisation system to preserve any knowledge about that user. However, credentials also allow one to reveal a subset

of the attributes contained in them and to make operations w.r.t. a pseudonym that can
be used to link a set of transactions of one user.

4.2   Approach II: Policy Extraction Approach

An authorisation system may meet the requirement of requesting the minimally necessary information about a subject willing to access a resource by communicating to
that entity the required access policy for a given resource/action tuple. However, such
communication is not foreseen in any authorisation system as they separate the process
of authentication (for requesting information about the subject) and authorisation. To
enable it, we introduce a server-side component, the so-called policy collection point
(PCP), which is able to extract an access policy from a specified resource/action combination. The PCP may interact with the PAP to retrieve the XACML authorisation policy
that it then converts into an authentication policy (e.g., ABC4Trust presentation policy [3], extended SAML token [1]) and returns it to the requesting entity. Using this
policy the service provider can request (tailored) authentication before taking an authorisation decision and we can retain the separation of authorisation and authentication to
a large extent.

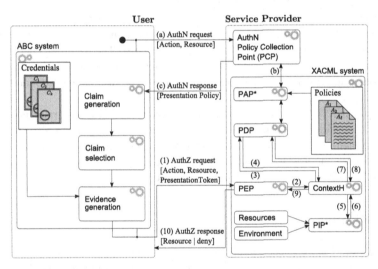

Fig. 3. Policy request (AuthN request) with appropriate policy collection point before performing
a mostly standard XACML authoirisation request

Figure 3 depicts the process of requesting an authentication policy from the PCP.
It also illustrates that the PAP and the PIP require slight modification from what they
perform in a standard XACML system (we thus denote them PAP* and PIP*, respectively). Concretely, the PAP* is able to output an authentication policy for a specific
resource/action combination. The derivation of such policies from the XACML format
poses challenges as some capabilities are unique to credential systems (e.g., proving
that an two attributes from distinct credentials have the same value). Further, the PIP*
is able to verify an authentication claim/evidence combination, possibly by using an
external component provided by the authentication system (as in Approach I, §4.1).

4.3 Comparison

Our first approach, using obligations to perform authentication during the authorisation process, requires only minor modifications to existing XACML implementations. It also allows for incremental adoption; data minimisation can be added at chosen points while not changing the behaviour for other existing policies. One drawback arising from this independence is that attributes communicated to the authorising entity need to be re-supplied on each new resource request, or the obligations service needs to implement caching, which is already done in the PIP. A further challenge is that the described approach requires system administrators to author XACML as well as authentication policies. We could mitigate this problem by deriving the authentication policy from the XACML policy, possibly relying on extensions of the specified format to support all desirable features. Clearly, such derivation process increases the ties between the authentication and authorisation – a property we tried to avoid in the first place. Further, we need to verify that the delay caused by the authentication transaction is acceptable to the entity who needs to maintain the state for the authorisation transaction.

The second approach mandates more changes to the standard XACML information flow. Through those changes it will be possible to maintain information about the subject as traditionally done in an XACML implementation. The (possible) re-use of this information may allow the service provider to increase the efficiency of the authorisation process assuming that many similar policies exist. The (required) derivation of authentication policies from the existing XACML access policies, however, may call for restrictions to and amendments of the latter to support the vast feature set of anonymous credential systems.

The approach of [1] is similar to the second approach but it integrates private credential concepts into the XACML language; the authorisation policies also specify the required authentication. Besides changing the policy language this combines drawbacks of the obligation approach (multiple policies; though specified in one document) with that of the policy extraction approach (changes needed to the architecture).

5 Conclusion

The data-minimisation principle allows a user to only reveal the minimal set of attributes or properties about attributes required for an operation at hand. This is conflicting with the traditional understanding of authorisation system implementations that require an entity that wants to access a resource to disclose all *possibly relevant* attribute values. Overcoming this challenge requires amending the information flow of current authorisation systems.

We presented two alternative approaches for integrating data-minimising authentication into an authorisation system. One method focuses on marginally changing the specified XACML system and has its advantages mainly in the ease of integration. The simplicity of implementation comes at the price of ending up with a system that is more complex in maintaining and we end up with interleaving the authentication and authorisation transaction. The second method aims at keeping those transactions separate, which forces us to extract authentication information from a XACML.

Future work will implement the described approaches to show their feasibility. Especially, contacting an entity during the authorisation decision may pose a problem as such interleaved transaction is currently not expected and it will increase the expected overall runtime. Further, the extraction of authentication information from XACML policies may not be possible to an extent that is desirable for maximal data minimisation. Extending the XACML standard at the foreseen extension points, however, may not allow extension with all functionality of anonymous credentials.

Another direction to be explored is the semantic interoperability between different domains. Extensions of XACML that introduce ontologies and trust management, e.g., [6], should be incorporated in the proposed integrated architecture.

References

1. Ardagna, C.A., De Capitani di Vimercati, S., Neven, G., Paraboschi, S., Preiss, F.S., Samarati, P., Verdicchio, M.: Enabling privacy-preserving credential-based access control with XACML and SAML. In: IEEE CIT 2010, pp. 1090–1095. IEEE Computer Society Press (2010)
2. Bichsel, P., Binding, C., Camenisch, J., Groß, T., Heydt-Benjamin, T., Sommer, D., Zaverucha, G.(Contributors): Cryptographic protocols of the Identity Mixer library. IBM Technical Report RZ 3730 (# 99740) (2009)
3. Bichsel, P., Camenisch, J., Dubovitskaya, M., Enderlein, R.R., Krontiris, I., Lehmann, A., Neven, G., Nielsen, J.D., Paquin, C., Preiss, F.S., Rannenberg, K., Stausholm, M., Zwingelberg, H.: H2.2 – ABC4Trust architecture for developers. In: ABC4Trust Heartbeat H2.2 (2013)
4. Bichsel, P., Camenisch, J., Preiss, F.S.: A comprehensive framework enabling dataminimizing authentication. In: Proc. of the 7th ACM DIM, pp. 13–22. ACM Press (2011)
5. Bichsel, P., Camenisch, J., Preiss, F.S., Sommer, D.: Dynamically-changing interface for interactive selection of information cards satisfying policy requirements. IBM Technical Report RZ 3756 (# 99766) (2009)
6. Böhm, K., Etalle, S., den Hartog, J.I., Hütter, C., Trabelsi, S., Trivellato, D., Zannone, N.: A flexible architecture for privacy-aware trust management. Journal of Theoretical and Applied Electronic Commerce Research 5(2), 77–96 (2010)
7. Brands, S.: Rethinking Public Key Infrastructures and Digital Certificates: Building in Privacy. MIT Press, Cambridge (2000)
8. Camenisch, J., Lysyanskaya, A.: An efficient system for non-transferable anonymous credentials with optional anonymity revocation. In: Pfitzmann, B. (ed.) EUROCRYPT 2001. LNCS, vol. 2045, pp. 93–118. Springer, Heidelberg (2001)
9. Camenisch, J., Mödersheim, S., Neven, G., Preiss, F.S., Sommer, D.: A card requirements language enabling privacy-preserving access control. In: SACMAT, pp. 119–128 (2010)
10. Chaum, D.: Untraceable electronic mail, return addresses, and digital pseudonyms. Communications of the ACM 24(2), 84–88 (1981)
11. OASIS: Assertions and protocols for the OASIS Security Assertion Markup Language (SAML) v2.0 (2005) OASIS Standard, http://docs.oasis-open.org/security/saml/v2.0/saml-core-2.0-os.pdf
12. OASIS: eXtensible Access Control Markup Language (XACML) V2.0 (2005) OASIS Standard, http://docs.oasis-open.org/xacml/2.0/access-control-xacml-2.0-core-spec-os.pdf
13. Samarati, P., di Vimercati, S.d.C.: Access control: Policies, models, and mechanisms. In: Focardi, R., Gorrieri, R. (eds.) FOSAD 2000. LNCS, vol. 2171, pp. 137–196. Springer, Heidelberg (2001)
14. Sandhu, R.S., Coyne, E.J., Feinstein, H.L., Youman, C.E.: Role-based access control models. Computer 29(2), 38–47 (1996)

Evaluating Trustworthiness through Monitoring: The Foot, the Horse and the Elephant

Vinh Bui, Richard Verhoeven, and Johan Lukkien

Department of Mathematics and Computer Science
Eindhoven University of Technology, The Netherlands
{t.v.bui,p.h.f.m.verhoeven,j.j.lukkien}@tue.nl

Abstract. This paper presents a framework for trust evaluation through monitoring, in particular, to address the question of how to derive trust from observations of certain properties. We propose a trust model based on subjective logic to represent trust through the notion of an opinion and to include aspects of uncertainty in a systematic fashion. Moreover, we analyze requirements for opinion generators and introduce novel parameterized generators that capture the requirements for opinion generators much better than current generators do. In addition, we show how a decision can be made based on trust monitoring within a certain context. The proposed trust evaluation framework is demonstrated with a case study of a Body Area Sensor Network. The results and examples show that the opinion generators can effectively work with various types of properties, including dependability, security and functionality related properties.

Keywords: trustworthiness, trust evaluation, monitoring, opinion generator, body area sensor networks.

1 Introduction

Trustworthiness, in general, refers to a relation among entities, where one relies on the other. At the user-system interaction level, trust is commonly based on a high transparency and a clear interaction, complemented with reliable and correct operation. When used inside the system, trust and trustworthiness refer to relations between entities in the system itself. Trust and a trust model form the basis of system decisions (e.g., whether or not an operating system accepts an application, how it asserts the quality of outcomes or decides to take an action).

As an example, a Body Area Sensor Network (BASN) consists of sensors, which record human body functions including physiological, emotional, and spatial aspects. BASNs can be used for diverse applications ranging from monitoring for medical purposes, sports coaching to computer gaming. The user acceptance of BASNs will largely be determined by the opinion that users have about the trustworthiness of such systems. To mention just a few examples, users trust that their data is safe and protected or that functions of the system (e.g., warning functions) work correctly. The doctor trusts the BASN to measure with a certain

T. Holz and S. Ioannidis (Eds.): TRUST 2014, LNCS 8564, pp. 188–205, 2014.

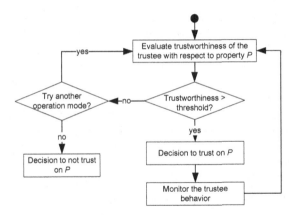

Fig. 1. The trust management scheme of software components in a BASN given in [4], including trust evaluation, monitoring, and the decision making processes with respect to property P

given accuracy and for a certain time. The user trusts his system to function within certain limits of use (e.g., duration without charging). This trust underlies the decisions stakeholders take. Decisions include, for example, to actually use the BASN or to select a particular application on it.

In [4], trust and trustworthiness were introduced as generic and pervasive concepts within a BASN. At the highest level, users of a BASN must be able to trust it, or more precisely, to trust it *to have some relevant properties.* Conversely, the BASN is said to be trustworthy *with respect to those properties.* Thus, the concept of trust is used to bound and guide changes in the system: the new state must be sufficiently trustworthy with respect to a given set of properties. Besides functionality, such properties can be qualities, including properties dependent on time. As an example, assume that a component is specified to use a certain maximum utilization. The acceptance of the component depends on the trust the system has in the truth of this. The pervasive nature comes from using this same model at all levels in the system. Figure 1 gives a trust management scheme to maintain the BASN as a trustworthy platform under changes in applications such as dynamic extension and configuration of the BASN applications.

In this paper, we regard trust as subjective: it is derived from the opinion of a trustor about a trustee[1]. This opinion of the trustor about whether a trustee has a property P has contributions from three different directions. First, there is an initial or base level of trust ranging from the trustor being credent to being suspicious. This base level determines trust in case of lack of knowledge or uncertainty. Second, trust derives from experience, i.e., from monitoring whether P holds or is endangered. Third, trust is obtained from recommendations by

---

[1] A note on terminology: we refer to trustor and trustee as the two parties under consideration. With the name 'trustee' we mean the subject of the opinion that the trustor has. We do not imply that a 'trustee' is automatically trusted.

other parties and thus is a combination of trust in this third party and its recommendation. Trust is built from composition of these three contributions, and is based on the property P that is expected. This suggests that in the evaluation of trust there are objective elements (facts like measurements, or the opinion of another entity on the subject matter) and subjective elements (the value a trustor assigns to such a fact).

This paper focuses on addressing the monitoring part, and in particular the question of how to derive trust from observations. We use the model of *subjective logic* [10,11] to represent opinions from which trust is derived, and to include the aspect of uncertainty in a systematic fashion. In subjective logic, deriving an opinion from observations is called *opinion generation*.

Contributions. We analyze requirements for opinion generators and we introduce novel parameterized generators that capture these requirements much better than current generators do. This work extends the work in [3] to include time; we also add a conceptual understanding of the continuous model and we give a general decision model, highlighted in the context of a BASN. In comparison to the original opinion generator in [11], we add the following: a) we deal in a natural way with the time of observation; b) we introduce parameters to define new categories of generators corresponding to particular requirements of a trustor; and c) we incorporate continuous observation rather than just discrete ones.

The paper is organized as follows. In Section 2, we discuss how we represent trust using subjective logic, in the form of an opinion. We explain how we derive a trust value and a confidence from an opinion, and how our trust-based decision scheme works. In Section 3, we present requirements for opinion generators. We then present and evaluate two types of opinion generators. One class is based on discrete observations (success, failure, and unknown) while the other class deals with continuous observations. Experiments and evaluation are discussed in Section 4 with a case study of a BASN. Related work is presented in Section 5. Finally, Section 6 gives conclusions and future work.

2   Trust Model

Trust Definition. Following the work in [4], we define trust as follows. *Trust is the degree of justifiable belief a trustor has that, in a given context, a trustee will live up to a given set of statements about its behavior.* Phrased differently, trust is a function of trustee, trustor, context and property that the trustee is supposed to have (i.e., the set of statements about its behavior). We put in the word 'justifiable' because we want to consider trust and trust computations that can be formalized and repeated. The codomain of trust is a scale of 0..100%; we also speak about a trust value.

Besides trust, we introduce the notion of confidence. *Confidence is the degree of certainty a trustor has about a trust value.* Its codomain is a scale of 0..100% as well.

Formalization. According to this definition, the subject of trust is a statement P consisting of trustee, context and behavior. Thus, a *trust statement* is a tuple

$P = (T, p, c, t)$ meaning 'trustee T will satisfy p in context c for a time t'. Both trust and confidence are calculated for a pair consisting of a trustor and a trust statement. We define this through the concept of an *opinion* a trustor A has about a trust statement P.

Opinions are part of a belief model defined in *subjective logic* [10,11]. Formally, an opinion denoted by $\omega_P^A = (b, d, u, a)$ expresses trustor A's belief in the truth of statement P. Here, b, d, and u represent belief, disbelief, and uncertainty respectively, where $b, d, u \in [0, 1]$ and $b + d + u = 1$. Uncertainty is caused by the lack of evidence to support either belief or disbelief. Parameter $a \in [0, 1]$ is called the base rate and represents the role of uncertainty in the computation of trust, viz., the percentage of uncertainty that is taken as belief. For a given opinion ω we define trust and confidence as follows.

$$\underline{t}(\omega) = \omega.b + \omega.a \cdot \omega.u. \tag{1}$$

$$\underline{c}(\omega) = 1 - \omega.u. \tag{2}$$

Hence, the trust contained in an opinion is the belief plus a percentage of the uncertainty. A credent trustor has this percentage equal to 1; a suspicious trustor has it 0; a neutral value is 0.5 which we will use most of the time.

Subjective logic defines methods to combine opinions into new ones. In this way, for example, opinions can be constructed based on an opinion of a recommender and the opinion about this recommender. Hence, the final opinion ω_P^A is the result of a series of such compositions. A discussion of this is beyond the purpose of this paper; the reader is referred to the references.

Decision Model. For taking decisions we assume that we have computed a number of trust values $\overline{tv} = (tv_1, \ldots, tv_n)$ and confidence values $\overline{cv} = (cv_1, \ldots, cv_n)$ from correspondent opinions. We then require that these values exceed certain given thresholds. More precisely, we assume that we are given a series of weight vectors $\overline{tw_1}, \ldots, \overline{tw_m}$ and $\overline{cw_1}, \ldots, \overline{cw_m}$ of dimension n and with a norm 1; and thresholds $tThr_1, \ldots, tThr_m$ and $cThr_1, \ldots, cThr_m$. Then the requirement is

$$\overline{tw_i} \cdot \overline{tv} \geq tThr_i, \quad \text{for } 1 \leq i \leq m, \tag{3}$$

$$\overline{cw_i} \cdot \overline{cv} \geq cThr_i, \quad \text{for } 1 \leq i \leq m. \tag{4}$$

Using matrix notation with the weight vectors as rows,

$$TW \, \overline{tv} \geq \overline{tThr}, \tag{5}$$

$$CW \, \overline{cv} \geq \overline{cThr}. \tag{6}$$

By taking $n = m$ and TW equal to unity we obtain an individual threshold per trust value. The general case gives a series of tradeoffs using the different weights. Thresholds may be context dependent. For example, trust thresholds corresponding to privacy protection may be lower if the wearer of the BASN has an acute condition.

We call a state safe if (5) and (6) hold. We can use this in a number of ways. Through monitoring, we can observe whether the current state is still safe, possibly leading to a decision to take action if it is not. Alternatively, an access control decision is based on computing whether a new state is safe.

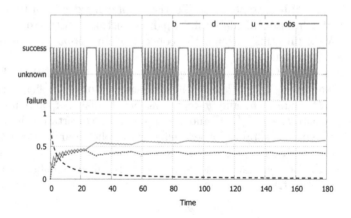

Fig. 2. Example of the evolution of (b, d, u) based on the classic definition of opinion generation in [11] with $\epsilon = 3$. The top line shows the observations with three values: failure, unknown (not used here), and success.

3   Opinion Generation

3.1   The Classic Generator

In this section we study the question of how to generate an opinion from observations. We assume here that we can observe the truth of a trust statement P; the outcomes are called success and failure. To start, the generator proposed in [11] is defined as follows. Discrete observations of successes and failures are collected in variables ns and nf, respectively, according to the following rules.

$$\text{Upon success: } ns \leftarrow ns + 1;$$
$$\text{Upon failure: } nf \leftarrow nf + 1. \tag{7}$$

A corresponding opinion (b, d, u, a) is defined as follows.

$$b = \frac{ns}{ns + nf + \epsilon}; \quad d = \frac{nf}{ns + nf + \epsilon}; \quad u = \frac{\epsilon}{ns + nf + \epsilon}. \tag{8}$$

With this definition, b and d are assigned the relative fractions of successes and failures respectively, while a number of uncertain observations, ϵ, is given as an initialization parameter. Base rate a remains a free parameter. Figure 2 shows an example. The observation sequence is plotted at the top with values ranging as failure (lowest), unknown (middle, not used here), and success (highest). This method, however, has the following limitations.

1. After many observations, new observations have little impact. This method might therefore be adequate to estimate a probability that an object has some static properties, but it does not work very well for properties that evolve over time.

2. Older observations get the same weight as more recent observations. The order of the observations in the past is in fact irrelevant for the current outcome. Other authors have observed this as well. In [14] a forgetting factor is introduced to address this issue.

3. Successes and failures are treated in the same way. Naturally, failures count heavier than success; sequences of failures typically decrease trust rapidly [2].

4. Although the horizontal axis in Figure 2 might be interpreted as time, it really represents an event count. In many cases, a correspondence to time is required. One way to achieve this is to perform periodic observations. In that case an observation may become missing, leading to an observation with the outcome 'unknown'.

3.2   Requirements for an Opinion Generator

From the above observations we obtain some requirements for an opinion generator as below.

1. Observations have different weight, e.g. more recent observations count heavier than older ones. This means that the observation order is relevant. Similarly, impact of success and failure can be different.

2. A long or infinite series of successes leads, in principle, to trust converging to 1. A property of interest is the time of convergence, which may depend on observed behavior in the past.

3. A series of failures must lead to trust converging to 0. In addition, a relatively frequent occurrence of failure must lead to a continuously low trust. It may even lead to recovery being possible only through a user intervention.

4. Uncertainty increases upon observing unknown values. There are two approaches for this: decreasing knowledge (reduction of knowledge of successes and failures) and increasing uncertainty. The latter makes recovery slower.

5. It takes time into account. While time passes without observations, uncertainty increases. This reduces confidence and most often trust decreases as well (trust decays over time).

6. Besides discrete observations, continuous observations (reflecting a 'distance' to failure) must be included.

7. It provides a set of parameters (a profile) can be tuned for different trust statements (and that, in fact, address the above requirements).

3.3   Proposed Opinion Generators

We retain a model with two variables nf and ns capturing failure and success; the definition of an opinion remains as in (8). In order to address the above requirements we modify the update rules. We present and evaluate two types of opinion generators as below.

---

[2] This is reflected in the expression: 'trust comes by foot but leaves by horse'.

Discrete Observations. This generator is based on the discrete values of observations 'success', 'failure', and 'unknown'. We introduce three parameters, γ, δ, and $\zeta \in [0,1]$, which are used to update the values of ns and nf using the following rules.

$$\begin{aligned}
&\text{Upon success: } ns \leftarrow ns + 1; nf \leftarrow \gamma \cdot nf; \\
&\text{Upon failure: } nf \leftarrow nf + 1; ns \leftarrow \delta \cdot ns; \\
&\text{Upon unknown: } ns \leftarrow \zeta \cdot ns; nf \leftarrow \zeta \cdot nf.
\end{aligned} \tag{9}$$

The original method in (7) is obtained with parameters[3] γ, δ and ζ set to 1. The γ and δ values indicate the level of pessimism and optimism and determine how fast disbelief or belief are lost when faced with a success or failure, respectively. With fluctuating successes and failures, both ns and nf remain small such that the uncertainty term ϵ plays a more important role. The linear increase, exponential decrease allows us to model the aspect of 'trust comes by foot but leaves by horse'.

These update rules address Requirement 1 since new observations have more impact. A long series of successes inevitably leads to a dominating value of ns addressing Requirement 2. A similar comment holds for a long series of failures, giving Requirement 3. The (ϵ, ζ) pair controls respectively how fast uncertainty is overcome and how fast it is introduced upon 'unknown' observations. For $\zeta < 1$, both ns and nf become small upon unknown observations. Thus, b and d go back to zero (thus increasing u) with the effect that the system is more or less reset. This satisfies Requirement 4. Requirement 5 is satisfied when observations are periodic. The parameters in the method provide the capability of customizing the trust evaluation (Requirement 7). For example, choosing δ to be zero, represents the policy that belief drops completely after a failure. If γ equals 1, the occurrence of failures is never forgotten (the model behaves like an elephant that never forgets), leading to a slower recovery after each failure. This opinion generator therefore can cope with a kind of on-off attacks, which the classic generator cannot do (see the example in Figure 2). In these on-off attacks, an object may alternate between periods of reporting success and failure or try to report a series of successes in order to acquire a high trust value and be allowed a number of successive failures without rasing an alarm. By choosing δ to be zero, belief drops completely after a failure leading to a correspondent drop in trust and confidence.

Figure 3 presents an example of using this method, in which the input data set has an occurrence of a failure after a long sequence of successes. The trust value is also shown using $a = 0.5$. Because the failures remain stored in nf, it leads to increasingly longer convergence of trust. The figure shows that (1) the observation order is relevant (more recent observations count heavier than older ones); (2) a success influences disbelief and uncertainty as well, in contrast to the independence in the original model; (3) the stability of long-term observation

---

[3] Actually, we could be more precise and use ζ_1 and ζ_2 to discriminate between adjustments after success or failure. We keep the parameters space limited though.

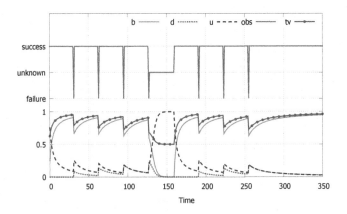

Fig. 3. Example of the evolution of (b, d, u) and the trust value based on the update rules (9). $\gamma = 1, \delta = 0.25, \zeta = 0.7, \epsilon = 3$ and a is fixed at 0.5.

towards the average is removed; (4) the slopes and shapes can be steered through several parameters.

One aspect is still to be improved. The figure shows that the increase of trust after a failure is convex. Intuitively, however, trust should increase slowly after a decrease and accelerate later. Therefore, the increase should be concave (with derivative 0) and only later become convex. We therefore adjust the update rules as follows.

$$\text{Define: } f(x) = \frac{x \cdot (\arctan(x \cdot \beta_2 - \beta_1) + \arctan(\beta_1))}{\pi/2 + \arctan(\beta_1)};$$

Upon success: $sc \leftarrow sc + 1; ns \leftarrow ns' + f(sc); nf \leftarrow \gamma \cdot nf;$ (10)
Upon failure: $nf \leftarrow nf + 1; ns \leftarrow \delta \cdot ns; sc \leftarrow 0; ns' \leftarrow ns;$
Upon unknown: $ns \leftarrow \zeta \cdot ns; nf \leftarrow \zeta \cdot nf; sc \leftarrow 0; ns' \leftarrow ns,$

where sc represents the count of successes since the last failure or unknown. New parameters β_1 and β_2 define the horizontal stretch (how long it takes for trust to increase again) and the slope, respectively. Figure 4 shows the result of the same observations as in Figure 3 with $\gamma = 1, \delta = 0.25, \beta_1 = 7, \beta_2 = 0.2$, and $\zeta = 0.7$.

Continuous Observations. The discrete values in the opinion generator are not always adequate. For some trust statements, failure might be a state that is never allowed. A possible approach is to have a safety boundary around the failed state and to regard all observations within the boundary as failures. A more precise approach is to let contributions to the opinion be determined by the distance to the failed state. An example is monitoring for sufficient resources, e.g., memory. The observation then represents how close the current memory availability is to the failed state.

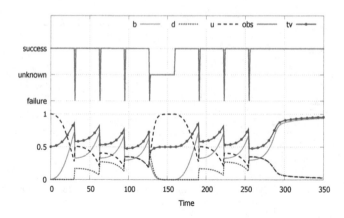

Fig. 4. Example of the evolution of (b, d, u) and the trust value based on update rules (10). $\gamma = 1, \delta = 0.25, \beta_1 = 7, \beta_2 = 0.2, \zeta = 0.7, \epsilon = 3$ and a is fixed at 0.5.

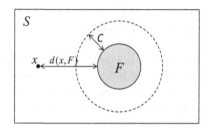

Fig. 5. The space F of failed states and its complement S. The cut-off distance C defines a border around F. The distance of an element x to F, $d(x, F)$, is given by the minimal distance to elements in F. s equals 0 in F and 1 outside C.

An observation s is now a value within the range $[0, 1]$; we also use $f = 1 - s$. We propose the following rules.

$$\begin{aligned} \text{Upon unknown: } & ns \leftarrow \zeta \cdot ns; nf \leftarrow \zeta \cdot nf; \\ \text{Otherwise: } & ns \leftarrow \delta^f \cdot ns + s; nf \leftarrow \gamma^s \cdot nf + f. \end{aligned} \quad (11)$$

For $(s, f) = (1, 0)$ and $(s, f) = (0, 1)$, this results in Equation (9), hence it is a true generalization of that. A correspondent generalization of (10) is not straightforward and needs further investigation beyond the scope of this paper.

A next question is how to model the computation of this s. In the discrete case, the space of observations O can be written as $O = F + S$, with F corresponding to failures and S to successes (defined by the trust statement P under consideration). In the continuous case, s is a mapping: $O \rightarrow [0, 1]$. In order to define it we still assume we have a set F where s equals 0 (hence, $S = O \setminus F$). We further assume that we have a metric $d(x, y)$ representing the distance between two elements $x, y \in O$. This metric is generalized to sets by taking the minimum distance over all members in the set, with the empty set having distance infinity.

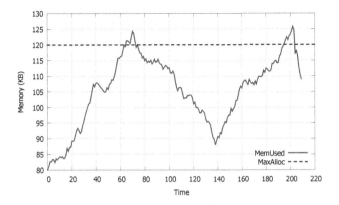

Fig. 6. Example of the actual memory usage of component T at run time. The dashed line shows the maximum admitted memory usage for T.

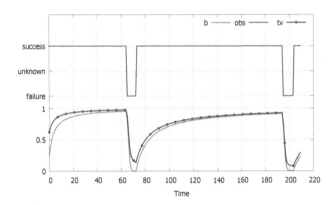

Fig. 7. Results of belief and trust values with the discrete observations and the update rules in Equation (9). $\gamma = 1, \delta = 0.25, \zeta = 0.7, \epsilon = 3$ and a is fixed at 0.5.

Hence, for $x \in S, d(x, F)$ represents the distance of x to F. In addition, we assume to have a cut-off distance C above which s equals 1 (see Figure 5). In this way, we let s be a function of the distance. An example is

$$s(x) = \begin{cases} (\frac{d(x,F)}{C})^{\alpha}, & \text{if } d(x, F) < C; \\ 1, & otherwise, \end{cases} \qquad (12)$$

where α is a parameter that determines the sharpness of the curve. More classes of functions are possible as well.

An Example. Let T be a software component running on a system. We consider an example of statement $P = (T, p_{mem}, c, t)$ about a memory usage property of T. Predicate p_{mem} indicates that '$MemUsed \leq MaxAlloc$', where $MemUsed$ and

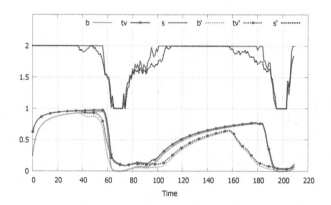

Fig. 8. Results of belief and trust values with the continuous observations and the update rules in Equation (11), with $C = 8, \alpha = 1$ (solid lines) and $C = 15, \alpha = 0.5$ (dashed lines). $\gamma = 1, \delta = 0.25, \zeta = 0.7, \epsilon = 3$ and a is fixed at 0.5.

MaxAlloc represent the memory used by the component and the given limit the component is supposed to stay under (e.g., 120 KB), respectively. Context c and time t are not relevant for this example. Thus, trust statement P becomes: the trustor (system manager) trusts T to have '$p_{mem} : MemUsed \leq MaxAlloc$'. Figure 6 shows the actual memory usage of component T at run time. The dashed line shows the maximum of the memory allocation, *MaxAlloc* = 120 KB. We compute the trustworthiness of statement P using both discrete and continuous observation models.

Discrete Observations: In this method, an observation gets a value of 'failure', 'success', or 'unknown' (not used here). When *MemUsed* > *MaxAlloc* the observation is 'failure', otherwise the observation is 'success'. Figure 7 shows the results of b and tv by applying the update rules in Equation (9). The top line shows the observations again. At time 65 and 195, the memory usage exceeds the value of 120 KB. Consequently, the belief b and trust value tv decrease.

Continuous Observations: In this method, the observation is represented by the value of $s \in [0, 1]$ computed using Equation (12) with $C = 8$ and $\alpha = 1$. Figure 8 shows the results of b and tv (the solid lines) by applying the update rules in Equation (11). The top line shows the value of s (which is added to 1 for presentation in the figure). At time 58 and 180, the memory usage exceeds the value of 112 KB ($MaxAlloc - C$) and s starts decreasing. Different from the above method, b and tv start decreasing when the memory usage is above 112 KB and they decrease faster when the memory usage is closer to *MaxAlloc*. In addition, the trust value takes a longer time to recover. This method, therefore, responds to the trend of the observed property. The parameters C and α can be customized for different types of quality properties. With a critical property, we should set C to a bigger value and α to a smaller value. For example, the dashed lines in Figure 8 show the values of s', b', and tv' with parameters $C = 15$ and $\alpha = 0.5$.

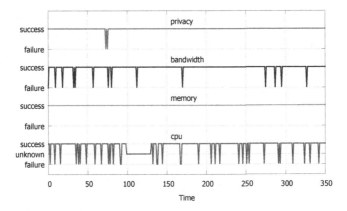

Fig. 9. Observations of the quality properties CPU usage, memory usage, bandwidth usage, and privacy using the three-valued observation model. There are unknown observations of the CPU usage in the period [100, 130].

4   A Case Study of a BASN

4.1   BASN Model

We demonstrate our trust model and opinion generators with a case study of a BASN, where the BASN platform plays the role of the trustor and a software component plays the role of the trustee. Our goal is to investigate the effectiveness of the opinion generators; for this work we focus on opinions of quality properties, and we restrict ourselves to the discrete model. Furthermore, we show how a decision can be made based on trust monitoring within a certain context.

We look at the example of a BASN that includes an ECG sensor, such that a component can monitor a patient and report relevant data to a doctor. Although the doctor would prefer the most accurate information (the raw ECG signal at 250Hz), other concerns forbid this, e.g., resource sharing, a long battery life or privacy concerns of the patient. The decision whether the system allows the component to run depends on its trustworthiness and the system context. For example, when a life threatening condition is detected or when the doctor requests a daily recording of the raw ECG signal for some period, the system context can change such that privacy and resource concerns are less important.

4.2   The Trust Model

We use the model proposed in the Trust4All framework [15] to describe the quality properties of a component as monitored by the platform. According to this model, a component has a *quality profile*, which consists of metrics of quality properties that are asserted to hold in a certain context. Such profile is attached to the component during development time. The quality properties can consist

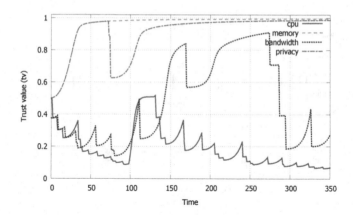

Fig. 10. Trust values of the quality properties CPU usage, memory usage, network bandwidth usage, and privacy using opinion generator (10)

of a number of (sub) quality properties, e.g., the performance property consists of CPU usage, memory usage, and network bandwidth usage. Moreover, the quality profile can have one or more *quality modes*, which correspond to qualities at different operational modes.

Let us assume that we are given a component T with a quality profile consisting of four properties: CPU usage, memory usage, network bandwidth usage (for which maximum values are specified), and privacy. Here, privacy is the degree to which unauthorized parties are prevented from obtaining sensitive information. From this profile we derive a set of trust statements $\{P_i\}$, where $P_i = (T, p_i, c_i, t_i)$ (in this example, we ignore for simplicity the roles of c_i and t_i). Suppose that T runs on platform A, then a trust relationship between A and T is established through a set of opinions, $\{\omega_{P_i}^A\}$. Predicates $p_i, i = 1, \ldots, 4$ are defined as follows.

p_1: CPU usage is less than 60%.
p_2: Memory usage is less than 40%.
p_3: Network bandwidth usage is less than 25%.
p_4: The degree of privacy is larger than 90%.

The opinion of A about statement P_i is $\omega_{P_i}^A = (b_i, d_i, u_i, a_i)$, the trust value is $tv_i = b_i + a_i u_i$, and the confidence value is $cv_i = 1 - u_i$. Thus, the trust and confidence values of A are $\overline{tv} = (tv_1, \ldots, tv_4)$ and $\overline{cv} = (cv_1, \ldots, cv_4)$, respectively.

An example series of observations of the properties at run time is shown in Figure 9, using the three-valued discrete observations. Observe that there are unknown observations in the period [100, 130]. The memory property has only success observations because the memory usage is always smaller than 40%.

We then apply opinion generator (10) to compute the trust and confidence values of the above observations. The parameters $\gamma = 1, \delta = 0.25, \beta_1 = 7, \beta_2 = 0.2, \zeta = 0.7, \epsilon = 3$, and $a = 0.5$ are chosen for all properties. The trust and confidence values of the properties are shown in Figure 10 and Figure 11, respectively. We observe the following:

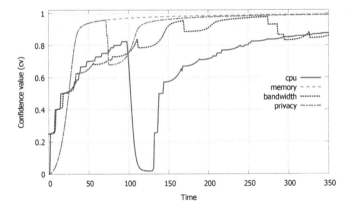

Fig. 11. Confidence values of the quality properties CPU usage, memory usage, network bandwidth usage, and privacy using (10)

- In general, the trust value of the CPU property is low (under 0.5) since failure observations occur frequently. The unknown observations in the period [100, 130] make the uncertainty value (u_1) increase, and thus the confidence value ($cv_1 = 1 - u_1$) decrease. The trust value is then increased by the contribution of $a_1 \cdot u_1$, which is controlled by parameter a_1, but it cannot become greater than 0.5 since $a_1 = 0.5$. However, when taking a decision, this trust value might not be considered since the corresponding confidence value is too small.
- Both trust and confidence values of the memory property go to 1 because of the all-success observations.
- The starting trust value of the network bandwidth property is smaller than 0.5 since the first observation is a failure. With a long sequence of success observations (e.g., in the period [160, 270]) the trust value increases significantly. The increase follows the behavior of the arctan() function of the update rules.
- Because of few failure observations, trust and confidence values of the privacy property are mostly high and close to 1.

4.3   Decision Making

The computed trust underlies decisions to be taken. These can be decisions to reconfigure, to stop an application, to raise an alarm or it can be a form of access control. The model we have introduced in Section 2 does this in the form of a series of tradeoffs between different trust values with respect to a threshold. These thresholds as well as these tradeoffs are dependent on the context, which is any information that can be used to characterize the situation of involved entities [5]. In our example this is typically a mode of operation of the system. For example, if the system is low on energy we are more strict on energy usage and require high trust in components staying within energy bounds. This is

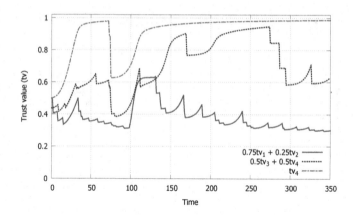

Fig. 12. Trust values are computed with the left-hand sides of Equation (13), (14), and (15), respectively

reflected in weights and thresholds. For the sake of the example we mention two tradeoff equations, where tv_i refers to the trust value of the mentioned properties.

$$0.75tv_1 + 0.25tv_2 \geq 0.9 \tag{13}$$

$$0.5tv_3 + 0.5tv_4 \geq 0.6 \tag{14}$$

$$tv_4 \geq 0.8 \tag{15}$$

The first equation represents a tradeoff between processing and memory usage and the second between network bandwidth usage and privacy. The last equation gives a minimal trust value to privacy. Figure 12 plots the left-hand sides of these equations.

When the patient has a heart condition and an emergency occurs, the privacy weight and threshold might be lowered. In this emergency mode, the raw ECG signal is recorded and made accessible to the doctor, which reduces privacy and gives intensive network communication. Trust thresholds for privacy and bandwidth properties will be small in this mode.

5   Related Work

Many trust management models and frameworks have been proposed for various applications, such as public key authentication [2,9], e-commerce [13], peer-to-peer networks [12,16], ad hoc and wireless sensor networks [19,14,18], and software systems [17,6,7]. According to the types of evidence that the trust value is based on, they can be classified into (1) certificate-based frameworks, in which the certificates are used as pre-deployment knowledge to establish a trust relationship; (2) behavior-based frameworks, in which a trustor continuously monitors the behavior of a trustee and builds the trust; and (3) hybrid frameworks that combine the previous approaches [1,18]. Also, trust can be evaluated in different ways [14], such as linguistic descriptions of trust relationships and the continuous or discrete numerical values assigned to the level of trustworthiness. In our work, we want to quantitatively evaluate the trustworthiness with respect to given properties based on the behavior of the trustee. Trust is built on compositions of properties, typically determined through monitoring, and is related to the service that is expected.

In [19], the concept of trustworthiness is extended to the notion of an opinion which a node has of any other nodes in mobile ad hoc networks. The trust value is computed as the mean of a distribution using Bayes' rule based on empirical observations. Besides trust, the concept of confidence is introduced that captures a belief that the value is correct. The work, however, focuses on developing metrics and mechanisms for establishing trust with respect to the objective of reliable packet delivery. In contrast, our trust evaluation approach can be applied in various applications; the trust and confidence values can be computed for arbitrary statements about an entity. Furthermore, the opinion generators can be customized through parameters and for the types of discrete observation and continuous observation.

The authors of [14] present a trust evaluation framework, which is employed in ad hoc networks for securing ad hoc routing and assisting malicious node detection. Trust is measured as uncertainty, thus the trust metric is defined based on entropy. Then, two trust models based on entropy and probability (the beta function) are introduced for trust propagation. Also, a forgetting factor is introduced to address the issue of the same weight for older and more recent observations. In our work, we further consider the unknown observations, the time, and the different effects of success and failure observations, and we introduce a decision model. This makes our approach more general.

In [18], a trust establishment and management framework for wireless sensor networks (WSNs) is presented. The framework is aimed at minimizing memory, computation and communication overheads involved in trust management in WSNs. The evaluation of the trust value is based on the successful and unsuccessful interactions within a time window. The recent trust value could be given more (or less) weight in the overall trust calculation. Similarly, paper [8] aims to develop a lightweight trust management for medical sensor networks. The trust value is computed based on the number of successful and failed interactions between sensor nodes in a time window. An aging factor is introduced to discriminate the importance of recent and older trust values. The work, however, supports only binary observations. Also, the trust-based operation (decision model) is not explicitly specified.

Yan et al. [17] propose an adaptive trust control model to evaluate, establish, and ensure the trust relationships among software system entities. The model concerns the quality attributes of the entity and a number of trust control modes supported by the system. During system runtime, quality attributes are monitored by observing the trustee's performance. The trust value of each quality attribute then can be generated based on the number of positive and negative points of the observation. The trust value generator is based on the original opinion generator of subjective logic, which has drawbacks as explained in this paper. The work, however, focuses more on providing control mechanisms to maintain the trust relationship than on improving the method of trust evaluation.

6   Conclusion

In this work, we have presented a framework to evaluate trustworthiness of general properties of an entity through monitoring, based on an extension of subjective logic. The generality implies that we can use this framework for monitoring dependability, security and functionality related properties. We stated requirements for opinion generators. Based on the requirements we have proposed novel parameterized generators that can be used with both discrete and continuous observations. It was shown that these opinion generation functions capture the requirements much better than current opinion generators do. In addition, the generator's parameters give a trustor the ability of customizing for various properties, e.g., to select an optimistic or pessimistic attitude. The combination of trust and confidence values helps to make a more precise decision. The confidence level can be associated with the criticality of the decision: a subject with a high trust value but with a low confidence value should not be trusted for higher-risk decisions.

We demonstrated the trust model and opinion generators for the case study of a Body Area Sensor Network platform, where the platform plays the role of the trustor and the software component plays the role of the trustee. The results show that the generation functions work effectively with various types of quality properties, such as CPU usage, memory usage, and privacy. Based on trust monitoring, decisions can be made according to a certain context. In future work, we investigate mechanisms to maintain and improve the trustworthiness. We focus on dependability related properties and decision structures that are controlled by the observed trust. An example is changing the mode of operation for reducing energy use in case the trust that sufficient energy remains available is too low. Another example is providing a sandbox environment in case correct behavior of a component is not sufficiently trusted.

Acknowledgements. This work has been conducted within the VITRUVIUS project supported by the Dutch Ministry of Economic Affairs under the Innovation Oriented Research Program.

References

1. Aivaloglou, E., Gritzalis, S.: Hybrid trust and reputation management for sensor networks. Wireless Networks 16(5), 1493–1510 (2010)
2. Blaze, M., Feigenbaum, J., Lacy, J.: Decentralized trust management. In: Proceedings of the 1996 IEEE Symposium on Security and Privacy, pp. 164–173 (May 1996)

3. Bui, V., Verhoeven, R., Lukkien, J., Kocielnik, R.: A trust evaluation framework for sensor readings in body area sensor networks. In: ICST International Conference on Body Area Networks, Boston, Massachusetts, USA (September 2013)

4. Bui, V.T., Lukkien, J.J., Verhoeven, R.: Toward a trust management model for a configurable body sensor platform. In: Proceedings of the 6th International Conference on Body Area Networks (BodyNets 2011), pp. 23–26 (2011)

5. Dey, A.K.: Understanding and using context. Personal Ubiquitous Computing 5(1), 4–7 (2001)

6. Ding, S., Ma, X.J., Yang, S.L.: A software trustworthiness evaluation model using objective weight based evidential reasoning approach. Knowledge and Information Systems, 1–19 (2011)

7. Hasan, Z., Krischkowsky, A., Tscheligi, M.: Modelling user-centered-trust (UCT) in software systems: Interplay of trust, affect and acceptance model. In: Katzenbeisser, S., Weippl, E., Camp, L.J., Volkamer, M., Reiter, M., Zhang, X. (eds.) Trust 2012. LNCS, vol. 7344, pp. 92–109. Springer, Heidelberg (2012)

8. He, D., Chen, C., Chan, S., Bu, J., Vasilakos, A.V.: Retrust: Attack-resistant and lightweight trust management for medical sensor networks. IEEE Trans. on Information Technology in Biomedicine 16(4), 623–632 (2012)

9. Herzberg, A., Mass, Y., Mihaeli, J., Naor, D., Ravid, Y.: Access control meets public key infrastructure, or: assigning roles to strangers. In: Proceedings of the 2000 IEEE Symposium on Security and Privacy, pp. 2–14 (2000)

10. Jøsang, A.: A logic for uncertain probabilities. International Journal of Uncertainty, Fuzziness and Knowledge-Based Systems 9(3), 279–311 (2001)

11. Jøsang, A., Hayward, R., Pope, S.: Trust network analysis with subjective logic. In: Proceedings of the 29th Australasian Computer Science Conference, ACSC 2006, Australia, pp. 85–94 (2006)

12. Kamvar, S.D., Schlosser, M.T., Garcia-Molina, H.: The Eigentrust algorithm for reputation management in P2P networks. In: Proceedings of the 12th International Conference on World Wide Web, pp. 640–651. ACM, NY (2003)

13. Manchala, D.: Trust metrics, models and protocols for electronic commerce transactions. In: Proceedings of the 18th International Conference on Distributed Computing Systems, pp. 312–321 (May 1998)

14. Sun, Y., Han, Z., Yu, W., Liu, K.: A trust evaluation framework in distributed networks: Vulnerability analysis and defense against attacks. In: Proceedings of the 25th IEEE International Conference on Computer Communications (INFOCOM), pp. 1–13 (2006)

15. Trust4All: Trust4All project (2007),
http://www.win.tue.nl/trust4all/summary.html

16. Xiong, L., Liu, L.: Peertrust: supporting reputation-based trust for peer-to-peer electronic communities. IEEE Transactions on Knowledge and Data Engineering 16(7), 843–857 (2004)

17. Yan, Z., Prehofer, C.: Autonomic trust management for a component-based software system. IEEE Trans. Dependable Secur. Comput. 8(6), 810–823 (2011)

18. Zhang, J., Shankaran, R., Orgun, M., Varadharajan, V., Sattar, A.: A dynamic trust establishment and management framework for wireless sensor networks. In: Proceedings of the 8th IEEE/IFIP International Conference on Embedded and Ubiquitous Computing (EUC), pp. 484–491 (December 2010)

19. Zouridaki, C., Mark, B.L., Hejmo, M., Thomas, R.K.: A quantitative trust establishment framework for reliable data packet delivery in manets. In: Proceedings of the 3rd ACM Workshop on Security of Ad hoc and Sensor Networks, SASN 2005, pp. 1–10. ACM, NY (2005)

Extending Development Methodologies
with Trustworthiness-By-Design
for Socio-Technical Systems
(Extended Abstract)

Nazila Gol Mohammadi[1], Torsten Bandyszak[1], Sachar Paulus[2], Per Håkon Meland[3],
Thorsten Weyer[1], and Klaus Pohl[1]

[1] paluno – The Ruhr Institute for Software Technology, University of Duisburg-Essen,
45127 Essen, Germany
[2] Department of Economics, Brandenburg University of Applied Sciences,
4770 Brandenburg an der Havel, Germany
[3] SINTEF ICT, Strindveien 4, N-7465 Trondheim, Norway
{nazila.golmohammadi,torsten.bandyszak,thorsten.weyer,
klaus.pohl}@paluno.uni-due.de, paulus@fh-brandenburg.de,
per.h.meland@sintef.no

1 Introduction

Socio-Technical Systems (STS) include humans, organizations, and the information systems that they use to achieve certain goals [1]. They are increasingly relevant for society, since advances in ICT technologies, such as cloud computing, facilitate their integration in our daily life. Due to the difficulty in preventing malicious attacks, vulnerabilities, or the misuse of sensitive information, users might not *trust* these systems. *Trustworthiness* in general can be defined as the assurance that the system will per-form as expected, or meets certain requirements (cf., e.g. [2]). We consider trustworthiness as a multitude of quality attributes. As a means of constructive quality assurance, development methodologies should explicitly address the different challenges of building trustworthy software as well as evaluating trustworthiness, which is not supported by development methodologies, such as User-Centered Design (UCD) [3].

2 Extension Approach and Application Example

Our focus is on enhancing a broad spectrum of general software development methodologies to incorporate the consideration of trustworthiness. We propose an extension of the Software Process Engineering Meta-model (SPEM) [4], which allows for tailoring certain "trustworthy" process chunks into the development methodologies. We utilize the SPEM concept of "Capability Patterns", i.e., process building blocks that are independent of specific phases, and represent best practices [4]. The analysis results for User-Centered Design (UCD) [3] indicate that it is important to understand which trustworthiness characteristics of the system will enhance stakeholder trust and how system design can help to circumvent any distrust-related concerns.

T. Holz and S. Ioannidis (Eds.): TRUST 2014, LNCS 8564, pp. 206–207, 2014.
© Springer International Publishing Switzerland 2014

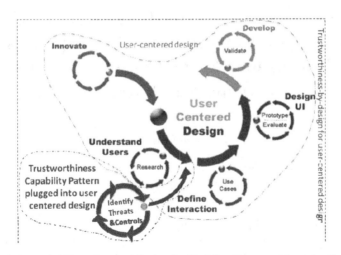

Fig. 1. Extended User-Centered Design for Enabling Trustworthiness-by-Design

Hence, it is not sufficient to elicit requirements w.r.t. the way in which people will use the system, as would be done in a standard user-centered design process. There is a need for eliciting and specifying requirements about which trustworthiness attributes will address potential trust issues that might affect the end users. Consequently, we exemplarily extended UCD by plugging the capability pattern "Identify Threats and Controls" into the early process stage of specifying user requirements (see Fig. 1). In order to provide tool support for designing, tailoring and sharing trustworthy development processes, we utilize the Eclipse Process Framework (EPF) [5], which has an underlying meta-model based on SPEM [4].

Acknowledgement. The research leading to these results has received funding from the European Union's FP7/2007-2013 under grant agreement 317631 (OPTET).

References

1. Sommerville, I.: Software Engineering, 9th edn. Pearson, Boston (2011)
2. Amoroso, E., Taylor, C., Watson, J., Weiss, J.: A Process-Oriented Methodology for Assessing and Improving Software Trustworthiness. In: 2nd ACM Conference on Computer and Communications Security, pp. 39–50. ACM, New York (1994)
3. Sutcliffe, A.G.: Convergence or Competition between Software Engineering and Human Computer Interaction. In: Seffrah, A., Gulliksen, J., Desmarais, M.C. (eds.) Human-Centered Software Engineering — Integrating Usability in the Software Development Lifecycle. Human-Computer Interaction Series, vol. 8, pp. 71–84 (2005)
4. Object Management Group: Software & Systems Process Engineering Meta-Model Specification, Version 2.0. Technical Report, Object Management Group (2008)
5. Eclipse Process Framework Project (EPF), http://www.eclipse.org/epf/

Challenges in Establishing Trustworthy Collaborations for Timely Responses to Emergency Animal Disease Incidents
(Extended Abstract)

John Žic

CSIRO Computational Informatics
Marsfield, NSW 2122
Australia

Developing and deploying authentication and authorization mechanisms and policies to control the flow of sensitive confidential information being shared between multiple organisations during a collaboration already represent technical and legal challenges.

We consider that there are three steps required to form a general *trustworthy collaboration*:

1. Formulation of a collaboration agreement that specifies how information is shared and controlled between the partners;
2. Proof of adherence of each partner against the collaboration agreement during critical (and agreed upon) events and
3. Non-repudiable evidence kept of partner behaviour during the collaboration.

In this presentation, we examine some of the challenges faced by state, commonwealth and independent research organizations within the Australian context in dealing with the formation of a committee in response to a biosecurity incident. This committee is a specific instance of a trustworthy collaboration, since inadvertent information disclosure may have significant national and international impact. However, this trustworthy collaboration needs to not only meet each of the three steps above, but needs to meet them with the significant additional constraint of *timeliness*.

Any Australian Commonwealth level emergency committee formed through the collaboration of multiple organizations immediately encounters the situation where each of the partners can be expected to have their respective organizations within separate legal (state or commonwealth) jurisdictions, each having their own implementatons of organizational policies and procedures for the control of sensitive information that comply with their respective jurisdiction.

Rapid resolution of inevitable differences between partners, as well as deploying technologies that are able to meet and implement enforceable collaboration agreement between the partners, have direct impact on the performance and responsiveness of the committee. Whereas the resolution may be done *a priori* to any incident, implementing a set of technologies (secure networking, storage and computation) that can support a collaboration agreement may vary depending on the incident and the mix of partners, the types of technologies that they

T. Holz and S. Ioannidis (Eds.): TRUST 2014, LNCS 8564, pp. 208–209, 2014.

implement in their respective organisations, and the way that they interoperate with other.

Each of the collaborating partners will run their own security (IT) systems that are governed by their respective policy implementations. Even though they adhere to a standard in principle, in practice there will be differences in their implementation and management, ranging from the preferred vendors used, to different management policies and different levels of compliance against "standard" procedures and processes.

The challenges faced are not always technical.

For example, implementing a federated identity solution across the states, commonwealth and independent research organisations such as that offered by the Australian Access Federation (AAF) (http://www.aaf.edu.au) is a policy (rather than technical) challenge because of the state-based legacy systems and each states desire to maintain a degree of independence from the Australian Commonwealth government. Any technical solutions must be light touch on each state system otherwise it will not be adopted (again, partly because of the legacy systems in place, partly because of the desire to remain independent). Nonetheless, the adoption of an inappropriate policy will have an impact on the timeliness and trustworthiness of the operation of the committee.

On the other hand, adoption of appropriate policies, and technologies and system architectures that fully comply with those policies yet try to change the fundamental operation of the committee, will also direct impact on the timeliness of response, and the general trustworthiness of the operation of the committee and its supporting infrastructure. The same can be said for the case where the supporting technology infrastructure alters the workflow of the committee - once again, having technologies and systems that fully comply with policy, yet interfere with the workflows of the committee will inevitably lead to worse timeliness and decreased trustworthiness of the operation of the committee.

To realise the vision of facilitating truly dynamic, real-time trustworthy collaborations requires an integrated approach to technologies sensitive to both policy and work practices within the trustworthy collaboration. A range of considerations needs to be examined: authentication of identity claims with high levels of assurance; authorization and access control policies and mechanisms; proof of integrity of information, equipment, and facilities; and finally, being able to deal effectively with exceptional cases through judicious provenance and compliance assurance mechanisms.

While some of these may be successfully done within a single enterprise, it is not the case when there are complex collaborations spanning multiple jurisdictions. To be truly effective in the context of managing a biosecurity incident, a system solution will consider the integration between three components: technology, policies and workflows and practices of collaborating partners.

Removing, or not addressing, any one of these can result in a sub-optimal solution and the failure to provide timely response to new biosecurity issues and threats.

Authentication System Using Encrypted Discrete Biometrics Data

Kazuo Ohzeki, YuanYu Wei, Masaaki Kajihara, Masahiro Takatsuka,
Yutaka Hirakawa, and Toru Sugimoto

Shibaura Institute of Technology, Graduate School of Engineering, Tokyo, Japan
{ohzeki,sugimoto}@sic.shibaura-it.ac.jp,
{m710101,ma14034,ma14067,hirakawa}@shibaura-it.ac.jp

Abstract. Biometric authentication has attracted attention because it has different characteristics from passwords. Biometric inputs are analog data and have a fixed fluctuation. Digitization is one possible measure to cope with the problems. Widening the quantization in step-size fashion to discriminate a personal distance is another possible measure. This paper proposes a biometric authentication system integrating these two measures. As biometric data are private, they are encrypted and saved on a server. Even if the server is attacked and the data are leaked, the private information concerning the biometric data is kept secret.

Keywords: biometrics, authentication, password, privacy, leakage.

1   Introduction

Biometric authentication has different characteristics from passwords composed of simple character strings. Biometric authentication has several features that need not be committed to memory, and one need not worry about forgetting, loss or theft of security information. However, the biometric technology of detecting the features of a human body image such as a face, fingerprints and iris is limited in that its discrimination ability is inadequate to cover the whole population. As the power of discrimination is limited, it is difficult to use solely biometric authentication, which is the first problem. On the other hand, a password for a specific ID has sufficient patterns that cannot be guessed and cracked. As the password should be memorized, many people use a short word or write the password down on a paper without memorizing it, which brings a low level of security. In this way, password authentication has the problem that the password can be leaked or stolen easily.

To cope with these two problems, embedding biometric authentication into a conventional password system will enhance the security level. To treat biometric information with appropriate concern for privacy, all biometric raw data should be enciphered. To perform encrypted authentication, the raw biometric data should be clearly discrete and quantized to the same vector for all trials. To realize clear and robust quantization of biometric data is the major technical problem for the proposed system.

T. Holz and S. Ioannidis (Eds.): TRUST 2014, LNCS 8564, pp. 210–211, 2014.

2   Related Works

Encrypting biometric data using a symmetric key is one of the biometric authentication methods [1]. The problem is that the symmetric key can be leaked to an outsider. Use of error correcting codes (ECC) is another idea to reduce ambiguity of biometric data. The ECC keeps the difference of two biometric data before and after encryption into a specified interval [2,3]. But the idea of maintaining similarity between raw and encrypted data means that the encryption is not a real cipher. Also, the ECC does not contribute to improving the ability to discriminate the user from other people.

3   Proposed System

To improve the security, in the public key infrastructure (PKI) a public key "K" and decoding key "D" are generated for encryption as shown in Fig.1. At registration, the decoding key "D" is not used at all and is removed. The biometric data are facial feature points and are denoted as vector $\mathbf{f}$. The vector $\mathbf{f}$ is encrypted by the key "K" and becomes $E_K(\mathbf{f})$. The encrypted biometric information $E_K(\mathbf{f})$ is stored in the file system. At the time of authentication, another facial vector $\mathbf{g}$ is input to the system and is encrypted by the same key "K" as used at registration, and becomes $E_K(\mathbf{g})$. $E_K(\mathbf{f})$ and $E_K(\mathbf{g})$ are matched for verification.

Combining this biometric authentication with the conventional password, the security level will be improved if the password is stolen. The private encrypted biometric information cannot be recovered because the decoding key is removed. To design robust quantization of feature points is an important object of our experiments.

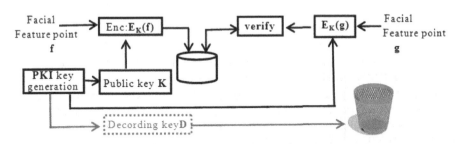

Fig. 1. Biometric authentication system using encrypted personal data

References

1. Raith, N.K., Connell, J.H., Bolle, R.M.: Enhancing security and privacy in Biometric-based authentication systems. IBM SYSTEMS Journal 40(3), 614–634 (2001)
2. Juels, A., Wattenberg, M.: A fuzzy commitment scheme. In: Proc. 6th ACM CCS, pp. 28–36 (November 1999)
3. Hao, F., Anderson, R., Daugman, J.: Combining Crypto with Biometrics Effectively. IEEE Trans on Computers 55(9), 1081–1088 (2006)

On the Development of Automated Forensic Analysis Methods for Mobile Devices

Panagiotis Andriotis[1], Theo Tryfonas[1], George Oikonomou[1], Shancang Li[1],
Zacharias Tzermias[2], Konstantinos Xynos[3], Huw Read[3],
and Vassilis Prevelakis[4]

[1] University of Bristol, MVB, Woodland Road, Clifton, Bristol BS8 1UB, UK
[2] FORTH-Institute of Computer Science, N. Plastira 100, 70013, Heraklion, Greece
[3] University of South Wales, Pontypridd, Wales, UK, CF37 1DL, UK
[4] Technical University, Hans-Sommer-Street 66, 38106, Braunschweig, Germany

Abstract. We live in a connected world where mobile devices are used
by humans as valuable tools. The use of mobile devices leaves traces that
can be treasured assets for a forensic analyst. Our aim is to investigate
methods and exercise techniques that will merge all these valuable information in a way that will be efficient for a forensic analyst, producing
graphical representations of the underlying data structures. We are using
a framework able to collect and merge data from various sources and employ algorithms from a wide range of interdisciplinary areas to automate
post-incident forensic analysis on mobile devices.

Keywords: Steganalysis, Smartphone, Sentiment Analysis, Post-
incident, SMS, Social Media, Forensics, Android.

1 Introduction

The basic types of data we can retrieve during a forensic analysis on devices
are text and images, the metadata for which are usually stored internally in
SQLite databases [1]. A forensic investigation deals with the problem of merging
all useful information, in order to provide evidence at a court of justice. In
this project we aim to automate this process and decrease the analysis time
using data mining methods to extract sentiment polarity from short messages.
Also, we highlight connections and interactions between entities that exist in
the Smartphone Ecosystem and in various social media communities, providing
graphical representations that demonstrate the proximity of their relationships
[3]. Finally, we propose a lightweight classification mechanism that distinguishes
suspicious JPEG images that might exist in the device's internal memory [2].

2 Methodology

The data aggregation mechanism, called DEViSE, provides a platform where the
data from various sources can be stored in a homogeneous format using XML
files. All these information can be stored in a central database and therefore, used

T. Holz and S. Ioannidis (Eds.): TRUST 2014, LNCS 8564, pp. 212–213, 2014.

upon the request of the visualization tools. For the social media module of our platform, we developed a crawler that can be enriched by data derived by mobile devices. Furthermore, we extended the functionality of a graph representation of interactions between entities by highlighting the 'closest friends' of the person under investigation. The short text messages can be further analysed to produce the Sentiment Timeline View and depict the emotional polarity between entities for a given timeframe. Our approach to this problem is the use of a bag-of-words schema that utilizes special features like the existence of emoticons and the lexicon's word valence evaluation. Finally, the automated system we propose is able to perform steganalysis on the JPEG images that exist in the internal memory of the mobile device, using our model for colour images derived by the empirical Benford's Law.

3   Results and Conclusion

Regarding the results derived from the JPEG images classification, our approach reaches hit rates of 70% - 100%, depending on the algorithm used to create the stego-carrier. The short text Sentiment Analysis module can correctly identify the emotional polarity of around 69% of the messages with a false positive rate reaching approximately an average of 25%. Finally the graphical representation of the entity linking, results to informative graphs which can be further enhanced by clustering algorithms that various visualization tools provide by evaluating measures like centrality. To conclude, we have developed an analysis automation platform able to perform specific tasks based on data collected from various sources. This system could be a helpful asset to the community of forensic analysts, but of course it cannot substitute their expert judgement to a court. It can instantly produce informative constructions derived from a wide data pool associated with the person under investigation, but it cannot act as a judgement tool in itself.

Acknowledgement. This work has been supported by the European Union's Prevention of and Fight against Crime Programme "Illegal Use of Internet" ISEC 2010 Action Grants, grant ref. HOME/2010/ISEC/AG/INT-002 and the Systems Centre of the University of Bristol.

References

1. Andriotis, P., Oikonomou, G., Tryfonas, T.: Forensic Analysis of Wireless Networking Evidence of Android Smartphones. In: WIFS, pp. 109–114 (2012)
2. Andriotis, P., Oikonomou, G., Tryfonas, T.: JPEG Steganography Detection with Benford's Law. Digital Investigation 9(3), 246–257 (2013)
3. Andriotis, P., Tzermias, Z., Mparmpaki, A., Ioannidis, S., Oikonomou, G.: Multi-level Visualization Using Enhanced Social Network Analysis with Smartphone Data. IJDCF 5(4), 34–54 (2013)

A Trusted Knowledge Management System for Multi-layer Threat Analysis

Thanasis Petsas[1], Kazuya Okada[2], Hajime Tazaki[3],
Gregory Blanc[4], and Paweł Pawliński[5]

[1] Institute of Computer Science, Foundation for Research & Technology – Hellas, Greece
petsas@ics.forth.gr
[2] Nara Institute of Science and Technology, Japan
kazuya-o@is.naist.jp
[3] The University of Tokyo, Japan
tazaki@nc.u-tokyo.ac.jp
[4] Télécom SudParis, CNRS UMR 5157 SAMOVAR, France
gregory.blanc@telecom-sudparis.eu
[5] CERT Polska, Research and Academic Computer Network, Poland
pawel.pawlinski@cert.pl

1 Motivation

In recent years, we have seen a surge of cybersecurity incidents ranging from widespread attacks (e.g., large-scale attacks against infrastructures or end points [1]) to new technological advances (i.e., new generations of malicious code are increasingly stealthy, powerful and pervasive [2]). Facing these incidents, the European Union, Japan, the United States or China have developed national cybersecurity programs, including training of professionals, development of roadmaps for new tools and services, and organization of national interest groups on the topic. *There is thus a shared need for a better understanding of this kind of large-scale threats.* Some of the basic requirements to better understand these large-scale incidents include handling large volumes of data collected from distributed probes and performing efficient cross-layer analysis.

2 System Description

In this paper, we introduce a trusted knowledge management system for multi-layer threat analysis (tKMS). tKMS is capable of supporting a great variety of sensors ranging from honeypots and spam detection systems to real-time intrusion detection systems and online web sources. Moreover, it provides actionable information for cyberdefense systems. Support for a wide array of sources is feasible thanks to the modular architecture and a common lightweight data sharing format – the *n6* API. tKMS is comprised of two basic components: the *Threat Information Sharing component* and the *Cross-layer Analysis module*, as shown in Figure 1. We have designed our system to meet the following requirements: (i) provision of trusted access to multiple sources of data, (ii) confidentiality of the security networks that provide the data, (iii) scalability, (iv) real-time analysis and (v) uniform programmability through support of multiple data types. What follows is a description of tKMS basic components.

T. Holz and S. Ioannidis (Eds.): TRUST 2014, LNCS 8564, pp. 214–215, 2014.

Fig. 1. Architecture of tKMS

Threat Information Sharing (TIS). This component manages threat information from *Analysis Modules*, *External Knowledge Systems* and *External Resources*. Originally, data posted by these components are unrelated and the system conjectures a relationship among them, turning them into knowledge.

Cross-Layer Analysis Module (CAM). The CAM aims at detecting cyber threats based on the analysis of data coming from the infrastructure and end point layers. The CAM consists of several components. Each component serves the purpose of detecting a certain threat or a number of threats that are somehow related. The analysis results are pushed to the TIS component via the n6 API.

External Knowledge System (EKS). This component designates external sources of cyber threat related information such as software vulnerabilities databases. The information is provided through an API using the common exchange format.

External Resources (ER). This component collects cyber threat information or related information not formatted in any standard scheme. The main difference with the EKS is that the resources do not provide any data sharing interfaces. That kind of information is gathered mainly by web crawlers and other automated data gathering mechanisms which are able to extract knowledge from external sources. Acquired knowledge is managed under the TIS.

The n6 API. n6 is a platform for processing security-related information and its API provides a common and unified way of representing data across the different sources that participate in our knowledge management system. n6 exposes a REST-ful API over HTTPS with mandatory authentication via TLS client certificates, to ensure confidential and trustworthy communications. Moreover, it uses an event-based data model for representation of all types of security information. Each event is represented as a JSON object with a set of mandatory and optional attributes.

Access control and encryption mechanisms are used in order to preserve confidentiality of data across the different components. Moreover authentication mechanisms are used in the components' communication to make our system resilient to hijacking.

References

1. Brown, M.: Pakistan hijacks youtube,
   http://www.renesys.com/2008/02/pakistan-hijacks-youtube-1/
2. Kushner, D.: The real story of stuxnet,
   http://spectrum.ieee.org/telecom/security/the-real-story-of-stuxnet

Diagraming Approach to Structure the Security Lessons: Evaluation Using Cognitive Dimensions

Ying He[1], Chris Johnson[1], Maria Evangelopoulou[1], and Zheng-Shuai Lin[2]

[1] School of Computing Science, University of Glasgow, UK
{yingh,johnson}@dcs.gla.ac.uk, m.evangelopoulou.1@research.gla.ac.uk
[2] School of Informatics, University of Edinburg, UK
z.lin@ed.ac.uk

Abstract. Currently, the lessons learned from the security incidents are documented in add-hoc means such as lengthy security reports, free-style textual news letters, emails or informal meetings. This makes it difficult to effectively communicate security lessons among peers and organisations. The diagraming approach such as the Generic Security Template (G.S.T.) has been proposed to address this problem. This paper extends the work by evaluating its usability using the Cognitive Dimensions and identifies some aspects that need to be improved.

1   Introduction

Healthcare information privacy and security have been a primary concern of the public [1]. Security incidents in healthcare happen across the world, such as the Veterans Affairs dataloss incidents in 2006/2007 in the US, NHS Surrey IT asset disposal incident in 2013, in UK. However, the security lessons have not been effectively communicated using the conventional add-hoc means such as lengthy security reports, free-style textual news letters, emails or informal meetings. The diagraming approach, Generic Security Template (G.S.T.), has been proposed to address this problem [2]. It presents the lessons learned in a structured manner by mapping them to the security requirements of the ISMS. The objective is to enhance existing techniques used to communicate lessons from security incidents. A controlled experiment with university students shows that it can better assist the communication of security lessons compared to the free-style security incident report [3]. A field study in a healthcare organisation shows that it can assist in feeding back the lessons to the improvements of the information security management in healthcare [4]. However, those studies have not systematically evaluate the usability of G.S.T. as graphical notations. The Cognitive Dimensions framework provides a generic approach to measure various usability characteristics of notations and their environments [5]. This paper adopts this framework to evaluate the G.S.T.

2   The Evaluation and Results

As a preliminary study, twelve university students with diversified background participated in this study voluntarily. The study lasted for approximately 40

T. Holz and S. Ioannidis (Eds.): TRUST 2014, LNCS 8564, pp. 216–217, 2014.

minutes including a tutorial of the Generic Security Template, and the evaluation of the Generic Security Template. The evaluation questionnaire was based on the Cognitive Dimensions of Notations Usability Framework [5]. There are fourteen dimensions in the full framework. For our study, we did not ask about the creation or modification of the notation. Therefore, we have selected five dimensions as is shown in Table 1.

Table 1. Evaluation using Cognitive Dimensions

Dimension	Suggested Improvements
CD-Visibility	"might be difficult to differentiate between goals & sub goals"; "color may help visual interpretation"
CD-Diffuseness	"too many words"
CD-Closeness of Mapping	"The recommendation part needs to be simplified or separate individually (under suitable category)".
CD-Hard Mental Operation	"the template is not generic enough"; "too many words within one notation"
CD-Role Expressiveness	"could use multiple templates"; "might be hard to see whether the user wants to work on the high or low level of the hierarchy"

Table 1 summarizes the representative suggestions identified during the evaluation of the G.S.T. using Cognitive Dimensions. This study has identified several aspects of the G.S.T. that need to be improved. One of the key questions for future work is to determine an appropriate level of abstraction for G.S.T. Too much information might affect the readers' motivation, and ability to analyse the causes of a previous incident. While too little information will make it difficult to understand why an incident occurred and may provide insufficient contextual information to focus future interventions. This provides the foundation for future work on customising the G.S.T. to fit into the needs of particular organisaitons.

References

1. Porteous, T., Bond, C., Robertson, R., Hannaford, P., Reiter, E.: Electronic transfer of prescription-related information: comparing views of patients, general practitioners, and pharmacists. The British Journal of General Practice 53(488), 204 (2003)
2. He, Y., Johnson, C.: An empirical study on the use of the generic security template for structuring the lessons from information security incidents. In: The 6th International Conference of Computer Science and Information Technology (2014)
3. He, Y., Johnson, C.: An empirical study on the use of the generic security template for structuring the lessons from information security incidents. In: The 8th IFIP WG 11.11 International Conference on Trust Management (2014)
4. He, Y., Johnson, C., Lu, Y., Lin, Y.: Improving the information security management: An industrial study in the privacy of electronic patient records. In: The 27th International Symposium on Computer-Based Medical Systems (2014)
5. Green, T.R.G., Petre, M.: Usability analysis of visual programming environments: a'cognitive dimensions' framework. Journal of Visual Languages & Computing 7(2), 131–174 (1996)

TRACER: A Platform for Securing Legacy Code

Kostantinos Stroggylos[1], Dimitris Mitropoulos[1], Zacharias Tzermias[2],
Panagiotis Papadopoulos[2], Fotios Rafailidis[3], Diomidis Spinellis[1],
Sotiris Ioannidis[2], and Panagiotis Katsaros[3]

[1] Department of Management Science and Technology
Athens University of Economics and Business
{circular,dimitro,dds}@aueb.gr
[2] Institute of Computer Science
Foundation for Research and Technology - Hellas
{tzermias,panpap,sotiris}@ics.forth.gr
[3] Department of Informatics
Aristotle University of Thessaloniki
katsaros@csd.auth.gr, frafaili@yahoo.gr

Keywords: Static Analysis, Software Security, Trusted Applications,
Legacy software.

Abstract

A security vulnerability is a programming error that introduces a potentially
exploitable weakness into a computer system. Such a vulnerability can severely
affect an organization's infrastructure and cause significant financial damage to
it. Hence, one of the basic pursuits in every new software release should be to
mitigate such defects.

A number of tools and techniques are available for performing vulnerability
detection in software written in various programming platforms. One of the most
common approaches to identify software vulnerabilities is *static analysis* [1]. This
kind of analysis is performed by automated tools either on the program's source
or object code and without actually executing it. However, since the formats
in which static analysis tools store and present their results vary wildly, it is
typically difficult to utilize many of them in the scope of a project. By automating
the process of running a variety of vulnerability detectors and collecting their
results in an efficient manner during development, the task of tracking security
defects throughout the evolution history of software projects can be simplified.

In this paper we present TRACER, a framework to support the development
of secure applications by constantly monitoring software projects for vulnerabilities. TRACER simplifies the integration of existing tools that detect software
vulnerabilities and promotes their use during development and maintenance.

Instead of designing and implementing TRACER from the ground up, we built
it on top of the open source *Alitheia Core* [2] platform, which is designed for
facilitating large scale quantitative software engineering studies. While Alitheia
Core aims for efficient estimation of the quality of software projects, TRACER

T. Holz and S. Ioannidis (Eds.): TRUST 2014, LNCS 8564, pp. 218–219, 2014.

was designed with a focus on software security. To support the specific objectives of TRACER, a set of new components was added at each level of the Alitheia Core architecture. These include a model for representing software vulnerabilities, a mechanism for automatic vulnerability detection triggering, a REST API for accessing the analysis results, and an archetype for plug-ins to integrate new vulnerability detection tools in the platform. Like Alitheia Core, TRACER monitors multiple data sources associated with the development of a software project, such as the source code repository and bug tracking system, and automatically analyzes each revision. Therefore it can be used to track security defects throughout the evolution of a project.

In most cases, the detection of vulnerabilities on a software artifact involves only two steps: invoking an external tool created for this purpose with specific arguments as required, and evaluating the results it generates. There is a vast number of software vulnerability detection tools available, each one having different operating requirements. Such a tool can be integrated in TRACER by creating a corresponding driver that implements these two steps and stores the results using the data model provided by the platform. Thus we can leverage the functionality provided by existing tools, without duplicating it.

Such an external tool driver is called a vulnerability detector plug-in, and it uses the Alitheia Core infrastructure to handle automatic activation, as well as storage and retrieval of results. Each vulnerability detector is associated with the set of vulnerability types it can detect and the different types of software artifacts or programming constructs that it can analyze. This allows the platform to automatically trigger it when needing to check if a software project or artifact is vulnerable to a specific type of attacks or a new artifact is submitted to the system for evaluation.

To demonstrate the efficiency and usability of the platform, we have created plug-ins to integrate two different tools for vulnerability detection, namely: *FindBugs* [3], and *Frama-C* [4]. The former analyzes applications written in Java, while the latter examines applications written in C. This highlights the fact that our platform does not depend on the programming language used to develop the project that is being analyzed, and that the simplicity of integrating third party tools leads to high levels of expandability of the platform.

References

1. Chess, B., West, J.: Secure programming with static analysis. Addison-Wesley Professional (2007)
2. Gousios, G., Spinellis, D.: Alitheia core: An extensible software quality monitoring platform. In: Proceedings of the 31st International Conference on Software Engineering, ICSE 2009, pp. 579–582. IEEE Computer Society, Washington, DC (2009)
3. Hovemeyer, D., Pugh, W.: Finding bugs is easy. SIGPLAN Not 39, 92–106 (2004)
4. Cuoq, P., Kirchner, F., Kosmatov, N., Prevosto, V., Signoles, J., Yakobowski, B.: Frama-c: A software analysis perspective. In: Eleftherakis, G., Hinchey, M., Holcombe, M. (eds.) SEFM 2012. LNCS, vol. 7504, pp. 233–247. Springer, Heidelberg (2012)

Facilitating Trust on Data through Provenance

Manolis Stamatogiannakis, Paul Groth, and Herbert Bos

VU University Amsterdam, The Netherlands
{manolis.stamatogiannakis,p.t.groth,h.j.bos}@vu.nl

Abstract. Research on trusted computing focuses mainly on the security and integrity of the *execution environment*, from hardware components to software services. However, this is only one facet of the computation, the other being the *data*. If our goal is to produce *trusted results*, a trustworthy execution environment is not enough: we also need *trustworthy data*. Provenance of data plays a pivotal role in ascertaining trustworthiness of data. In our work, we explore how to use state-of-the-art systems techniques to capture and reconstruct provenance, thus enabling us to build trust on both newly generated and existing data.

1.1 Motivation

Provenance is a record that describes the sources and agents involves in producing a piece of data [6]. This record can be analyzed e.g. to understand if data conforms designated standards or to calculate a level of trust on the data in order to assist decision making. Thus, knowing the provenance of data can play a central role in the trust we put on them. On the other hand, not having any provenance information on our data could undermine the benefits of using a trustworthy execution environment: if we cannot trust the data we process, we will also be unable to trust the produced results.

1.2 Capturing Provenance through Dynamic Instrumentation

We have developed a new system called DataTracker[1] [7] which uses Dynamic Taint Analysis (DTA) to capture *high-fidelity provenance* from *unmodified programs*. DataTracker is based on Intel Pin[2] Dynamic Binary Instrumentation framework and a modified version of the libdft [4] library which provides a reusable framework for Dynamic Taint Analysis.

The architecture of DataTracker is depicted in Fig. 1a. Its main components are a Pin tool and a converter written in Python. The former generates provenance information in raw format which are converted to the W3C PROV format [6] by the latter. After converting to PROV, existing tools can be used to further process and visualize the provenance.

Fig. 1b shows the provenance graph produced for a simple grep-like utility. DataTracker attributes the output to only two of the four input files, which is an improvement over state of the art techniques [3,1,2]. These treat programs as *black-boxes*, tracking only program-OS interactions but not the actual use of

---

[1] Source code available on: http://github.com/m000/dtracker
[2] https://software.intel.com/articles/pintool

T. Holz and S. Ioannidis (Eds.): TRUST 2014, LNCS 8564, pp. 220–221, 2014.

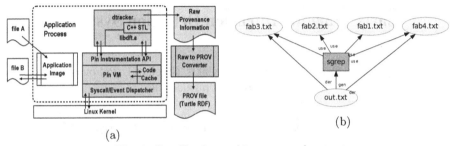

Fig. 1. DataTracker architecture and output

data. Thus, they would have attributed the output to all four inputs. In addition to eliminating such cases of false-positives, DataTracker captures provenance with byte-level granularity vs. the file-level granularity offered by comparable systems.

1.3   Post-hoc Provenance Reconstruction

We plan to explore using DataTracker for the post-hoc reconstruction of provenance. Our ultimate goal is to be able to reconstruct provenance relations between files and programs stored in a disk image. We plan to achieve this by: *a*) Collecting high-fidelity provenance information from live systems. *b*) Abstracting this information to generate "provenance behavior signatures" that reflect provenance patterns generated by specific programs. *c*) Matching these signatures with the files in the disk image. It is understood that reconstructed provenance will be of less fidelity than provenance directly captured by DataTracker during execution. We can improve the quality of this provenance by later applying heuristic-based methods (e.g. [5]).

References

1. Frew, J., Metzger, D., Slaughter, P.: Automatic capture and reconstruction of computational provenance 20(5) (2008)
2. Gessiou, E., Pappas, V., Athanasopoulos, E., Keromytis, A.D., Ioannidis, S.: Towards a Universal Data Provenance Framework Using Dynamic Instrumentation. In: Gritzalis, D., Furnell, S., Theoharidou, M. (eds.) SEC 2012. IFIP AICT, vol. 376, pp. 103–114. Springer, Heidelberg (2012)
3. Holland, D.A., Seltzer, M.I., Braun, U., Muniswamy-Reddy, K.-K.: PASSing the provenance challenge 20(5) (2008)
4. Kemerlis, V.P., Portokalidis, G., Jee, K., Keromytis, A.D.: libdft: Practical Dynamic Data Flow Tracking for Commodity Systems. In: Proceedings of VEE 2012 (2012)
5. Magliacane, S.: Reconstructing provenance. In: Cudré-Mauroux, P., Heflin, J., Sirin, E., Tudorache, T., Euzenat, J., Hauswirth, M., Parreira, J.X., Hendler, J., Schreiber, G., Bernstein, A., Blomqvist, E. (eds.) ISWC 2012, Part II. LNCS, vol. 7650, pp. 399–406. Springer, Heidelberg (2012)
6. Moreau, L., Missier, P.: PROV-DM: The PROV Data Model. Recommendation REC-prov-dm-20130430, W3C (2013)
7. Stamatogiannakis, M., Groth, P., Bos, H.: Looking Inside the Black-Box: Capturing Data Provenance using Dynamic Instrumentation. In: Proceedings of IPAW 2014, Cologne, Germany (2014)

Early Warning Intrusion Detection System

Panos Chatziadam, Ioannis G. Askoxylakis, Nikolaos E. Petroulakis,
and Alexandros G. Fragkiadakis

FORTHcert, Institute of Computer Science
Foundation for Research & Technology – Hellas (FORTH)
{panosc,asko,npetro,alfrag}@ics.forth.gr

1 Introduction

Early Warning Intrusion Detection System (EWIS) is a distributed global scoped
Internet threat monitoring system with the potential of detecting large scale malicious
events as early as possible.

The system's architecture includes a network of distributed low-interaction sensors
and a central server [1]. The sensors are small computing platforms [2] that by design
are easy to deploy in a distributed fashion to a large number of partner organizations.
They are preconfigured to be robust and secure and thus integrate non-intrusively to a
network infrastructure. Each sensor collects network activity flows of potentially
malicious intent from dark Internet address spaces and then relays this information to
the central server for logging and further analysis.

The system follows the design of a Network Telescope [3] which similarly to a
visual telescope, its resolution is relative to its size. As the number of deployed sensors grows, so does its resolution. EWIS's resolution is further enhanced by deploying
sensors to willing partner organizations.

2 Motivation

Proactive cyber-security tools provide basic protection as today's cyber-criminals
utilize legitimate traffic to perform attacks and remain concealed quite often until it is
too late. As critical resources, hidden behind layers of cyber-defenses, can still become compromised with potentially catastrophic consequences, it is of paramount
significance to be able to identify cyber-attacks and prepare a proper defense as early
as possible.

While traditional Honeypots can provide extensive information regarding an attack, they lack the ability of observing large scale events. Our vision was to establish
a system that would be cost effective to implement, easy to deploy and provide us
with sufficient data to create an Early Warning System that could potentially detect
large scale events such as Worm(s) and Distributed Denial of Service (DDoS) attacks
[4] on a global scale.

Furthermore, a globally scoped Network Telescope augmented by partner organization hosted sensors will expand EWIS's resolution beyond our national borders,
providing an aggregate view of Internet traffic across operational boundaries.

T. Holz and S. Ioannidis (Eds.): TRUST 2014, LNCS 8564, pp. 222–223, 2014.

3   Approach

The deployed sensors continuously capture data from dark space Internet addresses spaces. As these addresses are not in use, any traffic reaching them is considered to be of exploiting and therefore malicious intent. The data flows captured are relayed to the central server on a timely basis via encrypted network tunnels. The server stores the sensors' data to a local database in a way that it can be easily retrievable for analysis. A visualization interface provides several views of the collected data such as Historical packet traffic trends, Top 10 style statistics [Fig. 1], Protocol breakdown statistics and Backscatter traffic trends. Subsequent phases of the project will encompass a more advanced visualization framework, automated detection procedures, as well as the possible integration of wireless intrusion detection sensors [5] [6].

Source IP Addresses			Destination TCP/UDP Ports			Countries		
Source IP	Packet Count	Country	Destination Port	Packet Count	Trend	Total Packets	Country	Top IP
94.23.188.195 (?)	960		22 (?)	7991	▲	5153		61.147.103.142 (?)
188.138.125.48 (?)	944		5060 (?)	793	▼	2948		54.193.47.198 (?)
186.216.174.39 (?)	288		80 (?)	650	▼	1929		188.138.125.48 (?)
192.95.15.21 (?)	216		1433 (?)	509	▼	1140		94.23.188.195 (?)
54.193.47.198 (?)	204		8080 (?)	365	▼	698		186.216.174.39 (?)
61.147.103.142 (?)	200		3389 (?)	298	▼	501		89.248.172.195 (?)
218.2.22.107 (?)	192		23 (?)	291	▲	416		77.40.50.146 (?)
183.62.118.142 (?)	190		53 (?)	251	▼	396		192.95.15.21 (?)
89.248.172.195 (?)	168		21320 (?)	201	▼	316		180.225.203.220 (?)
207.244.66.108 (?)	151		443 (?)	148	▼	314		210.61.135.104 (?)

Fig. 1. Top 10 style statistics captured by an EWIS sensor

Acknowledgement. EWIS has been largely influenced by project NOAH.

References

1. Chatziadam, P., Askoxylakis, I., Fragkiadakis, A.: A Network Telescope for Early Warning Intrusion Detection. In: Proc. of the 2nd International Conference on Human Aspects of Information Security, Privacy and Trust, Heraklion, Greece, June 22-27 (2014)
2. Akram, R.N., Markantonakis, K., Mayes, K.: User centric security model for tamper-resistant devices. In: Proceedings - 2011 8th IEEE International Conference on e-Business Engineering, ICEBE 2011, pp. 168–177 (2011)
3. Irwin, B.: A framework for the application of network telescope sensors in a global IP network (January 2011), http://eprints.ru.ac.za/2557/ (retrieved)
4. Spyridopoulos, T., Karanikas, G., Tryfonas, T., Oikonomou, G.: A game theoretic defence framework against DoS/DDoS cyber attacks. Computers & Security 38, 39–50 (2013)
5. Fragkiadakis, A.G., Tragos, E.Z., Tryfonas, T., Askoxylakis, I.G.: Design and performance evaluation of a lightweight wireless early warning intrusion detection prototype. EURASIP Journal on Wireless Communications and Networking 2012(1), 73 (2012)
6. Fragkiadakis, A.G., Siris, V.A., Petroulakis, N.E., Traganitis, A.: Anomaly-based Intrusion Detection of Jamming Attacks, Local versus Collaborative Detection. In: Wiley Wireless Communications and Mobile Computing, pp. 1–19 (January 2013)

Author Index